A Guide to Programming the Commodore Computers

BRUCE PRESLEY

DISTRIBUTED BY

VAN NOSTRAND REINHOLD COMPANY

NEW YORK   CINCINNATI   TORONTO   LONDON   MELBOURNE

First published in 1983
Copyright © 1983
by

Library of Congress Catalog Card Number
83-50591

ISBN 0-422-27375-4

Educational orders may be placed by writing or calling:

Van Nostrand Reinhold Inc.
7625 Empire Drive
Attn: Department T
Florence, Kentucky 41042
Telephone 606-525-6600

Van Nostrand Reinhold Company
135 West 50th Street, New York, NY 10020

Macmillan of Canada
Division of Gage Publishing Limited
164 Commander Boulevard
Agincourt, Ontario M1S 3C7, Canada

Van Nostrand Reinhold Australia Pty. Ltd.
480 Latrobe Street
Melbourne, Victoria 3000, Australia

Van Nostrand Reinhold Company Ltd.
Molly Millars Lane
Wokingham, Berkshire, England RG11 2PY

16 15 14 13 12 11 10 9 8 7 6 5 4

ACKNOWLEDGMENT

The publication of this first edition of A GUIDE TO PROGRAMMING THE COMMODORE COMPUTERS represents the latest achievement of faculty and students at The Lawrenceville School in developing curricular materials to assist students in learning to program computers.

Because of our classroom experience over the past fifteen years, we are convinced that a structured, concisely written computer text is invaluable in teaching and learning programming. This latest manual, written specifically to instruct students in Commodore BASIC, not only retains but expands on the features which have resulted in the wide acceptance of our previous publications.

The production of this manual has involved the cooperation and talents of many individuals. Lester Waters, Robert Lynch, Eli Hurowitz and Donald Mikan have all made invaluable contributions to this publication. Each has authored and taken responsibility for specific areas of the manual. The clarity and accuracy of each chapter reflects their considerable effort and expertise. Marjorie Vining, of the Rhode Island School of Design, has produced the imaginative cover design, and James Adams, of The Lawrenceville School, has edited the text to ensure that it is both grammatically and stylistically correct. A very special thanks is due to Archie and Chris Browne and the staff at Browne Book Composition Inc. Their assistance in producing this text has been invaluable.

To all of these people I am deeply grateful. Thanks to their combined efforts we have produced what I believe to be one of the finest computer texts available today.

Bruce Presley

TABLE OF CONTENTS

INTRODUCTION

When discussing computers, it is convenient to divide the subject into two broad categories—hardware and software. Hardware refers to the computer itself and its peripheral devices—disk drives, printers, etc., whereas software refers to the programs or instructions which are entered into the computer to make it perform specific tasks. It is the purpose of this book to teach you how to program your computer. Therefore, it is a guide for producing software.

What is a computer?

A computer is a machine that accepts information, processes it according to specific instructions, and provides the results as new information. The computer differs from a simple calculator in several ways. It can store and move large quantities of data at very high speed and, even though it cannot think, it can make simple decisions and comparisons. For instance, the computer is capable of determining which of two numbers is larger or which of two names comes first alphabetically. Another major difference is that the computer can perform many varied tasks by changing its instructions. As you progress through this book, you will learn how to instruct the computer to perform increasingly sophisticated tasks by writing programs.

What is a program?

A program is a list of instructions that direct the computer in performing its operations. The computer never does any of its own thinking but merely repeats operations that it has been instructed to do. It is the program that instructs the computer as to which operations it will perform and in what sequence it will perform them.

The Development of the Computer

The modern computer evolved from simple calculating machines. Although for centuries simple arrangements of beads, wheels, and rods had been employed to perform addition and subtraction, the first large scale effort to design a machine capable of performing higher mathematical functions was the "Difference Engine" of Charles Babbage, first produced in 1820, which used a complicated system of gears and wheels. The British government later funded a project to make a large scale version of Babbage's machine, but the project was never successfully completed.

The first major breakthrough on the way to producing a modern computer occurred in the early nineteen forties when engineers started to use vacuum tubes to replace mechanical elements in calculating machines. This innovation resulted in the first fully electronic machine called the ENIAC (Electronic Numerical Integrator And Calculator), which was built at the University of Pennsylvania in 1946. Although considerably faster than its mechanical predecessors, the ENIAC had the major drawback of having its programs wired into the machine. Huge calculations might take only minutes to solve, but programming the machine could take many days.

John von Neumann proposed the idea of storing a program in a computer's memory rather than wiring it. This would eliminate the problem of rewiring the machine each time a new program was needed. The first computer to use the von Neumann concept was the EDSAC (Electronic Delay Storage Automatic Calculator) built at Cambridge University in 1949. Other computers quickly followed with increased speed and efficiency.

The next significant development occurred in the early nineteen sixties with the introduction of transistors into computers to replace the large and inefficient vacuum tubes. This innovation substantially decreased the size of a computer while increasing its speed and efficiency. But it is only within the last ten years with the development of integrated circuits to replace most of the computer's components that the computer has decreased both in size and in price to the point where it is now available to almost anyone desiring one. The computer you will program is considerably more powerful and efficient than the early computers built only twenty-five years ago, yet it costs only a tiny fraction of the early machines.

Computer Languages

The first modern computers used a group of commands called machine language. A command in machine language is just a group of specially coded numbers that the computer understands. This language is still used today within the computer, but few people ever program in it. Just as computers advanced, so did programming languages. Today there are hundreds of higher level programming languages with names like FORTRAN, BASIC, PASCAL, and PL/I. The computer translates the higher level programming language into machine language and then executes the program. The purpose of this manual is to present a comprehensive guide designed to teach the beginner the programming language called BASIC (Beginners All-purpose Symbolic Instruction Code), developed in the early nineteen sixties by John Kemeny and Tim Kurtz at Dartmouth College.

BASIC, as the name suggests, is well suited for the beginner. The commands are easy to remember because they describe the operations they represent. Like any programming language, BASIC has its specific commands and rules of syntax which determine the form of the commands submitted to the computer. In addition, the computer will only understand commands defined in the higher level language it is using. For instance, in the language BASIC the command PRINT will direct the computer to send information to the screen, but a similar command WRITE will not work at all. This similar command WRITE seems to have the same meaning as PRINT, but the computer will not understand it because WRITE is not defined in the language called BASIC.

This manual will teach you the specific commands and rules necessary to program your microcomputer in BASIC.

INTRODUCTION TO PROGRAMMING

Communicating with the computer requires a special language. The language described in this manual is Commodore BASIC, which consists of simple English words understood by the computer. In this chapter the user will be introduced to the most fundamental statements required to write a program on the Commodore computers.

Line Numbering

To establish the sequence of instructions for any given program, the programmer must assign numbers to each line within a program. This operation is essential because the computer reads instructions beginning with the lowest line number, then progresses to the next higher number and ends with the highest numbered line.

It is permissible to type the program lines out of order because the computer puts them back into their proper order. For example, line 20 may have been typed before line 10, but when the program is run, the computer automatically reads line 10 first. Such a system has the advantage of allowing any forgotten instructions, say between lines 10 and 20, to be entered later as lines 15, or 12, or 17, etc. For this reason it is best to number the lines of the program in units of ten (10, 20, 30, etc.) since this leaves nine possible line numbers that can later be inserted. It is also important to realize that the capital letter O cannot be used in place of zero.

An error in any instruction may be corrected at any time by depressing the RETURN key and retyping the entire line using the same line number. If two lines are given the same line number, the computer uses only the last one typed and erases the first. Typing only the line number followed by the RETURN key eliminates the line entirely. The highest line number allowed on the computer is 63999.

PRINT

There are two basic types of information which the computer can use: numbers and words. What distinguishes one from the other is that a number can be used in a mathematical calculation whereas a word cannot. The PRINT statement is used to print both numbers and words.

Program 1.1

This program uses the PRINT statement at each line to print the results shown below:

```
10 PRINT 5 * 3
20 PRINT 12 + 8
30 PRINT 7 / 2
40 PRINT "SAND"
50 PRINT "5*3"
RUN
 15
 20
 3.5
SAND
5*3

READY.
```

Line 10 instructs the computer to print the product of 5 and 3. Note than an asterisk (*) is used to indicate multiplication. Line 20 adds 12 and 8 whereas line 30 divides 7 by 2, with the slash (/) indicating division. At line 40 the word SAND is printed. When a word or any set of characters is printed, it must be enclosed within quotation marks. Line 50 prints "5*3" rather than 15 because quotation marks are used. Information enclosed in quotation marks is called a string; therefore, lines 40 and 50 contain strings.

The command RUN is typed after a program has been entered to execute the program, but it is not part of the program.

Typing Errors

An error in a program can be corrected in one of three ways. First, the program line can be retyped using the same line number. For example,

```
40 PRINT "ROCKS"

RUN
 15
 20
 3.5
ROCKS
5*3

READY.
```

changes only that part of the output which is produced by line 40. The second method of correcting an error involves the use of the key marked (DEL), which can be used if the error is detected while the line containing the error is being typed. Pressing the DEL key causes the computer to erase one character to the left of the cursor on the screen. The third method of error correction consists in the use of the built in editing feature. To learn how to use this feature refer to Appendix A.

LIST

The LIST command is used to print the program currently in the computer's memory. Typing LIST followed by striking the RETURN key will print the entire program; typing LIST followed by a line number and a RETURN will cause only that line to be printed. To list portions of a program, type LIST followed by the first and last line numbers of the portion desired, separating the two numbers with a hyphen (-). For example:

```
LIST
10 PRINT 5 * 3
20 PRINT 12 + 8
30 PRINT 7 / 2
40 PRINT "ROCKS"
50 PRINT "5*3"

READY.
```

```
LIST 50
50 PRINT "5*3"

READY.

LIST 20-40
20 PRINT 12 + 8
30 PRINT 7 / 2
40 PRINT "ROCKS"


READY.
```

NEW

Before entering a program into the computer the programmer should use the NEW command to clear the computer's memory. The use of this command insures that program lines from a previous program do not affect the new program:

```
LIST
10 PRINT 5 * 3
20 PRINT 12 + 8
30 PRINT 7 / 2
40 PRINT "ROCKS"
50 PRINT "5*3"

READY.

NEW

READY.

LIST

READY.
```

Observe that after the NEW command is used, a subsequent LIST shows that no program is currently in the computer's memory.

What is a variable?

One of the most useful properties of a computer is its ability to manipulate variables. A variable is a name which represents a value. On the computer, as in mathematics, X, Y, and Z are variables in the expression $Z = 10 + X + Y$ since they can assume many different values. The computer allows words as well as numbers to be represented by variables.

Numeric Variables

Numeric variables are represented by letters or by letters and numbers. A, D, A1, and B1 are all legal names for numeric variables. The computer allows the use of longer names for variables, but for the sake of simplicity only a single letter or a single letter followed by a single digit will be used in the early chapters of this manual.

To assign a value to a variable the following format is used:

$$\langle\text{variable name}\rangle = \langle\text{value}\rangle$$

For example, to assign X the value 5, the statement

$$20\ X = 5$$

could be used. Thus, when line 20 is reached, the variable X will be assigned the value 5. Internally, the computer stores values in memory locations. It is possible to compare these memory locations to boxes. In this case X is the name of the box, and 5 is the value in the box.

Variables can change in value as the name itself implies; however, it is important to realize that a variable can hold only one value at a time. Suppose a later statement such as

$$50\ X = 7$$

is entered. Then at line 50 the value of X will change from 5 to 7.

Thus, the value in the box named X is now 7:

The old value of X is lost and may not be retrieved again.

One numeric variable can be defined in terms of another in the computer, just as in algebra. For example, when the statement Y = 4∗X is executed by the computer, Y will be assigned the value 20 if X = 5, or Y will be assigned 28 if X = 7, and so on.

It is important to realize that the equal sign (=) is interpreted as "is assigned the value." Therefore, when assigning a value to a variable, the statement must be in the form: 'variable = value', *not* 'value = variable'. Therefore, the statement

$$50\ 7 = X$$

is invalid.

This program assigns values to the variables X and Y, the value of Y being dependent upon the value of X:

```
10 X = 12
20 Y = 3 * X + 5
30 PRINT X, Y
40 X = 15
50 PRINT X, Y
60 Y = 3 * X + 5
70 PRINT X, Y

RUN
 12              41
 15              41
 15              50

READY.
```

The value of X is originally 12 at line 10 and then becomes 15 at line 40. Y changes its value at line 60 because X changed at line 40. Note than when X and Y are printed at line 50, X is now 15, but Y is still 41 because the variable Y is not changed until it is reassigned at line 60. A comma is used in the PRINT statements at lines 30, 50, and 70 to allow the values of X and Y to be printed on a single line. On the Commodore-64 up to four variables can be printed on a single line of the display by the use of commas to separate each variable name; on the VIC-20 two variables can be printed on a single line.

String Variables

String variables are variables which are assigned values consisting of a sequence of characters. A character is a symbol found on the computer keyboard, which may be a letter, a number or any of the special graphic symbols.

String variable names are used in the same way as numeric variable names, except that a string variable name must end with a dollar sign ($). For example, A$, D$, A1$, C5$ all represent string variables. To assign characters to a string variable, the programmer must enclose the characters in quotation marks. For example, the statement

$$10 \ A\$ = \text{``HARRY''}$$

will assign "HARRY" to the string variable A$.

If the box analogy is used again, memory can be thought of as follows:

A$

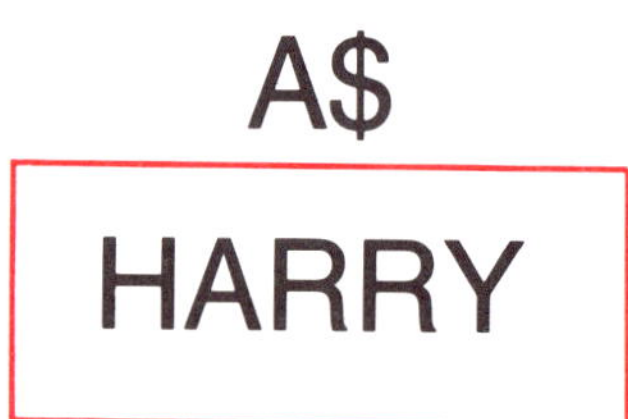

At some later point in a program it is possible to assign different characters to the same variable. For example, the statement

$$50 \; A\$ = \text{``SHERRY''}$$

will replace "HARRY" with "SHERRY." Thus, the box named A$ now contains "SHERRY."

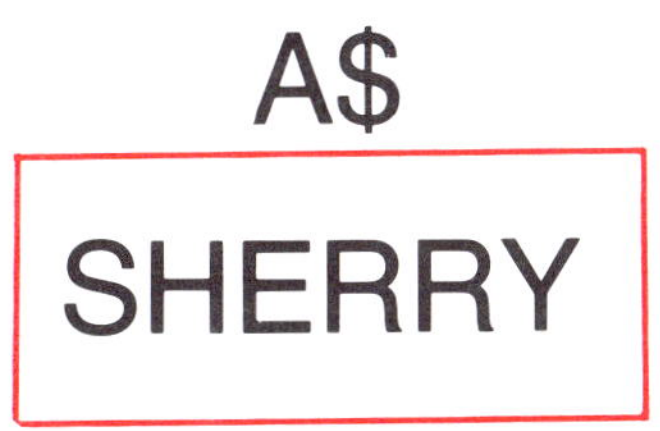

Program 1.3

This program assigns two different sets of characters to the string variable B$:

```
10 B$ = "GEORGE"
20 PRINT B$
30 B$ = "JUDY"
40 PRINT B$
50 PRINT "IT IS NICE TO SEE YOU, "; B$

RUN
GEORGE
JUDY
IT IS NICE TO SEE YOU, JUDY

READY.
```

Observe that at line 50 a sentence can be formed from two strings, the first of which in this case is not a variable.

Note that when a semicolon rather than a comma is used to separate items in a PRINT statement, the items will be printed next to each other on the same line.

Review

1. Write a program that will print the value of Y when X = 5 and Y = 5X + 7.

2. Write a program that will produce the following output by using string variables for "HARRY" and "SHERRY" but not for the other words.

```
RUN
HELLO, HARRY
SHERRY IS LOOKING FOR YOU.

READY.
```

A variable may be directly assigned its value not only by a statement such as X = 5 but also by a combination of READ and DATA statements.

Program 1.4

This program uses READ and DATA statements to assign values to numeric variables:

```
10 READ X, Y, Z
20 PRINT X + Y + Z
30 DATA 3, 2, 0.5

RUN
 5.5

READY.
```

The READ statement at line 10 instructs the computer to assign numbers to the variables X, Y, Z. The computer finds these numbers in the DATA statement at line 30 and assigns them in the order listed (X = 3, Y = 2, and Z = 0.5). If the program contains more than one DATA statement, the computer starts reading data from the first statement and continues sequentially through the remaining DATA statements.

In a DATA statement only numbers that are expressed in decimal or scientific form are acceptable. For example, the numbers .0032, -5.78, 1050, 2.9E5, and 4.76 E-12 are acceptable. The E stands for "times ten to the power" (e.g., 5.3 E3 = 5300 and 8.72 E−3 = .00872). However, data such as the arithmetic expressions 15/3, 3∗5, and 7+2 are not permitted in DATA statements since, unlike PRINT statements, DATA statements allow for no calculations.

GOTO

Suppose that a student has more than one set of values for the variables X, Y, Z in Program 1.4. To introduce the extra values, the student can retype line 30 as follows:

```
30 DATA 3, 2, 0.5, −7, 2.5, 1E2
RUN
 5.5

READY.
```

Note that only the first three numbers in the DATA statement are processed; the remaining numbers are not used. To overcome this problem, the programmer can retype line 30 each time a new set of data is to be used, but this involves unnecessary labor. A GOTO statement between lines 20 and 30 solves this problem by establishing a loop which allows line 10 to be used again.

```
LIST

10 READ X, Y, Z
20 PRINT X + Y + Z
25 GOTO 10
30 DATA 3, 2, 0.5, -7, 2.5, 1E2

READY.


RUN
 5.5
 95.5

?OUT OF DATA  ERROR IN 10
READY.
```

Observe that by typing the command LIST the computer prints the current version of Program 1.4 including the new line. Running Program 1.4 now allows all the data in line 30 to be processed.

Each time the computer reaches line 25 the GOTO statement causes the computer to return to line 10 where the next set of data is assigned to the variables. On the first pass through the loop X =3, Y = 2, Z = .5; on the second pass X = -7, Y = 2.5, Z = 1E2. However, on the third attempted pass, no additional data is available for assignment to the variables at line 10 and, therefore, an error message is printed.

The location of DATA statements within a program is not important, so they can be placed anywhere. Good programming style suggests that you place them at or near the end of a program. When the computer encounters a READ statement, it makes use of DATA statements regardless of their location. DATA statements may contain strings as well as numbers.

Program 1.5

This program reads the names and grades of three students and prints the averages of their grades:

```
5 PRINT "NAME", "AVERAGE"
10 READ N$, A, B, C, D
20 X = (A + B + C + D) / 4
30 PRINT N$, X
40 GOTO 10
50 DATA WATERS,83,95,86,80,KANE,56,97,66,89,MIKAN,61,83,42,90

RUN
NAME               AVERAGE
WATERS              86
KANE                77
MIKAN               69

?OUT OF DATA  ERROR IN 10
READY.
```

Examine this program carefully because it contains a number of important concepts. Line 5 produces the headings for the columns and is placed at the beginning of the program to insure that the headings will be printed only once. Line 10 assigns a student's name to the string variable N$ and the student's four grades to the numeric variables A, B, C, D. Unless the sequence of string variables and numeric variables in the READ statement is the same as the sequence of strings and numbers in the DATA statement, an error will occur. Line 40 returns the program to line 10 to read more data. What would happen if

$$40 \text{ GOTO } 5$$

were substituted for the current line 40?

Review

3. Write a program using READ, DATA statements to evaluate Y where $Y = 3X + 5$ and $X = 3$, 5, 12, 17, 8.

4. Write a program containing the DATA line from Program 1.5 which prints only the name and first grade of each student.

```
RUN
NAME                FIRST GRADE
WATERS                 83
KANE                   56
MIKAN                  61

?OUT OF DATA  ERROR IN 10
READY.
```

INPUT

In many instances it is preferable to introduce data from the keyboard rather than place it in a DATA statement. To do this an INPUT statement is used in place of the READ, DATA statements. When an INPUT statement is executed, the computer prints a question mark (?) and then waits for data to be entered.

Program 1.6

Data entered from the keyboard is used to assign a value to the variable X in the following program:

```
10 INPUT X
20 PRINT 5 * X * X + 3
30 GOTO 10
```

```
RUN
? 3
 48
? 6
 183
? 2
 23
?
```

The GOTO statement at line 30 creates a loop which will continue to run until it is halted. Ordinarily a program may be halted by pressing the STOP key; however, when a program is waiting for input from the keyboard, the computer must be reset in order to halt it. To reset the computer, press the RESTORE key while depressing the STOP key. This operation halts the run of the program, clears the screen and causes the computer to print READY.

Program 1.7

This program is a revision of Program 1.5. Here a student is asked for his or her name and four grades. The computer then prints the name and grade average. It is possible to have the INPUT statement print a question or a remark by enclosing the words to be printed in quotation marks followed by a semicolon and the variable names. Also, note that more than one variable can be entered by using a single INPUT statement:

```
10 INPUT "WHAT IS YOUR NAME"; N$
20 INPUT "WHAT ARE YOUR GRADES"; A, B, C, D
30 X = (A + B + C + D) / 4
40 PRINT N$, X
50 GOTO 10

RUN
WHAT IS YOUR NAME? TED
WHAT ARE YOUR GRADES?  87, 54, 76, 95
TED             78
WHAT IS YOUR NAME? JOHN
WHAT ARE YOUR GRADES?  78, 76, 47, 84
JOHN            81.25
WHAT IS YOUR NAME? SHERRY
WHAT ARE YOUR GRADES?  100, 95, 31, 60
SHERRY          71.5
WHAT IS YOUR NAME?
```

PRINT Formatting

There are a number of ways in which output can be formatted by the use of punctuation. A few of the more important uses of punctuation are demonstrated by the following program:

Program 1.8

The Commodore-64 is capable of printing 40 characters on a single line. This line is divided into four printing zones consisting of 10 characters each. When commas are used in a PRINT statement, the output is printed in successive zones.

```
5 PRINT "N A M E", "G R A D E S", "AVERAGE"
10 READ N$, A, B, C
20 X = (A + B + C) / 3
30 PRINT
40 PRINT N$, A; B; C, X
50 GOTO 10
60 DATA HAYES,90,87,93, GRAHAM,74,98,83, WATSON,53,76,18

RUN
N A M E           G R A D E S            AVERAGE

HAYES             90  87  93             90

GRAHAM            74  98  83             85

WATSON            53  76  18             49
?OUT OF DATA  ERROR IN 10
READY.
```

Note the output produced by line 5. Each word begins at the beginning of one of the zones because commas have been used to separate the words. The PRINT at line 30 is used to place a blank line between each of the printed lines. When printing a number, the computer places a single space in front of and behind the number. If the number is negative, the space in front is occupied by the minus $(-)$ sign.

When semicolons (;) are used in place of commas (as in line 40), the output of each variable begins in the next space following the last variable printed.

Note also that for the VIC-20 only 22 characters per line can be printed. This line is divided into 2 print zones consisting of 11 characters each.

Program 1.9

This program demonstrates the difference between commas and semicolons used in a PRINT statement:

```
10 PRINT "ZONE 1", "ZONE 2", "ZONE 3", "ZONE 4"
20 X = -14
30 PRINT "**"; X; "**"
40 T = 42
50 PRINT "**"; T; "**"
60 A$ = "86"
70 PRINT "**"; A$; "**"
80 PRINT X; T; A$; 99
```

```
RUN
ZONE 1      ZONE 2      ZONE 3      ZONE 4
**-14 **
** 42 **
**86**
-14   42 86 99

READY.
```

Note how the values -14 and 42 were printed by lines 30 and 50, respectively. Line 70 shows that strings are not printed with a leading or trailing space.

PRINT TAB

The PRINT TAB statement provides an easy way to format output and allows the programmer to begin portions of the printout at specified locations. The left edge of the Commodore-64 screen is TAB(0), and the right edge of the screen is TAB(39). The left edge of the VIC-20 is TAB(0), and the right edge is TAB(21). The printing of information at TAB positions 3, 11 and 17 is accomplished in the following manner:

```
10 PRINT TAB(3); "THIS"; TAB(11); "IS"; TAB(17); "TAB"

RUN
   THIS     IS     TAB

READY.
```

It is important to use semicolons in each instance after the TAB parentheses.

Program 1.10

The substitution of variables for the numbers in the TAB parentheses is permissible provided these variables have previously been assigned values.

```
10 READ X, Y, Z
20 PRINT TAB(X); "THIS"; TAB(Y); "IS"; TAB(Z); "TAB"
30 DATA 3, 11, 17
RUN
   THIS     IS     TAB

READY.
```

Program 1.11

This program draws a triangle on the display screen:

```
10 PRINT TAB(10); "*******"
20 PRINT TAB(11); "*"; TAB(16); "*"
30 PRINT TAB(12); "*"; TAB(16); "*"
40 PRINT TAB(13); "*"; TAB(16); "*"
50 PRINT TAB(14); "*"; TAB(16); "*"
60 PRINT TAB(16); "*"

RUN
         *******
          *     *
           *    *
            *   *
             *  *
                *

READY.
```

The PRINT TAB statement moves the cursor to the right only, never to the left. If a TAB position is specified which is to the left of the current TAB position, the cursor will remain where it is and the printing will proceed from there.

```
10 PRINT TAB(10); "##"; TAB(15); "##"
20 PRINT TAB(15); "##"; TAB(10); "##"

RUN
         ##    ##
               ####

READY.
```

Review

5. Write a program in which you input a value of X and have the computer calculate 5*X and X/5. The printout should appear exactly as shown below:

```
RUN
WHAT IS X? 12
5*X = 60
X/5 = 2.4
WHAT IS X? 20
5*X = 100
X/5 = 4
WHAT IS X? 64
5*X = 320
X/5 = 12.8
WHAT IS X?
```

6. Write a program which allows you to input your name and the name of a friend and then produces the printout as follows:

```
RUN
WHAT  IS  YOUR  NAME?  BRUCE
WHAT  IS  YOUR  FRIEND'S  NAME?  JUDY
JUDY  IS  A  FRIEND  OF  BRUCE

WHAT  IS  YOUR  NAME?  DON
WHAT  IS  YOUR  FRIEND'S  NAME?  SHERRY
SHERRY  IS  A  FRIEND  OF  DON

WHAT  IS  YOUR  NAME?
```

Immediate Mode

The computer may perform simple tasks using the immediate mode rather than a program. An immediate mode instruction is typed without a line number. When the computer receives a command without a line number, it recognizes that the command is not part of a program but is to be executed immediately. The following are examples of immediate mode statements:

```
PRINT (3*5) + 4
 19

READY.
PRINT 7/9
 .777777778

READY.
A = 5

READY.
B = 2

READY.
PRINT A + B + 4
 11

READY.
A$ = "BETTY"

READY.
PRINT A$; " BOO"
BETTY BOO

READY.
```

Note that a RUN command was not used in any of the preceding examples. Most commands are permissible in the immediate mode with the notable exception of the INPUT statement. In performing most tasks it is best to write complete programs and to reserve the use of immediate mode for simple calculations.

The REM statement is used in the body of a program to allow the programmer to introduce explanatory remarks. Everything to the right of a REM statement is ignored by the computer when the program is run. For example,

30 REM CALCULATE AREA OF CIRCLE

will be printed only when the program is listed. Remarks placed strategically within a program are useful in explaining the function of various parts of the program.

Program 1.12

This program incorporates the major topics covered in this chapter, which the reader should now be familiar with, and demonstrates how they might be used together in a single program.

```
10 PRINT "HOW FAR OVER IS EACH ITEM"
20 INPUT "TO BE PRINTED";T
30 READ A$
40   PRINT TAB(T);A$
50 GOTO 30
60 DATA THIS,IS,A,SAMPLE,OF,THE
70 DATA MATERIAL,IN,CHAPTER,ONE

RUN
HOW FAR OVER IS EACH ITEM
TO BE PRINTED? 7
       THIS
       IS
       A
       SAMPLE
       OF
       THE
       MATERIAL
       IN
       CHAPTER
       ONE

?OUT OF DATA  ERROR IN 30
READY.
```

EXERCISES

1. Write a program which prints the following:

```
RUN
A
  B
    C
ABCD

READY.
```

2. Write a program which makes the following calculations. Check the results by hand computation:

   (a) $8 * (19 - 4)$
   (b) $1 * 2 + 2 * 3 + 3 * 4 + 4 * 5$
   (c) $1 + 1 / 10 + 1 / 100$
   (d) $10 - 20 + 30 - 40 + 50 - 60$

3. What is the exact output for the following program?

```
10 A = 3
20 PRINT "THE VALUE OF B"
30 B = A + 4*4
40 PRINT B
```

4. How many lines of output does the following program produce before an error message appears indicating "?OUT OF DATA ERROR IN 10"?

```
10 READ A,B,C
20 PRINT (A+B+C)/3
30 GOTO 10
40 DATA 11,32,42,14,25,36,47
50 DATA 58,39,50,61,22,83,94
```

5. Peter Goodpepper has loused up once again. Here is a program of his which he says "mysteriously doesn't work." Give Peter a hand and correct this monstrosity for him so that the output looks like the following:

```
THE SUM IS 20
THE SUM IS 14
?OUT OF DATA ERROR IN 10
```

```
10 READ A B
20 PRINT THE SUM IS  A+B
30 GOTO 12
40 DATA 12,8,3*5,5
```

6. Write the output and check by running the program.

```
10 READ A$
20 PRINT A$
30 GOTO 10
40 DATA S,I,X!," 6",6
```

7. Write a program in which the price (P) in cents of a loaf of bread and the number (N) of loaves bought are entered from the keyboard. The total spent for bread is to be printed in dollars and cents.

8. Write a program which will enter your weight (W) in pounds and height (H) in inches and which then will print the quotient W/H followed by the words "POUNDS PER INCH."

9. Using an INPUT statement, write a program which produces the following output:

```
RUN
? 2,4
X = 2        Y = 4       X*Y = 8
? -8,70
X =-8        Y = 70      X*Y =-560
?
```

10. Predict the output of the following program. Check the answer by running the program:

```
10 P$ = "TOTAL PRICE"
20 P = .89
30 PRINT P$;" = $0";P
```

11. Predict the output and check by running the program:

```
10 READ A,B,C,D
20 PRINT A,B
30 PRINT C;"   ";D
40 DATA 3E2,510,3E-1,.51
```

12. Use immediate mode to print the following numbers:

(a) .05 (b) .005
(c) 123456789 (d) 1234567890
(e) −.065 (f) 4.62E5
(g) .086E-3 (h) −4,900

13. Self-proclaimed computer whiz Cecil Robert Clancy has typed the following gibberish in the immediate mode and has challenged anyone to guess the output correctly before he or she presses the RETURN key. Put Cecil in his place and correctly predict the answer.

```
PRINT "AAA";111,222;"AAA","333";"    ";16-3*2
```

14. Have the computer produce the following output:

```
RUN
12345678901234567890
*         9        ?

READY.
```

15. What is the exact output for the following program?

```
10 A$ = "ABCD"
20 B$ = "XYZ"
30 F = 7
40 G = -4
50 PRINT A$;B$
60 PRINT A$;F
70 PRINT F;B$
80 PRINT G;B$
```

16. Write a program to evaluate each of the following expressions for A = 10 and B = 7:

$$(7A + 10B)/2AB \qquad\qquad (1/2)A/(A-B)$$

17. In the first week of the season the cross country team ran the following number of miles each day: 2, 3, 4, 3, 5. Write a program to calculate and print the total mileage for the week.

18. A piece of pizza normally contains about 375 calories. A boy jogging one mile uses about 100 calories. Write a program that asks him how many pieces he wishes to eat and then tells him how far he must run to burn up the calories he will consume.

```
RUN
HOW MANY PIECES DID YOU EAT? 4
YOU MUST RUN 15 MILES.

READY.
```

19. Have the computer evaluate the expression $12x + 7y$ for the following data:

x	3	7	12
y	2	9	-4

20. Write a program that will allow a string A$ to be entered. Then have the computer print the string followed by " KEEPS THE DOCTOR AWAY."

21. Using an INPUT statement, write a program that will compute the volume of a room given its length, width, and height.

22. Write a program to compute the areas (cm^2) of circles with radii 5.0 cm., 3.0 cm. and 8.0 cm. Have the output in the form "AREA OF CIRCLE=" with two spaces between each of the printed lines.

23. Just as three-dimensional objects are measured by volume, so four-dimensional objects are measured by tesseracts. Have your program ask for the dimensions of a four-dimensional object (height, width, length, and "presence") and print the object's tesseract.

24. With the equation $E = MC^2$, Einstein predicted that energy could be produced from matter. If the average human hair weighs a tenth of a gram and the town of Woodsylvania uses 2×10^{11} units of energy in a day, find out how many hairs from Einstein's head would be required to supply the town for a day ($C = 3 \times 10^{10}$).

25. Use the computer to calculate your library fines. Enter the number of books you have borrowed and how many days late they are. Have the computer print the amount of your fine if you are charged 10¢ per day per book.

26. The perimeter of a triangle is equal to the sum of the lengths of the three sides of the triangle. The semiperimeter is one-half of the perimeter. A triangle has sides of lengths 13 cm, 8 cm, 11 cm. A second triangle has sides of 21 ft, 16 ft, 12 ft. Write a program that reads these measurements from a DATA statement and then prints the semiperimeter of each triangle, showing the correct units. The output should look like this:

SEMIPERIMETER OF FIRST TRIANGLE 16 CM.

SEMIPERIMETER OF SECOND TRIANGLE 24.5 FT.

27. Professional athletes have succeeded in making staggering sums of money through careful negotiations. Of course, the real winner is Uncle Sam, who does not negotiate at all. Write a program which asks for a player's name and salary and then prints the player's name, take-home salary and taxes if the tax rate for his income bracket is 44%

```
RUN
WHAT IS THE PLAYER'S NAME?
RUN
WHAT IS THE PLAYER'S NAME? JUGGIE RACKSON
WHAT IS JUGGIE RACKSON'S WAGE 150000
JUGGIE RACKSON WOULD KEEP $ 84000
HE WOULD PAY $ 66000 IN TAXES.

READY.
RUN
WHAT IS THE PLAYER'S NAME? BABE RUTH
WHAT IS BABE RUTH'S WAGE 42000
BABE RUTH WOULD KEEP $ 23520
HE WOULD PAY $ 18480 IN TAXES.

READY.
```

28. Sale prices are often deceptive. Write a program to determine the original price of an item, given the sale price and the discount rate.

```
RUN
SALE PRICE? 3.78
DISCOUNT RATE? 10
THE ORIGINAL PRICE WAS $ 4.2

READY.
```

29. The area of a triangle can be found by multiplying one-half times the length of the base times the length of the altitude (A — .5 * base * height). Write a program that allows the user to enter from the keyboard the base and altitude of a triangle and then skips a line before printing out the area of the triangle.

```
RUN
WHAT IS THE BASE? 10
WHAT IS THE ALTITUDE? 5

THE AREA IS 25

READY.
```

30. A state has a 7 percent sales tax. Write a program that will allow you to INPUT the names and prices (before taxes) of different items found in a department store and then print the item, tax, and the price of the item including tax.

```
RUN
ITEM'S NAME? COAT
WHAT IS ITS PRICE? 65
COAT HAS A TAX OF $ 4.55 AND COSTS $ 69.55
ITEM'S NAME? TENNIS RACKET
WHAT IS ITS PRICE? 23
TENNIS RACKET HAS A TAX OF $ 1.61 AND COSTS $ 24.61
ITEM'S NAME?
```

31. In an election in Grime City candidate Sloth ran against candidate Graft for mayor. Below is a listing of the number of votes each candidate received in each ward. What total vote did each candidate receive? What percentage of the total vote did each candidate receive?

Candidate	Sloth	Graft
Ward 1	528	210
2	313	721
3	1003	822
4	413	1107
5	516	1700

32. A Susan B. Anthony dollar of diameter 2.6 centimeters rests on a square postage stamp as shown. Have the computer find the area in square centimeters of the part of the stamp not covered by the coin.

33. Given the assumption that you sleep a healthy 8 hours a night, have the computer print the number of hours of your life which you have spent sleeping. Input the date of your birth and today's date in numeric form (e.g., 6, 4, 62). Use 365 days in each year and 30 days in a month.

34. Using an INPUT statement, write a program which averages each of the following sets of numbers: (2, 7, 15, 13); (8, 5, 2, 3); (12, 19, 4); (15, 7, 19, 24, 37). Note that the sets do not contain the same number of elements.

DECISIONS AND LOOPS

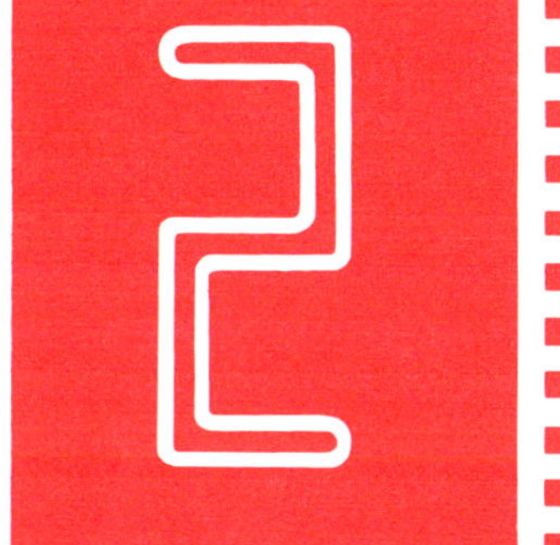

IF...THEN
AND OR
END
FOR...TO
STEP
NEXT
RESTORE
IF...THEN
AND OR
END
FOR...TO
STEP
NEXT
RESTORE
IF...THEN
AND OR
END
FOR...TO
STEP
NEXT
RESTORE
IF...THEN
AND OR
END
FOR...TO
STEP
NEXT
RESTORE

The statements presented in Chapter 1 allow the user to perform routine calculations and to print numbers or strings in different formats. The computer executes routine calculations according to specific rules of precedence called Order of Operations. The higher capabilities of a computer are not called upon until the computer is used to make decisions or to carry out a process many times. This chapter will first outline the Order of Operations and then present the conditional statement IF . . . THEN, which allows the computer to make simple decisions. Finally this chapter will introduce the statements FOR . . . TO . . . STEP, NEXT, which allow loops to be established in a convenient manner.

Order of Operations

What is the value of 2 + 20/4? Should the 2 be added first to the 20 and then the division performed afterward, or should the 20 first be divided by 4 and then be increased by 2? The latter procedure is correct because division is carried out before addition. When parentheses are used, the operations in the innermost parentheses are completed first. For example, (2 + 20)/4 = 22/4 = 5.5.

The computer performs arithmetic operations in the same order as that employed by mathematicians. Quantities in parentheses are evaluated first (starting from the innermost), followed by raising to a power, then by multiplication and division, and finally by addition and subtraction. Operations of equal priority are carried out from left to right. For example:

6/3*2	The result is 4. Although the answer might seem to be 6/6 = 1, the computer starts at the left and performs the division first and then the result of the division is multiplied by 2.
3*(5 + 6)	The result is 33. The computer first adds 5 and 6 and then multiplies the sum by 3.
5 + (3*(6/2))	The result is 14. The computer first divides 6 by 2, the operation within the innermost parentheses. Next it multiplies that result by 3 and finally adds 5.
12 + 4/0	The result is an error message. The computer does not divide by zero.
2↑3↑2	The result is 64, just as it would be for (2↑3)↑2. Again, the left-to-right rule is in operation. Remember that ↑ is used to raise to a power, and appears on the screen as an inverted V.

IF . . . THEN

The statements introduced in Chapter One (GOTO, PRINT, etc.) are called unconditional because the computer will always execute them. In contrast, the IF . . . THEN statement is conditional because the action taken depends upon whether the condition is found to be true.

The simplest form of the IF . . . THEN statement is:

IF <condition> THEN <line number>

The 'condition' portion of the statement compares two quantities which must be separated by one of the symbols indicated in the table below:

SYMBOL	MEANING
$=$	equal to
$>$	greater than
$<$	less than
$>=$	greater than or equal to
$<=$	less than or equal to
$<>$	not equal to

An example of an IF . . . THEN statement is:

20 IF $X > 5$ THEN 60

When the condition in line 20 (X is greater than 5) is true, the computer jumps to line 60. When the condition is false, as when X is less than or equal to 5, the computer proceeds to the next line of the program.

Program 2.1

This program determines whether the value entered for X is the solution to the equation $2X - 18 = 0$. The computer decides which of two messages is to be printed:

```
10  INPUT X
20  IF 2*X-18=0 THEN 50
30  PRINT X;"IS NOT THE SOLUTION"
40  GOTO 10
50  PRINT X;"IS THE SOLUTION"

RUN
? 15
  15 IS NOT THE SOLUTION
? 4
  4 IS NOT THE SOLUTION
? 9
  9 IS THE SOLUTION

READY.
```

Note the necessity of line 40. Without it, the program would print "IS THE SOLUTION" even when the solution was not X. The line number sequence that the computer follows when X is the solution is 10, 20, 50; and when X is not the solution, it follows the line number sequence 10, 20, 30, 40, 10.

The IF . . . THEN statement can be used to compare two strings. Here the symbols greater than ($>$), less than ($<$), equal to ($=$), etc., now refer to an alphabetical rather than a numerical order.

Program 2.2

The following program determines if A$ is alphabetically before, the same, or after B$:

```
10 PRINT
20 INPUT "ENTER TWO STRINGS";A$,B$
30 IF A$=B$ THEN 70
40 IF A$>B$ THEN 90
50 PRINT A$; " IS BEFORE ";B$
60 GOTO 10
70 PRINT A$; " IS EQUIVALENT TO ";B$
80 GOTO 10
90 PRINT A$ " IS AFTER ";B$
100 GOTO 10

RUN

ENTER TWO STRINGS? VIC,COM
VIC IS AFTER COM

ENTER TWO STRINGS? A,C
A IS BEFORE C

ENTER TWO STRINGS? SYSTEM,SYSTEM
SYSTEM IS EQUIVALENT TO SYSTEM

ENTER TWO STRINGS?
```

Line 30 directs the computer to line 70 if A$ and B$ are equivalent. Line 40 causes a jump to line 90 if A$ comes after B$ in the alphabet. Line 50 is reached only if both conditions in lines 30 and 40 fail and, therefore, A$ comes before B$ in the alphabet.

Extended Use of the IF . . . THEN Statement, Multiple Statement Lines

In the preceding section the simplest form of the IF . . . THEN statement was given as:

$$IF\ <condition>\ THEN\ <line\ number>$$

More flexible usage of IF . . . THEN permits a statement instead of a line number to follow the word THEN. This means that the statement after the condition will be executed only if the condition is true. The form is:

IF $<$condition$>$ THEN $<$statement$>$

The following examples illustrate legal use of the IF . . . THEN statement:

IF X $< >$ 0 THEN PRINT X
IF Z$>$1 THEN PRINT ''IT IS LARGER THAN ONE''
IF R$< =$ 0 THEN R $=$ X $+$ 2

The computer allows a series of statements to be entered on a single program line if they are separated from each other by colons (:). Multiple statement lines have special meaning when used with IF . . . THEN. *All* statements following THEN will be executed when the condition following IF is true. *No* statements following THEN will be executed when the condition is false. For example,

60 IF X $=$ 5 THEN PRINT ''GOOD'': GOTO 80

has two statements on one line. If the condition X $=$ 5 is true, then "GOOD" will be printed and program control will be passed to line 80. If the condition is false, neither of these actions is taken. Instead, the program will continue on to the line following line 60. This means either the PRINT "GOOD" and the GOTO 80 statements are executed, or neither is executed. Whichever of the two occurs depends upon whether the condition X $=$ 5 is true.

Program 2.3

Program 2.1 can be shortened by using multiple statement techniques:

```
10  INPUT X
20  IF 2*X-18=0 THEN PRINT X;"IS THE SOLUTION": GOTO 10
30  PRINT X;"IS NOT THE SOLUTION": GOTO 10

RUN
? 15
 15 IS NOT THE SOLUTION
? 2
 2 IS NOT THE SOLUTION
? 9
 9 IS THE SOLUTION
?
```

Note that the statement GOTO 10 in line 20 is executed *only* if the condition in the IF . . . THEN statement is true. Otherwise the program proceeds to line 30. The statement GOTO 10 in line 30 will always be executed if line 30 is reached since it is not preceded by an IF . . . THEN statement on the same line.

Review

1. Allow two numbers, A and B, to be entered in the computer and then print the two numbers in descending order.

2. Allow two names to be entered and then printed in alphabetical order.

```
RUN
ENTER TWO LAST NAMES? PATRICK,GREER
GREER
PATRICK
ENTER TWO LAST NAMES?
```

AND, OR

The statement modifiers AND and OR can be used in the IF ... THEN statement when more than one condition is to be considered. The statement

$$20 \text{ IF } X > 5 \text{ AND } Y = 3 \text{ THEN } 50$$

will cause a transfer to line 50 only if *both* conditions are true. On the other hand, the statement

$$20 \text{ IF } X > 5 \text{ OR } Y = 3 \text{ THEN } 50$$

will cause program control to be transferred to line 50 if *either or both* conditions are true.

Program 2.4

The following program uses the OR modifier and reviews much of what has been presented:

```
10 INPUT "WHO ARE YOU";N$
20 IF N$="JAMES BOND" OR N$="007" THEN 50
30 PRINT "THIS MISSION IS NOT MEANT FOR YOU!"
40 PRINT : GOTO 10
50 PRINT "THESE ORDERS ARE FOR YOUR EYES ONLY!"
60 INPUT "ARE YOU ALONE";A$
70 IF A$<>"YES" THEN PRINT "TRY LATER." : GOTO 10
80 PRINT : PRINT "DR. SHIVAGO HAS ESCAPED! YOUR"
90 PRINT "MISSION, SHOULD YOU DECIDE TO ACCEPT"
100 PRINT "IT, IS TO SEEK OUT SHIVAGO AND"
110 PRINT "RETURN HIM TO THE SPANDAU PRISON"
```

```
RUN
WHO ARE YOU? BRAVE SIR ROBIN
THIS MISSION IS NOT MEANT FOR YOU!

WHO ARE YOU? JAMES BOND
THESE ORDERS ARE FOR YOUR EYES ONLY!
ARE YOU ALONE? NO
TRY LATER.
WHO ARE YOU? 007
THESE ORDERS ARE FOR YOUR EYES ONLY!
ARE YOU ALONE? YES

DR. SHIVAGO HAS ESCAPED! YOUR
MISSION, SHOULD YOU DECIDE TO ACCEPT
IT, IS TO SEEK OUT SHIVAGO AND
RETURN HIM TO THE SPANDAU PRISON

READY.
```

Line 10 asks the user for a name. The name entered as N\$ is compared with the two names at line 20. If N\$ is either 'JAMES BOND' or '007', then the program skips to line 50. Otherwise, a message is printed by line 30 and the program returns to line 10. At line 50 a warning message is printed whereas line 60 inquires whether Mr. Bond is alone. Note that in line 70 any response other than 'YES' will cause the program to print 'TRY LATER' and jump back to line 10. Otherwise, the mission description is printed by lines 80 through 110.

END

The END statement is used to terminate the run of a program. For example,

$$80 \text{ END}$$

will cause the run of a program to stop when line 80 is reached. It is possible to place END statements at more than one location within a program, including insertion in an IF ... THEN statement.

Program 2.5

This program uses the END statement to terminate program execution when the name KERMIT is input:

```
10 INPUT "WHAT IS YOUR NAME";N$
20 IF N$="KERMIT" THEN END
30 PRINT "IT'S GOOD TO MEET YOU, ";N$
40 PRINT : GOTO 10

RUN
WHAT IS YOUR NAME? CYNTHIA
IT'S GOOD TO MEET YOU, CYNTHIA

WHAT IS YOUR NAME? KERMIT

READY.
```

3. Write a program that will allow a number N to be entered. If the number is between 25 and 112, then the computer should indicate this; otherwise, the computer should say that the number is out of range.

```
RUN
ENTER A NUMBER? 14
  14 IS OUT OF RANGE
ENTER A NUMBER? 54
  54 IS BETWEEN 25 AND 112
ENTER A NUMBER? 112
  112 IS OUT OF RANGE
ENTER A NUMBER?
```

4. Write a program in which the user enters a string N$. If it comes alphabetically before Garbage or after Trash, then have the computer print "YES"; otherwise have it print "NO".

FOR ... TO ... STEP, NEXT

The FOR ... TO ... STEP, NEXT statements provide a simple way of establishing a loop. A loop is a section of a program designed to be executed repeatedly. The FOR ... TO ... STEP, NEXT loops provide a method for generating a large sequence of numbers in a case where each number in the sequence differs from its predecessor by a constant amount. The general form of the FOR ... TO ... STEP, NEXT statement is:

```
    FOR <variable> = <starting value> TO <ending value> STEP <increment>
        .
        .
        .
    NEXT <variable>
```

Note that the 'variable' after FOR and NEXT must be the same. A string variable cannot be used in FOR ... NEXT loop. The STEP portion may be omitted if the increment equals +1.
For example:

```
    10 FOR X = 2 TO 6
        .
        .
        .
    40 NEXT X
```

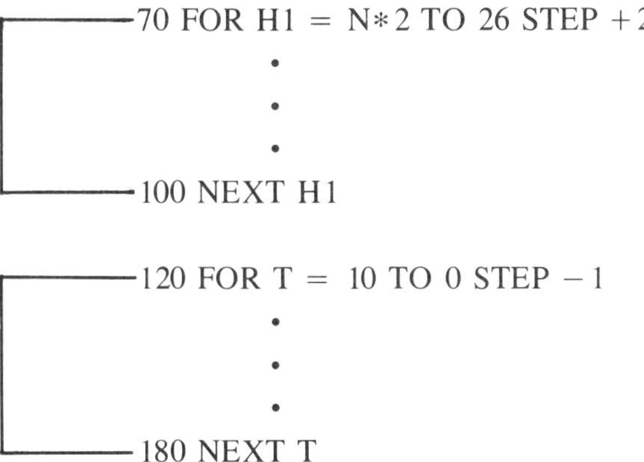

Note that a loop is formed by the FOR ... TO ... STEP and NEXT statements. In the example,

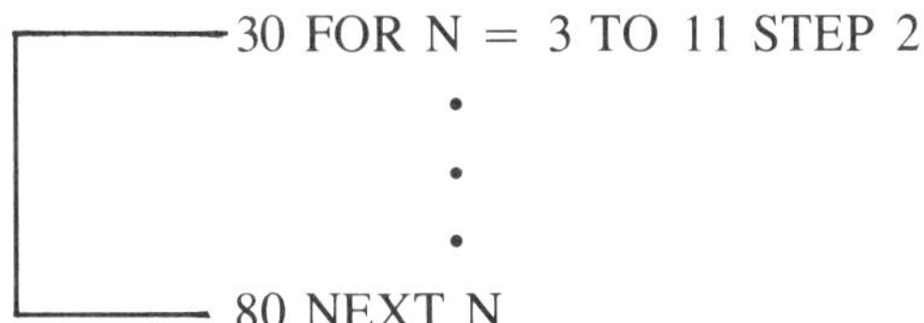

the variable N starts at line 30 with a value of 3. N retains the value of 3 until the NEXT N statement is encountered at line 80. At this point N is increased by the STEP value. In this example N changes from 3 to 5 to 7, etc. All the statements in the lines occurring between lines 30 and 80 are executed in sequence during each consecutive pass through the loop. The program continues to return from line 80 to the line immediately following line 30 until N exceeds the specified limit of 11. At this point the program exits from the loop and moves on to the line following 80.

Program 2.6

This program uses READ, DATA, whereas Program 2.7 uses a FOR ... TO ... STEP, NEXT loop to print all integers between 10 and 30, inclusive.

```
10  READ N
20  PRINT N;
30  GOTO 10
40  PRINT "   DONE"
50  DATA 10,11,12,13,14,15,16,17,18
60  DATA 19,20,21,22,23,24,25,26,27
70  DATA 28,29,30

RUN
  10   11   12   13   14   15   16   17   18   19
  20   21   22   23   24   25   26   27   28   29
  30
?OUT OF DATA  ERROR IN 10
READY.
```

Program 2.7

```
10 FOR N = 10 TO 30
20    PRINT N;
30 NEXT N
40 PRINT "   DONE"

RUN
 10   11   12   13   14   15   16   17   18   19
 20   21   22   23   24   25   26   27   28   29
 30     DONE

READY.
```

Program 2.6 continues to read data until all of it is exhausted. Since N is incremented by 1, the STEP portion is omitted. Program 2.7 generates all of the values of N between 10 and 30. Note that the loop in Program 2.7 is completed by a NEXT statement, not a GOTO statement. Therefore, unlike Program 2.6, Program 2.7 can proceed to line 40.

Indentation is used in program 2.7 to clarify the contents and boundaries of the FOR . . . NEXT loop. This practice is recommended since it clarifies the program's structure. After typing the line number you can indent the contents of the line by typing the letter I while depressing the Commodore (C=) key. This will cause a graphic character to appear, which may be ignored since it will not appear when the program is listed. The space bar may now be used to indent the line to the desired position.

Program 2.8

This program finds solutions to the compound condition $5X + 3 < 100$ and $2X^2 - 1 > 50$ and tests all odd integers from 1 to 25:

```
10 FOR X = 1 TO 25 STEP 2
20    IF 5*X+3<100 AND 2*X^2-1>50 THEN PRINT X;
30 NEXT X
40 PRINT "   DONE"
50 END

RUN
 7   9   11   13   15   17   19     DONE

READY.
```

Note that the symbol ($\uparrow$) is used to denote 'raised to the power' (e.g., $X \uparrow 2$ means $X*X$). Lines 10 and 30 create a loop for testing the conditions located at line 20. The loop starts at line 10 with $X = 1$. Each time the program reaches the NEXT X statement at line 30, X is incremented by the STEP value, which is 2. The program will then return to line 20 unless the value of the loop variable X has exceeded its maximum value of 25, at which point the loop will be exited. Remember that a FOR loop is not completed by a GOTO statement but by a NEXT statement.

Program 2.9

The following program illustrates the use of a negative STEP value. The integers from 1 to 10 are printed in descending order:

```
10 FOR X = 10 TO 1 STEP -1
20   PRINT X;
30 NEXT X
40 PRINT
50 END

RUN
 10  9  8  7  6  5  4  3  2  1

READY.
```

Review

5. Write a program that prints the integers between 1 and 25, inclusive.

6. Using a FOR ... TO ... STEP, NEXT loop, have the computer print the following:

```
RUN
 20   18   16   14   12   10

READY.
```

7. Write a program that will allow a number N to be entered. Using N as a STEP value, print numbers between 8 and 20.

```
RUN
STEP VALUE? 2
 8   10   12   14   16   18   20

READY.
```

RESTORE

At times the user might find it desirable to employ a set of data more than once. The RESTORE statement makes it possible to read data again starting at the beginning of the data. For example,

40 RESTORE

causes the next READ statement encountered to read data starting with the first item in the first DATA statement.

Program 2.10

This program searches DATA statements for a specific student and then prints the student's grades. It employs the RESTORE statement so that each time a student's name is entered a searching process starts at the beginning of the first DATA statement. How would the program run if line 20 were deleted?

```
5 PRINT
10 INPUT "NAME"; B$
20 RESTORE
30 FOR P = 1 TO 6
40   READ N$,A,B,C,D
50    IF N$=B$ THEN 80
60 NEXT P
70 PRINT "STUDENT ";B$;" NOT FOUND" : GOTO 5
80 PRINT N$;" HAS THE FOLLOWING GRADES:"
90 PRINT A;B;C;D
100 GOTO 5
110 DATA WATERS,83,75,92,80,TRANTER,74,81,92,76
120 DATA SAVAGE,72,81,63,60,RICKARD,99,84,92,87
130 DATA MULRYAN,100,93,82,89,LEMONE,94,93,85,94
140 END

RUN

NAME? RICKARD
RICKARD HAS THE FOLLOWING GRADES:
 99  84  92  87

NAME? LEMONE
LEMONE HAS THE FOLLOWING GRADES:
 94  93  85  94

NAME? BROWNE
STUDENT BROWNE NOT FOUND

NAME? MULRYAN
MULRYAN HAS THE FOLLOWING GRADES:
 100  93  82  89

NAME? SAVAGE
SAVAGE HAS THE FOLLOWING GRADES:
 72  81  63  60

NAME? WATERS
WATERS HAS THE FOLLOWING GRADES:
 83  75  92  80

NAME?
```

Program 2.11

This program incorporates the major topics covered in this chapter, which the reader should now be familiar with, and demonstrates how they might be used together in a single program.

```
10 INPUT "WORD TO SKIP";S$
20 FOR W=1 TO 10
30   READ W$
40    IF W$=S$ THEN 60
50    PRINT W$
60 NEXT W
70 PRINT
80 INPUT "REPEAT";R$
90 IF R$<>"YES" THEN END
100 RESTORE
110 PRINT
120 GOTO 10
130 DATA THIS,IS,A,SAMPLE,OF,THE
140 DATA MATERIAL,IN,CHAPTER,TWO

RUN
WORD TO SKIP? CHAPTER
THIS
IS
A
SAMPLE
OF
THE
MATERIAL
IN
TWO

REPEAT? YES

WORD TO SKIP? THE
THIS
IS
A
SAMPLE
OF
MATERIAL
IN
CHAPTER
TWO

REPEAT? NO

READY.
```

EXERCISES

1. Write a program to allow two numbers (A and B) to be entered. Have the computer compare them and print a message stating whether A is less than, equal to, or greater than B.

2. Write a program which allows three names to be entered as A\$, B\$ and C\$. Have the computer print the name which is alphabetically last.

3. Perform each of the following computations on paper. Check your results by using immediate mode on the computer.

   (A) 3↑2↑3   (B) 5 - 4↑2
   (C) 3*(5 + 16)   (D) 5 + 3 * 6/2
   (E) 640/10/2 * 5   (F) 5 + 3 * 4 - 1
   (G) 2↑3↑2   (H) 2↑(3↑2)
   (I) 64/4 * 0.5 + ((1 + 5) * 2↑3) * I/(2 * 4)

4. Write a program which prints six exclamation marks if BIGWOW is entered for the string X\$ but which otherwise prints six question marks. The program is run until interrupted by the user.

5. Use only one line number to enter two strings (A\$ and B\$) and to print output similar to the following:

```
RUN
? START,FINISH
START     FINISH
FINISH    START

READY.
```

6. Allow a number (X) to be entered. Print the message "NOT BETWEEN" if X is either less than -24 or greater than 17. Only one IF . . . THEN statement is permitted.

7. Allow a string (A\$) to be entered. Print the message "A\$ IS BETWEEN" If A\$ comes between "DOWN" and "UP" alphabetically. Only one IF . . . THEN statement is permitted.

8. Allow a number (X) to be entered. Print "IN THE INTERVAL" if X satisfies the inequality 25 < X < 75, but otherwise print "NOT IN THE INTERVAL." Only one AND and one IF . . . THEN statement are to be used.

9. Rewrite the program of the preceding exercise, using OR instead of AND.

10. Use only one PRINT statement to produce the following rectangle:

```
RUN
************
************
************

READY.
```

11. Print the cubes of the odd integers from 11 to -11, inclusive, in descending order.

12. Print all the integers which end in 4 from 4 to 84, inclusive.

13. Use a loop to print a line of 20 asterisks.

14. Write a one line Immediate Mode command for each of the following:
   (A) Find the value of 143 x 74.
   (B) Find the average of 53. 72, 81 and 76.
   (C) Find which is larger, $X \uparrow Y$ or $Y \uparrow X$, when X = 4 and Y = 5.

15. Print all of the integers in the set 10, 13, 16, 19, . . . , 94, 97.

16. Using a loop, have the computer print a letter I as follows:

```
RUN
*****
 ***
 ***
 ***
 ***
 ***
 ***
*****

READY.
```

17. Below is a list of various creatures and the weapon necessary to destroy each:

Creature	Weapon
Lich	Fire Ball
Mummy	Flaming Torch
Werewolf	Silver Bullet
Vampire	Wooden Stake
Medusa	Sharp Sword
Triffid	Fire Hose

Using READ and DATA, have the computer state what weapon is to be used to destroy a given creature.

18. Marvelous Matilda has written the following program using too many GOTO statements
    and cannot figure out in what order the lines of the program will be executed. Assist her by
    listing the line numbers in the sequence in which the computer will execute them:

```
10 READ A,B
20 IF A>4 OR B>4 THEN 50
30 IF A<1 AND B<1 THEN 60
40 GOTO 70
50 X = A+B : GOTO 80
60 X = A*B : GOTO 80
70 X = A/B
80 IF X>1 THEN PRINT X : GOTO 10
90 DATA 5,3,-1,-2,0,2
```

19. John Doe's brother Jim has been assigned the following program for homework. Jim is not
    in shape today, so assist him by stating the exact order in which the lines of the following
    program are to be executed:

```
10 READ A,B,C
20 S = A+B*C
30 IF S=10 THEN RESTORE : READ S
40 PRINT S,
50 IF S=14 THEN END
60 GOTO 10
70 DATA 4,2,3,6,0,2,7
```

20. Write a program which asks for a person's age. If the person is 16 years or older, have the
    computer print "YOU ARE OLD ENOUGH TO DRIVE A CAR." Otherwise, have the com-
    puter indicate how many years the person must wait before being able to drive.

```
RUN
HOW OLD ARE YOU? 16
YOU ARE OLD ENOUGH TO DRIVE A CAR.

READY.
```

21. The Happy Holiday Motel has 10 rooms. Have the computer print a label for each room's
    door indicating the room number. For example:

```
RUN
```

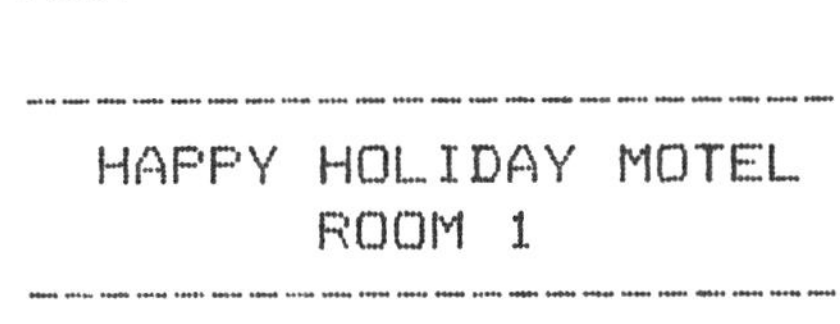

22. As candidate for mayor, you are very busy. Use the computer to print thank you letters to
    10 people who have contributed money to your election campaign. Be sure to mention the
    exact amount each person has contributed.

```
RUN

DEAR RICH BRYBURRY,
    THANK YOU FOR YOUR GENEROUS CONTRIBUTION
OF 25000 DOLLARS TO MY ELECTION CAMPAIGN. MAYBE
NEXT YEAR WE WILL HAVE BETTER LUCK!
                              SINCERELY,

                              SMILEY R. POLITICO
```

23. Write a program which will produce the following table:

```
RUN
 X            X^2           X^3

 2            4             8
 4            16            64
 6            36            216
 8            64            512
 10           100           1000

READY.
```

24. The Bored Auto Company has done it again! Some models of their cars may be difficult to drive because their wheels are not exactly round. Cars with model numbers 102, 780, 119, 229, 189, and 195 have been found to have a defect. Write a computer program that allows 10 of their customers to enter the model number of their car to find out whether or not it is defective.

25. Using only two print statements, write a program to print a triangle that in N lines high and N columns wide. For example:

```
RUN
? 5
*
**
***
****
*****

READY.
```

26. Write a program that will produce the following triangle. The figure is centered on TAB(10):

```
RUN
             *
           *   *
         *       *
       *           *
     *               *
   *                   *
 *                       *
*************

READY.
```

27. The following table contains employee performance data for the Tippecanoe Typing Company:

Employee	Performance
Oakley	69%
Howe	92%
Anderson	96%
Wolley	88%
Goerz	74%

Tippecanoe Typing is suffering from financial difficulties and needs to cut back on its staff. Using READ, DATA and a loop, have the computer print notices of dismissal for any employee whose production performance is below 75%.

```
RUN

DEAR OAKLEY,
   I AM SORRY THAT I MUST FIRE YOU.
YOU HAVE BEEN SUCH A FINE EMPLOYEE
WITH A PERFORMANCE RATING OF 69 %
I'M SURE YOU'LL HAVE NO TROUBLE
FINDING ANOTHER JOB.
                    SINCERELY,

                    GEORGE SHWABB


DEAR GOERZ,
   I AM SORRY THAT I MUST FIRE YOU.
YOU HAVE BEEN SUCH A FINE EMPLOYEE
WITH A PERFORMANCE RATING OF 74 %
I'M SURE YOU'LL HAVE NO TROUBLE
FINDING ANOTHER JOB.
                    SINCERELY,

                    GEORGE SHWABB


READY.
```

28. Wayne Peber bought stock two years ago and wants to use the computer to calculate his profit or loss. He bought 200 shares of Consolidated Technologies at $85.58 per share and 400 shares of American Amalgamated Securities at $35.60 per share. Today C.T. is worth $70.82 a share and A.A.S. is worth $47.32 a share. What is his profit or loss?

29. The Exploitation Oil Company uses the computer to determine the weekly wages of its employees by inputting the hours worked and the hourly wage for each employee. If the employee works over 40 hours, he or she is paid one and a half times the hourly rate for each additional hour.

```
RUN
HOURS WORKED? 45
HOURLY WAGE? 10.00
THE WAGE FOR THE WEEK IS $ 475

READY.
```

30. The Last Chance Finance Company is charging a rate of 2% per month on all loans it is making. Write a program that allows Last Chance to calculate the monthly payments charged a customer using the following formula:

$$\text{Monthly Payment} = \frac{L * I}{1 - (1 + I)^{-m}}$$

$$\text{where } L = \text{Amount loaned}$$
$$I = \text{Interest (monthly)}$$
$$m = \text{Number of months to be loaned}$$

```
RUN
THE AMOUNT OF THE LOAN? 100
LENGTH OF THE LOAN IN YEARS? 5
THE MONTHLY PAYMENT IS $ 2.87679654
TOTAL AMOUNT PAID WILL BE $ 172.607792

READY.
```

31. You have $200.00 to spend on a buying spree. Write a program that, as you buy merchandise, subtracts the cost and the appropriate sales tax (5%) from your remaining money and shows your present total. The program should prevent you from buying items that cost more than you have.

```
RUN
HOW MUCH DOES THE ITEM COST? 10.00
YOUR TOTAL IS NOW $ 189.5

HOW MUCH DOES THE ITEM COST? 250.00
YOU DON'T HAVE ENOUGH MONEY.
HOW MUCH DOES THE ITEM COST? 25.00
YOUR TOTAL IS NOW $ 163.25

HOW MUCH DOES THE ITEM COST? 0

READY.
```

32. Have the computer find all odd integers from 5 to 25 which are simultaneous solutions of the inequalities $X^3 > 500$ and $X^2 + 3X + 2 < 700$. Print only the solutions.

COMPUTER GAMES

3

RND
INT
POS
TIME
GET
RND
INT
POS
TIME
GET
RND
INT
POS
TIME
GET
RND
INT
POS
TIME
GET
RND
INT
POS
TIME
GET
RND
INT
POS

This chapter will introduce material which should be interesting, practical and entertaining. In fact, the emphasis will be placed on techniques to involve the user in computer games, which are often the most enjoyable way to learn computer programming.

RND

In many computer simulations that involve science problems and also in a variety of computer games, the process of generating random numbers is essential. The RND function generates random numbers on the computer. The statement

$$X = RND(0)$$

will assign X a random number such that $0 < X < 1$.

Program 3.1

This program will print 4 random numbers:

```
10 FOR I = 1 TO 4
20    PRINT RND(0),
30 NEXT I

RUN
 .335939109              .0234396458
 .218750238              .15234524

READY.
```

INT

The statement A = INT(X) sets A to the largest integer that is not greater than X. This function does not round off a positive number but simply truncates its decimals. In the case of a negative number, it takes the next lower negative integer. For example:

$$INT\ (3.7640) = 3 \qquad INT\ (5.9) = 5$$
$$INT\ (-1.7) = -2 \qquad INT\ (-3.01) = -4$$

At times it is preferable to have the computer pick random integers instead of long random decimals. This can be accomplished by using INT. The following formula can be used to assign X a random integer between A and B, inclusive:

$$X = INT\ ((B - A + 1)*RND(0) + A)$$

For example, the statement

$$X = INT(26*RND(0) + 75)$$

will assign X a random integer between 75 and 100, inclusive.

Program 3.2

This game program selects a random number from 1 to 100 and then gives the player an unlimited number of chances to guess it. After each guess the computer informs the player that the guess is too high, too low or correct.

```
10 PRINT "I'M THINKING OF A RANDOM NUMBER FROM 1 TO 100."
20 R = INT(100 * RND(0) + 1)
30 INPUT "WHAT IS YOUR GUESS"; G
40 IF G<R THEN PRINT "TOO LOW!" : GOTO 30
50 IF G>R THEN PRINT "TOO HIGH!" : GOTO 30
60 PRINT "THAT IS CORRECT!!!"
RUN
I'M THINKING OF A RANDOM NUMBER FROM 1 TO 100.
WHAT IS YOUR GUESS? 50
TOO LOW!
WHAT IS YOUR GUESS? 75
TOO LOW!
WHAT IS YOUR GUESS? 86
TOO LOW!
WHAT IS YOUR GUESS? 90
THAT IS CORRECT!!!

READY.
```


Review

1. Write a program that will generate 2 random integers between 50 and 150 and find their product.

```
RUN
 134 MULTIPLIED BY 110 IS 14740

READY.
```

2. Write a program similar to Program 3.2 which picks a random number between 1 and 50, inclusive, and gives the player only five attempts to guess it.

```
RUN
I'M THINKING OF A RANDOM NUMBER FROM 1 TO 50.
WHAT IS YOUR GUESS? 25
TOO LOW!
WHAT IS YOUR GUESS? 37
TOO LOW!
WHAT IS YOUR GUESS? 44
TOO HIGH!
WHAT IS YOUR GUESS? 40
TOO LOW!
WHAT IS YOUR GUESS? 41
TOO LOW!
YOU'VE HAD 5 GUESSES NOW.
THE NUMBER WAS 42

READY.
```

Summation

If the programmer decides to keep score for the number guessing game (Program 3.2), some technique will have to be devised to keep count of the number of guesses taken. One possible technique is to use a summation statement of the form:

$$30 \ A = A + 1$$

The statement $A = A + 1$ makes no sense in mathematics since A can equal A but not A + 1. The computer, however, interprets the equal sign to mean "is replaced by" rather than "equal to", and each time it encounters line 30 above, it takes the present value of A, adds 1 to it, and makes that sum the new value of A.

Program 3.3

This program demonstrates how the summation statement works by printing the values of the variable A until the program is halted with the STOP key:

```
10 A = A + 1
20 PRINT A;
30 GOTO 10

RUN
 1   2   3   4   5   6   7   8   9   10   11   12
 13   14   15   16   17   18
BREAK IN 20
READY.
```

If line 10 is replaced with

$$10 \ A = A + 5$$

then 5 will be added to A each time the statement is encountered.

```
10 A = A + 5
RUN
 5   10   15   20   25   30   35   40   45   50
 55   60   65   70   75   80
BREAK IN 20
READY.
```

In this problem the initial value of A is zero for both runs because the computer sets any undefined numeric variables to zero at the start of a run.

Program 3.4

Here, Program 3.2 has been modified to record the number of turns required to guess the random number. In this case the variable A acts as a counter, increasing in value by 1 after each guess:

```
10 PRINT "I'M THINKING OF A RANDOM NUMBER FROM 1 TO 100."
20 R = INT(100 * RND(0) + 1)
30 INPUT "WHAT IS YOUR GUESS"; G
35 A = A + 1
40 IF G<R THEN PRINT "TOO LOW!" : GOTO 30
50 IF G>R THEN PRINT "TOO HIGH!" : GOTO 30
60 PRINT "THAT IS CORRECT!!!"
70 PRINT "THAT TOOK YOU";A;"GUESSES."

RUN
I'M THINKING OF A RANDOM NUMBER FROM 1 TO 100.
WHAT IS YOUR GUESS? 50
TOO LOW!
WHAT IS YOUR GUESS? 75
TOO HIGH!
WHAT IS YOUR GUESS? 67
TOO HIGH!
WHAT IS YOUR GUESS? 59
THAT IS CORRECT!!!
THAT TOOK YOU 4 GUESSES.

READY.
```

Rounding Errors

Because the computer has a finite capacity, any numerical computations involving infinitely repeating decimals cannot be accurate (for example, $1/3 = .3333\ldots$, which the computer truncates to a limited number of digits). Since the computer uses binary numbers (0 and 1), any fraction whose denominator is not an integral power of 2 (2, 4, 8, 16) will be an infinitely repeating decimal and therefore will be truncated by the computer. In Chapter Eight binary numbers are examined in greater detail.

Program 3.5

This program illustrates the processes of summation and rounding error:

```
10 FOR X = 1 TO 1500
20    A = A + (1/2)
30    B = B + (1/3)
40 NEXT X
50 PRINT "A =";A
60 PRINT "B =";B

RUN
A = 750
B = 500.000023

READY.
```

The final value of A is the result of adding ½ 1500 times, which comes out to exactly 750. B, however, which is the result of adding ⅓ 1500 times, does not come out to exactly 500 because of the rounding error. At times the computer does not recognize an equality when one in fact exists. If the line

$$70 \text{ IF } B = 500 \text{ THEN PRINT ``EQUAL''}$$

were added to the above program, then the computer would not print the word "EQUAL."

Review

3. Select 50 random integers between 0 and 9, inclusive, and have the computer tell how many of the numbers were from 0-4 and how many were from 5-9.

```
RUN
THERE WERE 22 NUMBERS BETWEEN 0 AND 4.
THERE WERE 28 NUMBERS BETWEEN 5 AND 9.

READY.
```

POS

The POS function is used to find the current horizontal position of the cursor. The statement

$$X = POS(0)$$

will assign X a value corresponding to the horizontal position (the current TAB position) of the cursor on the screen. On the Commodore-64, X = 0 for the left edge and 39 for the right edge. On the VIC-20, X = 0 for the left edge and 21 for the right edge.

The variable TIME is set by the computer to the number of "jiffies" which have elapsed since the computer was turned on. A jiffy is equal to 1/60 of a second. For example,

$$T = TIME$$

sets the variable T equal to the number of jiffies accumulated since the computer was turned on.

Program 3.6

This program checks how long it takes a student to respond to a multiplication problem, awarding 100 points if the student answers correctly within 1 second and subtracting 20 points for each additional second taken:

```
10 X = INT(12*RND(0) + 1)
20 Y = INT(12*RND(0) + 1)
30 PRINT "WHAT IS";X;"*";Y
40 T1 = TIME
50 INPUT A
60 T2 = TIME
70 IF A<>X*Y THEN PRINT "INCORRECT, YOU GET 0 POINTS" : END
80 T = INT((T2-T1)/60 + .5)
90 PRINT "THAT TOOK YOU";T;"SECONDS."
100 IF T>5 THEN PRINT "YOU GET 0 POINTS." : END
110 PRINT "YOU GET";20*(6-T);"POINTS."

RUN
WHAT IS 6 * 7
 42
THAT TOOK YOU 2 SECONDS.
YOU GET 80 POINTS.

READY.
```

When the computer executes line 40, the current time in jiffies is assigned to the variable T1. After the answer has been entered at line 50, the current time at that point is assigned to T2 at line 60. The elapsed time in jiffies, the time taken to respond, is the difference between T2 and T1. Line 80 converts this elapsed time from jiffies to the nearest second.

GET

The GET statement is used to input a single digit or character from the keyboard. Its format is:

$$GET \text{ } \langle variable \rangle$$

Unlike the INPUT statement, the character struck is not printed and it is not followed by striking the RETURN key. When a GET statement is executed, the computer immediately checks the keyboard to see what key is being pressed and assigns the variable that value. If no key has been struck when a GET statement is executed, then numeric variables are assigned 0, and string variables are assigned a null("") character. For example,

$$100 \text{ GET A\$}$$

assigns A$ a single character which was typed on the keyboard.

Program 3.7

This program requires the user to type an X to complete the printing of a limerick. Note the use of the GET statement at line 70:

```
10 PRINT "THERE ONCE WAS A CAT"
20 PRINT "NAMED HARRY,"
30 PRINT "WHO WISHED HE COULD"
40 PRINT "CATCH A CANARY,"
50 PRINT
60 PRINT "  (PRESS X TO CONTINUE)"
70 GET A$
80 IF A$ <> "X" THEN 70
90 PRINT "ONE DAY IN THE HOUSE,"
100 PRINT "HE SAW A MOUSE,"
110 PRINT "AND SOON THE TWO"
120 PRINT "WERE MARRIED"

RUN
THERE ONCE WAS A CAT
NAMED HARRY,
WHO WISHED HE COULD
CATCH A CANARY,

   (PRESS X TO CONTINUE)
ONE DAY IN THE HOUSE,
HE SAW A MOUSE,
AND SOON THE TWO
WERE MARRIED

READY.
```

Game Programs

Two game programs are presented here which the programmer should study carefully and then attempt to modify to write other game programs.

Program 3.8

In the game of NIM, two players in turn take matches from a pile originally containing twenty matches. Each player may take either 1 or 2 at a time. The player who takes the last match wins the game. The computer's strategy is simple. If the computer goes first, it will take 2 matches. If the player is allowed to go first, then the computer will match the player's first move. Thereafter, in either case, the computer will select a number of matches so that the total of the player's previous selection and the computer's is 3. For example, if the player picks 2, the computer will pick 1. The following program plays NIM with the user, randomly deciding who goes first:

```
1 REM   M - NUMBER OF MATCHES
2 REM   C - COMPUTER'S SELECTION
3 REM   P - PLAYER'S SELECTION
4 REM
10 PRINT " HERE I HAVE TWENTY MATCHES."
20 PRINT "EACH PLAYER MAY TAKE EITHER"
30 PRINT "1 OR 2 AT A TIME. THE PLAYER"
40 PRINT "WHO TAKES THE LAST MATCH WINS"
50 M = 20   : REM START WITH 20 MATCHES
60 IF RND(0) < 0.5 THEN PRINT "YOU GO FIRST." : GOTO 130
70 PRINT "I'LL GO FIRST."
80 C = 2 : GOTO 110  : REM COMPUTER GOES FIRST
90 IF M > 17 THEN C = P : GOTO 110
100 C = 3-P  : REM COMPUTER'S MOVE
110 PRINT "COMPUTER TAKES"; C
120 M = M - C  : REM REMAINING MATCHES
130 PRINT M; "MATCHES REMAIN."
140 IF M = 0 THEN PRINT "YOU LOSE." : END
150 PRINT "HOW MANY MATCHES DO YOU WANT?";
160 GET P
170 IF (P<1) OR (P>2) OR (P>M) THEN 160
180 PRINT P
190 M = M - P  : REM DEDUCT PLAYER'S CHOICE
200 IF M > 0 THEN 90  : REM ANY MATCHES LEFT?
210 PRINT "YOU WIN!"
220 END

RUN
 HERE I HAVE TWENTY MATCHES.
EACH PLAYER MAY TAKE EITHER
1 OR 2 AT A TIME. THE PLAYER
WHO TAKES THE LAST MATCH WINS
YOU GO FIRST.
 20 MATCHES REMAIN.
HOW MANY MATCHES DO YOU WANT? 2
COMPUTER TAKES 2
 16 MATCHES REMAIN.
HOW MANY MATCHES DO YOU WANT? 2
COMPUTER TAKES 1
 13 MATCHES REMAIN.
```

```
HOW MANY MATCHES DO YOU WANT? 2
COMPUTER TAKES 1
  10 MATCHES REMAIN.
HOW MANY MATCHES DO YOU WANT? 2
COMPUTER TAKES 1
   7 MATCHES REMAIN.
HOW MANY MATCHES DO YOU WANT? 2
COMPUTER TAKES 1
   4 MATCHES REMAIN.
HOW MANY MATCHES DO YOU WANT? 2
COMPUTER TAKES 1
   1 MATCHES REMAIN.
HOW MANY MATCHES DO YOU WANT? 1
YOU WIN!

READY.
```

The random number generated at line 60 determines who will go first. If the computer goes first, then lines 70 and 80 are executed, forcing the computer to select 2 matches. Otherwise, if the player goes first, control is passed to line 130. A GET is used at line 160 to input the player's choice. Note that a PRINT statement is used at line 180 so that the player can see his or her response. Remember that the GET statement does not print the keyboard input. Line 170 insures that only 1 or 2 matches are taken by the player and that the number of matches selected does not exceed the number of matches remaining. The computer's choice, based on the player's previous choice, is calculated at line 100. The sum of the two moves should be 3.

Program 3.9

This program simulates a roulette wheel, which has two colors (red and black) and thirty numbers. The player is asked to make a bet and pick a color and number. Picking the correct color returns the bet; picking the correct number but wrong color wins thirty times the bet, and picking the correct number and color wins the player sixty times the bet. Why would a casino using this roulette wheel be highly unprofitable?

```
1 REM   N - NUMBER CHOSEN BY PLAYER
2 REM   C - CONVERSION OF C$ TO A NUMBER (1 OR 2)
3 REM   B - PLAYER'S BET
4 REM   M - MONEY MADE BY PLAYER
5 REM N1 - ROULETTE WHEEL NUMBER
6 REM C1 - ROULETTE WHEEL COLOR
7 REM C$ - COLOR CHOSEN BY PLAYER
8 REM
10 REM PROMPT PLAYER FOR GUESS & BET
20 INPUT "WHAT NUMBER (1-30)"; N
30 PRINT "WHAT COLOR, (R)ED OR (B)LACK? ";
40 GET C$ : IF C$ = "" THEN 40
50 PRINT C$ : C = 2 : REM ASSUME BLACK
60 IF C$ = "R" THEN C = 1 : REM RED CHOSEN
70 INPUT "WHAT IS YOUR BET"; B
80 IF B < 0 THEN PRINT "NO CHEATING!" : GOTO 70
90 IF B > 1000 THEN PRINT "HOUSE LIMIT: $1000" : GOTO 70
```

```
100 REM
110 REM SPIN ROULETTE WHEEL
120 N1 = INT(30*RND(0) + 1)
130 C1 = INT(2*RND(0) + 1)
140 PRINT "THE WHEEL STOPPED ON:"; N1;
150 IF C1 = 1 THEN PRINT "RED" : GOTO 200
160 PRINT "BLACK"  : REM C = 2
200 REM
210 REM COMPUTE WINS OR LOSSES
220 M = -B  : REM ASSUME PLAYER LOST
230 IF N1 = N THEN AND C1 = C THEN 270
240 IF N1 = N THEN PRINT "YOU GOT THE NUMBER" : M = 30*B : GOTO 300
250 IF C1 = C THEN PRINT "YOU GOT THE COLOR" : M = B : GOTO 300
260 PRINT "YOU LOSE. BETTER LUCK NEXT TIME!" : GOTO 300
270 PRINT "CONGRATULATIONS! YOU GOT BOTH!" : M = 60*B
300 REM
310 REM TELL PLAYER OF WINS OR LOSSES
320 IF M < 0 THEN PRINT "YOU LOST $";-M : GOTO 340
330 PRINT "YOU NOW HAVE $"; M+B
340 PRINT "WHY NOT TRY AGAIN?" : END

RUN
WHAT NUMBER (1-30)? 27
WHAT COLOR, (R)ED OR (B)LACK? R
WHAT IS YOUR BET? 200
THE WHEEL STOPPED ON: 6 RED
YOU GOT THE COLOR
YOU NOW HAVE $ 400
WHY NOT TRY AGAIN?

READY.
RUN
WHAT NUMBER (1-30)? 32
WHAT COLOR, (R)ED OR (B)LACK? B
WHAT IS YOUR BET? 100
THE WHEEL STOPPED ON: 3 RED
YOU LOSE. BETTER LUCK NEXT TIME!
YOU LOST $ 100
WHY NOT TRY AGAIN?

READY.
```

Lines 20 through 70 prompt the gambler for a number between 1 and 30, a color (red or black), and his or her bet. Line 80 insures that the gambler does not attempt to defraud the bank by placing a negative bet. This simulated roulette table has a $1000 limit, which is strictly enforced by line 90. The actual 'spin' of the roulette wheel takes place at lines 120 and 130. The player's winnings (or losses) are computed in lines 220 through 270. Note that line 270 is reached only if both conditions are satisfied in the IF . . . THEN statement at line 230, which determines if both the color and number were matched by the player. Line 260 is reached only if the player incorrectly guessed both the color and the number, conditions which are checked by lines 240 and 250. Lines 320 and 330 inform the gambler of his or her good (or bad) fortune.

Note that a GET is used at line 40 rather than INPUT so that only a single letter can be entered. If INPUT were used and the user responded by typing 'RED' rather than just 'R' as instructed, the comparison at line 60 would fail.

EXERCISES

1. Generate ten random numbers between 0 and 1, but print only those which are greater than 0.5.

2. Generate three random numbers between 0 and 1, and print their sum.

3. Input a number (N). Print it only if it is an integer. (Hint: compare N with INT(N)).

4. Allow a user to guess a random integer between -3 and 4, inclusive. Print whether the guess was correct or not. If the guess was wrong, the correct value is also to be printed.

5. Determine randomly how many coins you find on the street. You are to find from 2 to 5 nickels, 1 to 4 dimes and 0 to 3 quarters. Lunch costs 99 cents. The program is to report the amount that you found and whether you are able to buy lunch with it.

```
RUN
YOU FOUND $ .95
SORRY, YOU CAN'T BUY LUNCH

READY.
RUN
YOU FOUND $ 1.15
YOU CAN BUY LUNCH

READY.
```

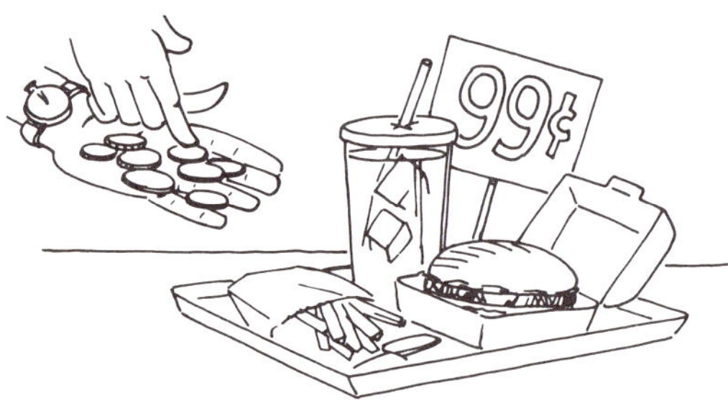

6. Input an integer (N), and print the sum of N random numbers between 0 and 1. Also print N/2 for comparison with the sum.

7. A child puts pennies into a piggy bank once each week for four weeks. The bank already contains 11 pennies in it when the child first receives it. Write a program to allow pennies to be added each week and to print the dollar value of the bank's contents after each addition.

8. Write a program that will act as a stopwatch. Use the GET and TIME commands to produce output similar to the following:

```
RUN
PRESS S TO START AND AGAIN TO STOP
THE STOPWATCH IS RUNNING
ELAPSED TIME = 6.35 SECONDS

READY.
```

9. Write a program that will print ten random integers from -10 to 10, inclusive.

10. Write a program to flip a coin 50 times and print the total number of heads and tails. Run the program ten times to get a comparison among the runs.

11. Brad Browne wrote both of the following programs but has forgotten what their output is. Determine the output and check your answer by running the program.

```
(a) 10 FOR Z = 1 TO 3
    20    A = A+Z
    30      PRINT A
    40 NEXT Z
    50 A = A+Z
    60 PRINT A
```

```
(b) 10 G = 123.456
    20 PRINT INT(10 * G)/10,  INT(10 * G + .5)/100
    30 PRINT INT(100 * G)/100,  INT(100 * G + .5)/100
    40 END
```

12. Write a program that generates 10 random integers betwen 8 and 25, inclusive, and prints them on the same line. The output should be similar to the following:

```
17   12   22   25   8   17   19   11   21   23
```

13. Make a chart showing in their correct order the values taken by the variables X and Y. Circle those values that are printed by the computer. Check by running the program.

```
10 FOR X = 1 TO 3
15    READ Y
20    IF Y>0 THEN 35
25    Y = Y + X
30    IF X=2 THEN Y = Y - 1 : GOTO 40
35    PRINT X,Y
40 NEXT X
45 DATA 5,0,-1
```

14. (a) Determine a possible output for the program below:
    (b) Rewrite the program so that the message LEARN THE MULTIPLICATION TABLE is printed if three wrong answers are given:
    (c) Rewrite the program so that five different questions are asked and the message NICE GOING, HOTSHOT is printed if all five questions are answered correctly:

```
10 A = INT(10 * RND(0) + 1)
20 B = INT(10 * RND(0) + 1)
30 PRINT TAB(7);A;"*";B;"=";
40 INPUT C
50 IF C = A * B THEN 80
60 PRINT "YOU ARE WRONG, TRY AGAIN."
70 GOTO 30
80 PRINT TAB(12);"CORRECT"
```

15. Write a program that contains one FOR ... NEXT loop which finds the sum of all the odd integers from 13 to 147, inclusive. The output should be as follows:

$$THE\ SUM = 5440$$

16. Suzy Sunshine wrote the following program. It allows the user to enter at the keyboard any integer greater than 1 and to have the computer tell the user whether or not the integer is prime. A prime number is an integer that contains only itself and 1 as factors. The computer tests the integer by repeatedly dividing it by integers smaller than itself but larger than 1 and checking whether the quotient is whole. If so, the integer entered by the user is not prime. The program contains three errors. Find them, rewrite the program and run it. The output should look like this:

```
RUN
INTEGER > 2 PLEASE? 12
THAT INTEGER IS NOT PRIME.

READY.
RUN
INTEGER > 2 PLEASE? 17
THAT INTEGER IS PRIME.

READY.
```

```
20 READ "INTEGER > 2 PLEASE";N
30 FOR X = 2 TO N-1
40    IF N/X = INT(N/X) THEN 70
50 NEXT N
60 PRINT "THAT INTEGER IS PRIME."
70 PRINT "THAT INTEGER IS NOT PRIME."
80 END
```

17. Generate 1000 random integers between 1 and 9, inclusive, and print how many were even and how many were odd. The output should be similar to the following:

```
RUN
THERE WERE 559 ODD INTEGERS.
THERE WERE 441 EVEN INTEGERS.

READY.
```

18. Write a program that allows the user and computer to select alternately integers between 3 and 12, inclusive, keep a sum of all the integers selected and declare the winner to be the one who selects that integer which makes the sum greater than 100. Have the program ask the user if he or she would like to proceed first or second.

19. A bank pays interest once a year at a yearly rate of 5%. A man deposits $1000 on January 1, 1983 and wishes to leave it there to accrue interest until the balance is at leat $2000. Compute the balance on Jan. 1 of each year, starting with 1984 and ending in the year when the balance exceeds $2000. The output should resemble the following:

```
DATE                        BALANCE
JAN 1,  1985                $ 1050
JAN 1,  1986                $ 1102.5
. . .                       . . .
. . .                       . . .
. . .                       $ 1979.93
. . .                       $ 2078.93
```

20. Input a positive integer N, and print all positive integers that are factors of N. The output should resemble the following:

```
RUN
A POSITIVE INTEGER, PLEASE? 1.4
YOUR NUMBER WAS NOT AN INTEGER
A POSITIVE INTEGER, PLEASE? 12
  1   2   3   4   6   12
READY.
```

21. Print the radius (cm.) of a sphere, given its volume (cm.^{3}). Round off the results to the nearest hundredth:

$$\text{DATA: } 690, 720, 460, 620$$
$$\text{Note: Volume} = (4/3)\,(\pi)\,R^3, \text{ where } \pi = 3.14159$$

22. (a) Print twenty random integers between 0 and 100, inclusive.
    (b) Change the program so that sixty percent of the twenty integers printed will be less than 25.

23. Using the POS function, write a program that determines the length of a string.

```
RUN
YOUR STRING? OZ-1335
OZ-1335
THE LENGTH OF OZ-1335 IS 7

READY.
```

24. Write a program to simulate the rolling of a pair of dice. (Each has six sides labeled with the numbers 1 through 6.) For each of the rolls add the two values obtained, calling the sum S (note that S may vary between 2 and 12). Roll the dice 100 times and print the average value of S.

25. Write a program that will pick 20 random integers from 1 to 100, inclusive, and print only
    those numbers that are prime. A prime number is one that can be only divided exactly (i.e.
    no remainder) by itself and 1.

26. You are to write a program to simulate a simplified version of the game 21. A deck of cards
    numbered from 1 to 10 are used and any number can be repeated since the deck contains
    many cards. the computer starts by asking you how many cards you want. It then deals you
    the cards, which are randomly picked, and totals their value. If the value exceeds 21, you
    automatically lose. If your value is under 21, the computer deals itself *three* randomly
    picked cards. The winner is the one with the highest score equal to or less than 21. Write
    your program so that the game can be played 10 consecutive times with the winner of each
    game winning one dollar. At the end of the 10 games print out the total winnings for you and
    the computer. The example below shows only the last three of the ten games:

```
HOW MANY CARDS DO YOU WANT? 4
YOU : 8   1   9   3
ME  : 1   4   8
I HAVE 13 AND YOU HAVE 21 SO YOU WIN.

HOW MANY CARDS DO YOU WANT? 3
YOU : 2   3   7
ME  : 8   10  1
I HAVE 19 AND YOU HAVE 12 SO I WIN!

HOW MANY CARDS DO YOU WANT? 3
YOU : 1   9   2
ME  : 8   8   6
I HAVE 22 AND YOU HAVE 12 SO YOU WIN.
MY WINNINGS = 4
YOUR WINNINGS = 6

READY.
```

27. Have the computer randomly select a number of quarters (from 0 to 7), dimes (from 0 to 4)
    and pennies (from 0 to 9) and print the exact number of coins and their total value. The user
    has three chances to determine how many quarters, dimes and pennies were selected.

28. The following table shows production output per day for each employee of Fazioli's Pizza
    Parlor. Plot a bar graph showing the output for the week for each of Fazioli's employees:

Employee	Pizza Production
Papa	18, 12, 9, 10, 16, 22, 14
Dellacona	12, 21, 19, 16, 28, 20, 22
Ricardo	18, 20, 14, 19, 11, 16, 23
Ferrara	23, 27, 18, 16, 21, 14, 24

```
RUN
SCALE:  * = 5 PIZZAS

PAPA        *******************
DELLACONA   ****************************
RICARDO     *************************
FERRARA     ******************************

READY.
```

NESTED LOOPS AND SUBSCRIPTED VARIABLES

DIM
CLR
DIM
CLR
DIM
CLR
DIM
CLR
DIM
CLR
DIM
CLR
DIM
CLR
DIM
CLR
DIM
CLR
DIM
CLR
DIM
CLR
DIM
DIM
CLR
DIM

We have previously observed that the FOR... TO... STEP, NEXT statements set up loops. This chapter proceeds further by showing how to combine two or more loops in such a way as to place one loop inside another.

The second part of this chapter deals with subscripted variables, which use a fixed variable name in conjunction with a variable subscript (e.g. A(N), where A is fixed and N varies). This technique enables a program to deal conveniently with a large amount of data. Subscripted variables usually employ FOR... NEXT loops to generate the values for the subscripts.

Nested FOR... NEXT Loops

The concept of a FOR... NEXT loop was presented in Chapter Two. In this chapter, the concept of nested FOR... NEXT loops (that is, one loop placed, or 'nested' within another) is introduced. For example:

```
10 FOR P = 1 TO 20
20      FOR Q = 3 TO 10
30      NEXT Q
40 NEXT P
```

By definition nested loops must never cross. One loop must be contained entirely within another or be entirely separated from another. For example, the following arrangement is not permissible because the loops cross each other:

```
10 FOR P = 1 TO 20
20 FOR Q = 3 TO 10
30 NEXT P
40 NEXT Q
```

When this program is run, the following error message will result:

?NEXT WITHOUT FOR ERROR IN 40

Program 4.1

This program uses nested loops to print a portion of the multiplication table:

```
10 FOR X = 1 TO 5
20    FOR Y = 2 TO 3
30       PRINT X; "*"; Y; "="; X*Y,
40    NEXT Y
50    PRINT
60 NEXT X
RUN
 1 * 2 = 2          1 * 3 = 3
 2 * 2 = 4          2 * 3 = 6
 3 * 2 = 6          3 * 3 = 9
 4 * 2 = 8          4 * 3 = 12
 5 * 2 = 10         5 * 3 = 15

READY.
```

Line 10 establishes the outer X loop and starts X with the value 1. X retains this value until it is incremented by the execution of line 60. Line 60 is not executed, however, until the inner Y loop, lines 20-40, has run its entire course. X therefore retains the value 1 while Y changes from 2 to 3. When the Y loop has finished its cycle of two passes, line 60 is executed, incrementing X to 2. The program returns to line 20 and starts the Y loop over again at its initial value of 2. Whenever a program encounters the FOR ... TO statement of a loop, the loop variable is reset to its initial value. Since this program does not return to line 10, the X loop is never reset to 1. Notice that Y will take on its values of 2 and 3 five times. Indentation is used in the above program in order to clarify the program's structure, and the contents of each loop are indented to clarify the boundaries of the loop. Remember, to indent a line, type the I key while depressing the Commodore (C=) key immediately after typing the line number. The space bar may then be used to indent the line to the desired position.

Program 4.2

This program calculates and prints all possible combinations of quarters, dimes and nickels that add up to fifty cents:

```
10 PRINT "QUARTERS","DIMES","NICKELS"
20 FOR Q = 0 TO 2 : REM QUARTERS
30    FOR D = 0 TO 5 : REM DIMES
40       FOR N = 0 TO 10 : REM NICKELS
50          IF Q*25+D*10+N*5=50 THEN PRINT Q, D, N
60       NEXT N
70    NEXT D
80 NEXT Q

RUN
QUARTERS        DIMES           NICKELS
   0              0               10
   0              1               8
   0              2               6
   0              3               4
   0              4               2
   0              5               0
   1              0               5
   1              1               3
   1              2               1
   2              0               0


READY.
```

Q represents the number of quarters, D the number of dimes and N the number of nickels. There may be anywhere from 0 to 2 quarters in a combination. Similarly, there may be anywhere from 0 to 5 dimes and from 0 to 10 nickels. Three nested loops ensure that every possible combination that *might* work is checked at line 50.

Review

1. Use nested loops to produce the following output. The outer loop runs from 20 to 24, and the inner loop runs from 1 to 3:

```
RUN
OUTER LOOP: 20
INNER: 1              INNER: 2              INNER: 3
OUTER LOOP: 21
INNER: 1              INNER: 2              INNER: 3
OUTER LOOP: 22
INNER: 1              INNER: 2              INNER: 3
OUTER LOOP: 23
INNER: 1              INNER: 2              INNER: 3
OUTER LOOP: 24
INNER: 1              INNER: 2              INNER: 3

READY.
```

The Need for Subscripted Variables

The major purpose of subscripted variables is to store easily and later retrieve large quantities of data. Programs 4.3 and 4.4 do not use subscripted variables but demonstrate when contrasted with later programs how useful subscripted variables are.

Program 4.3

This program generates ten random numbers from one to twenty, inclusive:

```
10 FOR X = 1 TO 10
20 Y = INT(20 * RND(0) + 1)
30    PRINT Y;
40 NEXT X

RUN
 5   14   1   16   20   13   20   11   17   17
READY.
```

Every time a new value is assigned to Y, it replaces the previous value for Y. Since the previous values of Y are not remembered, it is impossible to prevent repetition by comparing the old values of Y with the new value of Y. If a box analogy is used here, the first two cycles of Program 4.3 would appear as follows:

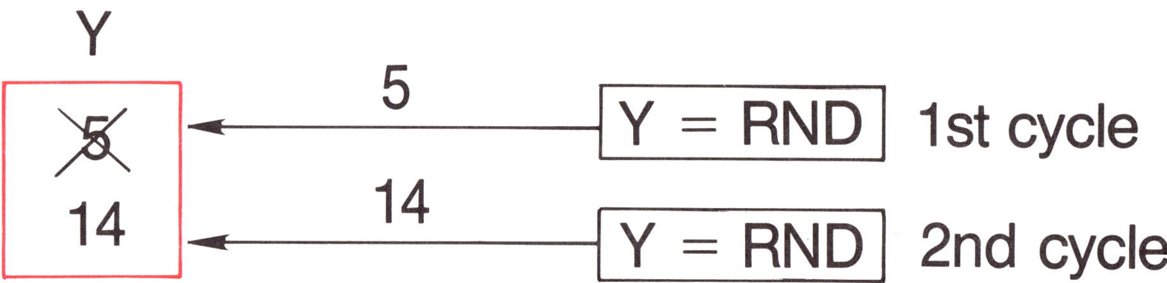

Program 4.4

This program prints four random numbers between 1 and 20, inclusive, without any repetition. The technique can be expanded to have the program choose 10 numbers if the user is willing to type the program lines required:

```
10 Y1 = INT(20 * RND(0) + 1)
20 PRINT Y1;
30 Y2 = INT(20 * RND(0) + 1)
40 IF Y2 = Y1 THEN 30
50 PRINT Y2;
60 Y3 = INT(20 * RND(0) + 1)
70 IF Y3 = Y2 OR Y3 = Y1 THEN 60
80 PRINT Y3;
90 Y4 = INT(20 * RND(0) + 1)
100 IF Y4 = Y3 OR Y4 = Y2 OR Y4 = Y1 THEN 90
110 PRINT Y4

RUN
 13   17   12   18

READY.
```

The similarity between the three sets of lines 30-50, 60-80 and 90-110 is obvious. In each set the first line selects a random number between 1 and 20, inclusive, and the second line checks to see if the number is a repetition of a number previously chosen. If this is the case, then execution goes back to the first line in the set so that another number may be chosen. Finally, the third line of the set prints the random number selected. The use of subscripted variables will eliminate the need for the repetition of these sets.

Single Subscripted Variables

In mathematics a set of single subscripted numeric variables (e.g., X_1, X_2, X_3, ...) is symbolized by a letter and a subscript, which is written below the line of the letter. On the computer the same set of subscripted variables would be referred to as X(1), X(2), X(3) and so on, where the integer enclosed in parentheses is the subscript.

The name for a set of single subscripted numeric variables consists of one of the usual numeric variable names, followed by the parenthesized subscript. For example, A(1), B2(17) and X(8) are all legal subscripted variable names. Similarly, single subscripted string variables names such as Z$(5), Y1$(20) and M$(14) are acceptable.

The subscript variable L(2) is *not* the same as the variable L2. Furthermore, the subscript is a part of the variable name and must not be confused with the value of the variable. For example, in the statement L(5) = 32 the subscript is 5 and the value of L(5) is 32.

Program 4.5

This program illustrates the difference between the subscript and the value of a subscripted variable:

```
10 L(1) = 7
20 L(2) = 5
30 L(3) = 4
40 PRINT "L(1) ="; L(1), "L(2) =";L(2), "L(3) ="; L(3)
50 PRINT "L(1 + 2) ="; L(1 + 2)
60 PRINT "L(1) + L(2) ="; L(1) + L(2)
70 X = 2
80 PRINT "L(X) ="; L(X)

RUN
L(1) = 7                 L(2) = 5                 L(3) = 4
L(1 + 2) = 4
L(1) + L(2) = 12
L(X) = 5

READY.
```

Lines 10 through 30 set the value of L(1) through L(3) as follows:

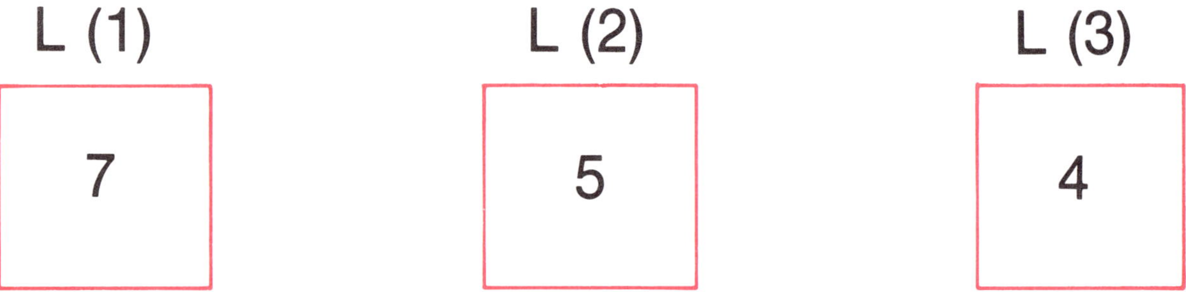

Lines 50 and 60 point out the difference between adding two subscripts and adding the values of two variables. L(1 + 2) is identical to L(3) and therefore has a value of 4. L(1) + L(2) calls for the values 7 and 5 to be added, thus producing a total of 12. Since the subscript X equals 2 in line 80, a value of 5 is printed. As can be seen, it is permissible to use a numeric variable as the subscript of a subscripted variable.

Program 4.6

Like Program 4.3, this program selects 10 random numbers between 1 and 20 and makes no attempt to prevent repetition. Yet unlike Program 4.3, it stores the numbers chosen in a subscripted variable:

```
10 FOR X = 1 TO 10
20   R(X) = INT(20 * RND(0) + 1)
30 NEXT X
40 PRINT "TEN RANDOM NUMBERS HAVE BEEN STORED IN R()."
50 PRINT
60 FOR N = 1 TO 10
70   PRINT "R(";N; ") HAS A"; R(N); "STORED IN IT."
80 NEXT N
```

```
RUN
TEN RANDOM NUMBERS HAVE BEEN STORED IN R().

R( 1 ) HAS A 15 STORED IN IT.
R( 2 ) HAS A 6 STORED IN IT.
R( 3 ) HAS A 6 STORED IN IT.
R( 4 ) HAS A 11 STORED IN IT.
R( 5 ) HAS A 18 STORED IN IT.
R( 6 ) HAS A 2 STORED IN IT.
R( 7 ) HAS A 2 STORED IN IT.
R( 8 ) HAS A 18 STORED IN IT.
R( 9 ) HAS A 19 STORED IN IT.
R( 10 ) HAS A 11 STORED IN IT.

READY.
```

This program has two loops which are not nested but which follow one another. Each loop is executed 10 times. In the first loop line 20 chooses a random number and stores it in one of the subscripted R() variables. The first time through this loop (X = 1) a random number is stored in R(1); the second time (X = 2), a new number is stored in R(2) and so on repeating 10 times. After the above run of this program, the R() boxes had contents as follows:

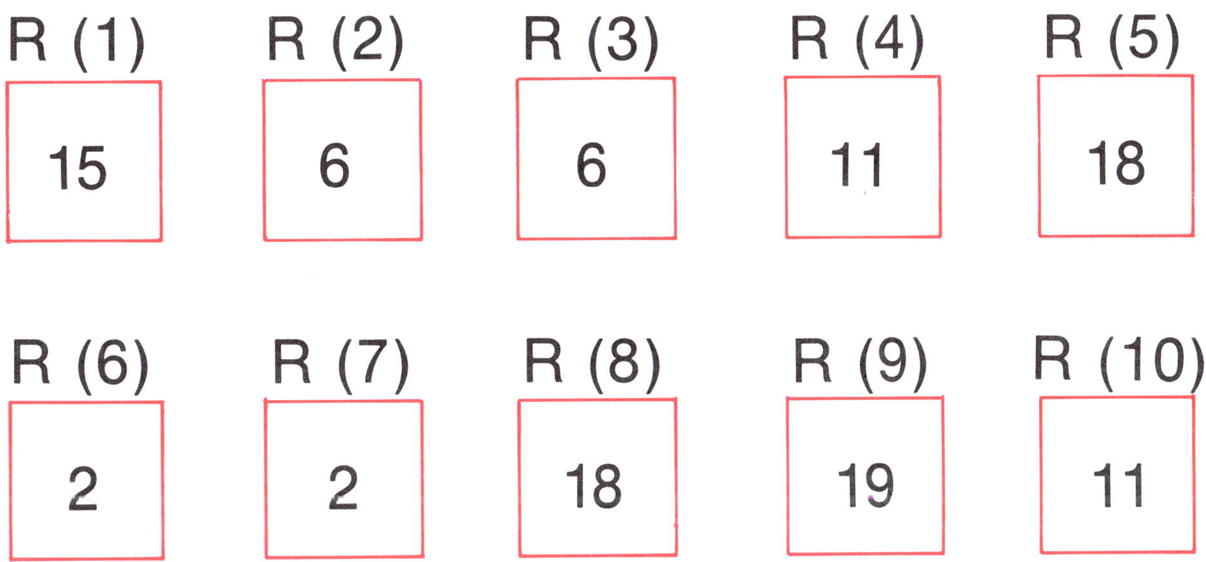

The second loop (lines 60 through 80) prints the contents stored in the boxes.

The ability to store numbers in this way will allow the writing of a new program to choose 10 random numbers *without* repetition. By checking whether a chosen random number equals any of those previously selected, a program can determine whether to accept the random number chosen or to make another selection.

Program 4.7

This program uses nested loops and subscripted variables to pick 10 random numbers between 1 and 20 without repetition:

```
10 FOR X = 1 TO 10
20    Y(X) = INT(20 * RND(0) + 1)
30    IF X = 1 THEN 70
40    FOR Q = 1 TO X-1
50      IF Y(X) = Y(Q) THEN 20
60    NEXT Q
70    PRINT Y(X);
80 NEXT X

RUN
 2  20  12  4  11  9  14  5  19  6
READY.
```

Line 20 selects a random number between 1 and 20, inclusive, and stores it in one of the subscripts of Y(). Since Y(1) is the first random number, line 30 is included to insure Y(1) will be printed immediately because it is obviously not a repeat of another number. Lines 40 to 60 constitute a nested loop which determines if a number just chosen, Y(X), is equal to any of the previously chosen numbers, Y(1) through Y(X-1). The X-1 in line 40 insures that Y(X) is not rejected by being checked against itself. If X rather than X-1 were used, then Q would eventually equal X. Line 50 would determine that Y(X) was a repeated number when Q equalled X and would then mistakenly return to line 20.

There is an additional reason for including line 30. When X and Q are equal to 1, Y(X) will equal Y(Q), and without line 30, program flow would continuously return to line 20.

Program 4.8

The following program will randomly read a list of 5 names into a subscripted string variable N$() without repeating any of the names:

```
10 FOR X = 1 TO 5
20    Y = INT(5 * RND(0) + 1)
30    IF N$(Y)<>"" THEN 20
40    READ N$(Y)
50 NEXT X
60 FOR Z = 1 TO 5
70    PRINT N$(Z)
80 NEXT Z
90 DATA TED,JOHN,MARY,DON,SUSAN

RUN
SUSAN
DON
JOHN
TED
MARY

READY.
```

```
RUN
MARY
SUSAN
TED
JOHN
DON

READY.
```

This program reads the names in the DATA statement in order but randomly places them in N$(1) to N$(5). Repetition is avoided by checking each new box as it is selected to discover whether it contains a name. If it is full, a new box is tried by selecting a new random number. The consecutive double quotation marks ("") at line 30 are used to check whether the box is empty. Unassigned subscripted string variables, which are empty, are represented on the computer by ("").

Review

2. Using subscripted variables, write a program in which 3 numbers are input. Then have the computer type them back in reverse order.

```
RUN
? 4
? 6
? 1
 1
 6
 4

READY.
```

3. Six words are to be entered from the keyboard. Have the computer randomly select and print four of the words as a "sentence" (which may or may not make sense). Repetition of words is allowed.

```
RUN
? JACK
? AND
? JILL
? RAN
? AWAY
? SCREAMING
JACK SCREAMING AWAY AWAY .

READY.
```

4. Modify the program of the previous exercise so that words are not repeated.

```
RUN
? JACK
? AND
? JILL
? RAN
? AWAY
? HAPPILY
AND AWAY RAN JACK .

READY.
```

Whenever the highest subscript of a subscripted variable exceeds 10, the computer must be informed. The DIM statement is used to direct the computer to reserve enough space in memory to accommodate the anticipated input. Its format is:

$$\text{DIM} <variable>(<dimension>)$$

For example, Program 4.8 could be changed to store 100 names by making the appropriate changes in several lines and adding the following line:

$$5 \text{ DIM N\$(100)}$$

The dimension may be either a numeric constant or a numeric variable. For example,

$$5 \text{ N} = 100 : \text{DIM N\$(N)}$$

is equivalent to line 5 above.

If the ages of the people were also to be stored, a numeric subscripted variable would have to be added and the DIM statement modified:

$$5 \text{ DIM N\$(100), A(100)}$$

It is possible to request more space (i.e. boxes) in memory than the computer can supply. This results in the following error message:

$$?\text{OUT OF MEMORY ERROR}$$

It is a good idea to place DIM statements at the beginning of a program because the DIM statement must be executed before more than 10 subscripts of a subscripted variable have been used. Though it is possible to have several DIM statements in a program, each subscripted variable may only be dimensioned once. If there are two DIM statements for the same variable or if a DIM statement is executed more than once, the error message

$$?\text{REDIM'D ARRAY ERROR}$$

will result.

CLR

In programs where available memory usage is limited it is sometimes useful to be able to clear variables which are no longer needed. This can be done using the CLR statement. For example,

$$100 \text{ CLR}$$

will remove all variables, including subscripted variables, from memory.

Program 4.9

This program demonstrates the effect of CLR on variables stored in the computer's memory:

```
10 A=47.9
20 R$="THIS IS AN EXAMPLE OF CLR"
30 T(4)=3.1416
40 PRINT A;R$;T(4)
50 CLR
60 PRINT
70 PRINT A;R$;T(4);"WHAT HAPPENED TO THE VARIABLES?"

RUN
 47.9 THIS IS AN EXAMPLE OF CLR 3.1416

 0   0 WHAT HAPPENED TO THE VARIABLES?

READY.
```

Double Subscripted Variables

The computer can also use double subscripts to name a variable. This is similar to single subscripting except that there are two numbers within the parentheses instead of one. For example,

$$A(1,5) \quad B3(7,3) \quad C\$(4,9)$$

are all double subscripted variables. The programmer can visualize the space in memory for a double subscripted variable as an array of rows and columns, rather than in a single column (as in the case with a single subscripted variable). This procedure provides a convenient technique for dealing with problems in which the data are two-dimensional in nature, such as the location of seats in a theater.

The box analogy will help the programmer understand more clearly how the double subscripted variable operates. The first integer in the subscript identifies the row and the second the column in which the variable is located. For example, A(2,3) is located at the second row, third column:

	Col. 1	Col. 2	Col. 3	Col. 4
Row 1	A (1, 1)	A (1, 2)	A (1, 3)	A (1, 4)
Row 2	A (2, 1)	A (2, 2)	A (2, 3)	A (2, 4)
Row 3	A (3, 1)	A (3, 2)	A (3, 3)	A (3, 4)

Program 4.10

A classroom has 5 rows of seats with 3 seats to a row. The following program randomly assigns a class of 14 students to seats, leaving one seat empty:

```
10  DIM N$(5,3)
20  FOR X = 1 TO 14
30     READ A$
40     R = INT(5 * RND(0) + 1)
50     C = INT(3 * RND(0) + 1)
60     IF N$(R,C)<>"" THEN 40
70     N$(R,C) = A$
80  NEXT X
90  FOR R1 = 1 TO 5
100    FOR C1 = 1 TO 3
110      IF N$(R1,C1)="" THEN PRINT "EMPTY", : GOTO 130
120      PRINT N$(R1,C1),
130    NEXT C1
140    PRINT
150  NEXT R1
160  DATA ANNE, DON, SHERRY, MAGGIE, TED, LIZ, ROB
170  DATA MARY, DAVID, MARK, KEVIN, SUSAN, WENDELL, CINDY
```

```
RUN
MARY       ROB         EMPTY
CINDY      DON         MAGGIE
DAVID      SHERRY      SUSAN
WENDELL    LIZA        KEVIN
MARK       TED         ANNE

READY.
```

The computer also allows 3, 4, etc., all the way up to 46 dimensions in a subscripted variable (e.g., DIM X(5,5,8,2,3,1)). However, the more dimensions that a subscripted variable has, the smaller each dimension must be because of the limited amount of space available in the computer's memory.

Review

5. Six numbers are to be input from the keyboard and stored in the subscripted variable X(). These are subsequently to be printed in a vertical column, and then a second time, closely spaced on a single line.

```
RUN
?  23
?  67
?  128
?  37
?  42
?  143
  23
  67
  128
  37
  42
  143

  23   67   128   37   42   143

READY.
```

6. Use the double subscripted variable X$(I,J) for which the row variable I runs from 1 to 5 and the column variable J from 1 to 3. Enter the letters A, B, C as the first row, D, E, F as the second, up to M, N, O as the fifth. Have the program print the following, making the rows become columns (Hint: Use READ, DATA):

```
RUN
A  D  G  J  M
B  E  H  K  N
C  F  I  L  O

READY.
```

Some Final Notes on Subscripted Variables

Subscripted string and numeric variables greatly enhance the programmer's ability to store and deal with large quantities of data within any one program run. It must be remembered, however, that if the program is run again, all of the stored data in the computer's memory is erased. This means that all of the boxes become either null ("") or zero at the start of the next run. A method for permanently storing data is presented in Chapter 9.

Extended Variable Names

Previously, variable names have consisted of a single letter or a single letter followed by a digit. As was pointed out in this chapter, these names may also be subscripted. Actually, variable names may be of any length. For example, ALPHABET, HAROLD, SCARE and BLACKBEARD23 are all permissible variable names. There are, however, drawbacks in these names. Nowhere in the name of a variable may any key word occur. For example, SCORE, FORTUNE, SAND and DIMWIT are all unacceptable variable names because they contain the words OR, FOR, AND and DIM, respectively. Also, no matter how long the variable name may be, the Commodore considers only the first two characters. This means the variable names XMIN and XMAX are considered the same because they both start with XM. Because of these drawbacks, it is recommended that extended variable names not be used except where they are useful in identifying what a variable represents.

EXERCISES

1. Using a nested loop, have the computer print a rectangle consisting of eight lines of thirty asterisks each.

2. Show the output of the following program and check by running it. Rerun the program after removing line 50:

```
10 FOR I = 1 TO 5
20    FOR J = 1 TO 2*I - 1
30       PRINT ".";
40    NEXT J
50    PRINT
60 NEXT I
```

3. Enter values of X(I) for I = 1 to 6. Print the values of I and X(I) in two columns with I proceeding in the order 1, 3, 5, 2, 4, 6.

4. Enter 15 letters of the alphabet (not necessarily different) and print them in reverse order as a single block of letters.

5. Have the computer compute the values of A(I,J), where A(I,J) = 3 * I + J * J, I varies from 1 to 4, and J varies from 1 to 12. The user is to input a number N from 1 to 4 so that all values of A(N,J) can be printed.

6. Using a DATA statement, have the computer enter one letter of the alphabet for each member of A$(I,J), where I runs from 1 to 11 and J from 1 to 3. The letters are first to be printed in the form of an 11 word sentence, each word consisting of 3 letters. Then, the letters are to be printed again as a 3 word sentence, each word consisting of 11 letters. The words may or may not make sense.

7. Carol, who has forgotten where the computer is, needs to know the output for the following programs. Predict the output in each case and check by running the program.

```
10 FOR L1 = 1 TO 3
20    FOR L2 = 5 TO 6
30       PRINT L1,L2
40    NEXT L2
50 NEXT L1
```

```
(b) 10 FOR X = 10 TO 15 STEP 2
    20    FOR Y = 15 TO 10 STEP -2
    30       IF Y=X THEN 99
    40       IF X<Y THEN PRINT X : GOTO 60
    50       PRINT Y
    60    NEXT Y
    70 NEXT X
    99 END

(c) 10 FOR S = 1 TO 10
    20    READ A(S)
    30 NEXT S
    40 PRINT A(3),A(7),A(10)
    50 DATA 23,12,45,2,87,34,89,17,2,35,70
```

8. Suzy Sunshine has done it again and has written another program that will not run properly. Assist her by correcting the program. The output should look like this:

```
RUN
 3          4
 4          3
 4          4
 5          3
 5          4

READY.

10 FOR A = 3,5
20    FOR B = 1,4
30       IF A * B <= 10 GOTO 50
40       PRINYAB
50    NEXT A
60 NEXT B
```

9. The following program is designed to print the numbers in the DATA statement in decreasing order. However, there are some errors in the program. Correct and run the program to produce this output:

```
RUN
 40   37   27   27   16   9   8   5   2   1
READY.

10 FOR X = 40 TO 1
20    FOR Y = 1 TO 10
30       READ N
40       IF N = X THEN PRINT N;
50    NEXT X
60 NEXT Y
70 DATA 5,27,37,16,27,8,2,40,1,9
```

10. What is the exact output for the following program?

```
10 READ B1,B2,B3,B4,B5,B6
20 FOR X = 1 TO 6
30    READ B(X)
40 NEXT X
50 PRINT "B4=";B4;" BUT B(4)=";B(4)
60 PRINT B1 + B2 + B3,
70 PRINT B(1) + B(2) + B(3),B(1+2+3)
80 DATA 3,7,4,1,8,12
90 DATA 14,42,69,86,12,111
```

11. The following program is designed to generate random integers between 1 and 99, inclusive, until it encounters a duplicate. At that point it should print how many numbers it has found and then print all of them. However, there are a number of errors in the program. Correct them to produce output similar to:

```
RUN
DUPLICATE AFTER 9 NUMBERS
 95   47   71   87    1   25   12   10   95
READY.
```

```
20 FOR X = 1 TO 100
30    N(X) = INT(99*RND(0)+1)
40    FOR Y = 1 TO 100
50       IF N(X) <> N(Y) THEN 70
60       PRINT "DUPLICATE AFTER";X;"NUMBERS"
70       FOR Z = 1 TO X : PRINT N(X); : NEXT Z
80    NEXT Y
90 NEXT X
```

12. Write a program that reads the names, street addresses, towns and zip codes of five people into subscripted variables N$(X), A$(X), T$(X) and Z$(X). The user enters a name, and the program prints the full name and address of that person. If the name is not there, have the program print PERSON NOT FOUND.

13. A Pythagorean triple is a set of three integers which are the lengths of the sides of a right trangle ($C^2 = A^2 + B^2$). Find all sets of three integers up to $C = 50$ which are Pythagorean triples. For example, $A = 3$, $B = 4$, $C = 5$ is a solution. (Note that due to rounding errors, it is better to use $A*A + B*B = C*C$ rather than $A\uparrow2 + B\uparrow2 = C\uparrow2$ to check for equalities.)

14. Stan's Grocery Store has 3 aisles and in each aisle there are five items. Write a program that will read 15 items into the subscripted variable I$(X,Y), dimensioned 3×5. Let his customers type in the item they want to buy and be informed by the computer of the aisle and the item's number.

```
RUN
WHAT ARE YOU LOOKING FOR? CHERRIES
YOU WILL FIND CHERRIES IN AISLE # 1   ITEM # 4
WHAT ARE YOU LOOKING FOR? MILK
YOU WILL FIND MILK IN AISLE # 2   ITEM # 2
WHAT ARE YOU LOOKING FOR? BROCCOLI
I'M SORRY, WE DON'T HAVE BROCCOLI
WHAT ARE YOU LOOKING FOR?
```

15. Pick 20 random integers between 10 and 99, inclusive. Print the odd integers on one line and the even integers on the next line. The output should look like this:

```
RUN
ODD INTEGERS: 15  81  89  33  97  23  23  55  55  11
EVEN INTEGERS: 84  72  76  44  52  84  88  58  66  78
READY.
```

16. Find the average of four grades for each of five students. The output should give in columns on consecutive lines each student's name, four grades and average. Each column should have a heading. The last student's average should be underlined and the class average printed below it in the same column.

```
RUN
STUDENT # 1 ? DON
ENTER FOUR GRADES:? 42,86,99,99
STUDENT # 2 ? LESTER
ENTER FOUR GRADES:? 50,55,45,34
STUDENT # 3 ? LIZ
ENTER FOUR GRADES:? 100,98,99,97
STUDENT # 4 ? ROB
ENTER FOUR GRADES:? 67,72,71,68
STUDENT # 5 ? SUE
ENTER FOUR GRADES:? 89,91,93,90
NAME        1     2     3     4      AVE.
DON         42    86    99    99     81.5
LESTER      50    55    45    34     46
LIZ         100   98    99    97     98.5
ROB         67    72    71    68     69.5
SUE         89    91    93    90     90.75
                                     ------
                                     77.25

READY.
```

17. Marcus Welby wants you to program the computer to keep track of his busy schedule.
(a) Write a program to allow a patient to choose the day and time he or she wants to see the doctor. There are 5 days and 6 time slots for each day. If the desired slot is empty, the patient enters his or her name. If it is full, the program asks for another slot.
(b) Add the steps needed to allow Dr. Welby to print his schedule for any particular day.

18. Marilyn Monroe has 3 skirts—red, green, and purple; 2 pairs of jeans—white and electric purple; 4 blouses—blue, pink, orange, and black; and 2 sweaters—yellow and green. Have the computer print a list of all possible combinations of the articles she can wear (e.g., red skirt and blue blouse, or white jeans and yellow sweater).

19. Write an extended version of the game high-low. In this game, the computer picks a secret random number from 1 to 100 and gives the player an unlimited number of chances to guess it. For each wrong guess the computer tells whether to guess higher or lower and stores the guess in a subscripted variable. If the player guesses the same number twice, the computer should produce the message WAKE UP! YOU GUESSED THAT NUMBER BEFORE.

20. Betty Davis has written the following two programs to sort data. Read the programs carefully and predict the output:

```
(a) 10 DIM A(10)
    20 FOR B = 1 TO 10
    30    READ A(B)
    40 NEXT B
    50 FOR C = 2 TO 10
    60    FOR D = 1 TO C-1
    70       IF A(D) <= A(C) THEN 90
    80       E = A(D):A(D) = A(C): A(C) = E
    90    NEXT D
    100 NEXT C
    110 FOR F = 1 TO 10
    120    PRINT A(F)
    130 NEXT F
    200 DATA 1,3,7,2,4,9,0,2,5,8
```

```
(b) 10 DIM Q$(10)
    20 FOR M = 1 TO 10
    30    READ Q$(M)
    40 NEXT M
    50 FOR R = 5 TO 10
    60    FOR Z = 5 TO R-1
    70       IF Q$(Z) <= Q$(R) THEN 90
    80       T$ = Q$(Z):Q$(Z) = Q$(R):Q$(R) = T$
    90    NEXT Z
    100 NEXT R
    110 FOR I = 10 TO 1 STEP -1
    120    PRINT Q$(I)
    130 NEXT I
    200 DATA JON,KIM,SUE,ELIZABETH,KIRSTIE
    210 DATA ZERO,HANS,SCOTT,WINSTON,MATILDA
```

21. The game Penny Pitch is common in amusement parks. Pennies are tossed onto a checkerboard on which numbers have been printed. By adding up the numbers in the squares on which the pennies fall, a score is accumulated. Write a program which simulates such a game in which ten pennies are to be randomly pitched onto the board shown below:

Have the computer print the board with an X indicating where each penny has landed and then the score. Below is a sample run. Note that more than one penny can land in one square:

```
RUN
 1   X   1   1   1   X
 1   2   2   2   2   1
 1   2   X   3   2   X
 1   2   X   X   2   1
 1   2   X   X   X   1
 1   1   1   1   X   1

SCORE =   19
```

22. Write a program that rolls two dice 1000 times and prints the number of times each different point total (2, 3, 4, 5 . . . , 12) appeared. The output should resemble the following:

```
POINT TOTAL              TIMES APPEARING
     2                        29
     3                        75
     4                        66
     5                       114
     6                       114
     7                       183
     8                       160
     9                       103
    10                        88
    11                        45
    12                        23
```

23. Write a program which makes up 15 "words" (i.e. groups of letters, whether pronounceable or not) composed of from one to seven randomly chosen letters and prints them. (Hint: use addition of strings. For example, if A$(2) = "B" and A$(12) = "L", then A$(2) + A$(12) = "BL".)

24. Use the computer to play a modified game of Othello. Have it randomly fill an 8 × 8 subscripted string variable with X's and O's and print the array by row (horizontal) and column (vertical). Examples are shown below. The X's are for player 1, the O's for player 2. Have the program ask the players alternately for the row and column of the opponent's piece that should be flipped (changed from an X to an O or vice versa). All of the opponent's pieces along the horizontal or vertical line passing through the flipped piece are also flipped. For example, if player 1 flipped the 0 at 1,8, board A would be changed to board B.

```
(a)     1 2 3 4 5 6 7 8          (b)     1 2 3 4 5 6 7 8
    1   X X O O X O X O              1   X X X X X X X X
    2   O O O X X O X X              2   O O O X X O X X
    3   X O X X O X O O              3   X O X X O X O X
    4   O O X O X O X O              4   O O X O X O X X
    5   O O X X X O X O              5   O O X X X O X X
    6   O O X O O X X O              6   O O X O O X X X
    7   O O X X O X O X              7   O O X X O X O X
    8   X X O X X O X X              8   X X O X X O X X
```

25. Mr. and Mrs. Charles Windsor want to start a bank account for their newborn son, William. They open the account with $500. At the beginning of each successive year they deposit $60 more. When William is 21, how much money will be in the account? (Assume the interest rate to be 6% compounded quarterly).

PROGRAMMING TECHNIQUES

5

GOSUB
RETURN
ON…GOTO
ON…GOSUB
STOP
CONT
GOSUB
RETURN
ON…GOTO
ON…GOSUB
STOP
CONT
GOSUB
RETURN
ON…GOTO
ON…GOSUB
STOP
CONT
GOSUB
RETURN
ON…GOTO
ON…GOSUB
STOP
CONT
GOSUB
RETURN
ON…GOTO
ON…GOSUB

Writing long, complex programs may require special programming techniques. It is often helpful to divide these programs into sections, called subroutines. Subroutines are useful because they perform a specified task and may be accessed from anywhere in the program. A long program may be divided into a main section and a series of subroutines. The main section directs the order in which the subroutines do their specialized jobs. This type of organization usually reduces the size of a program because the lines needed to perform a certain task have only to be placed once in a program, even though the task may be performed several times.

GOSUB, RETURN

In the case of programs whose various portions are repeated at different places, it may be efficient to use a subroutine. A subroutine is entered by the statement

$$\text{GOSUB } <\text{line number}>$$

and exited by the statement

$$\text{RETURN}$$

For example:

```
10  . . . . . . . .
20  GOSUB 200
30  . . . . . . .
40  . . . . . . .
200 . . . . . . .
210 . . . . . . .
220 . . . . . . .
230 RETURN
999 END
```

The skeleton program illustrates the use of a subroutine. At line 20 the program jumps to the subroutine, which begins at line 200, executes the subroutine and then returns from line 230 to the body of the program at line 30. It is legal to use more than one RETURN statement within a subroutine. You should remember that the computer always returns to the first statement after the GOSUB statement which caused the subroutine to be executed. The major difference between GOSUB and the GOTO statement is that GOSUB permits the use of RETURN. Subroutines are usually placed towards the bottom of a program. They may be written so that one subroutine can access another.

Program 5.1

Given the numbers of pennies, nickels, dimes and quarters as input, this program will output the total amount of money represented by these coins. One subroutine processes and reports the amount of money involved for each of the four types of coins:

```
10 A$ = "PENNIES": V = 1
20 GOSUB 200
30 A$ = "NICKELS": V = 5
40 GOSUB 200
50 A$ = "DIMES": V = 10
60 GOSUB 200
70 A$ = "QUARTERS": V = 25
80 GOSUB 200
90 PRINT "THE TOTAL VALUE WAS $";T/100
100 END
200 REM     SUBROUTINE
210 PRINT "NUMBER OF ";A$;
220 INPUT N
230 PRINT N;A$;" =";N*V;"CENTS"
240 T = T + N*V
250 RETURN

RUN
NUMBER OF PENNIES?  4
 4 PENNIES = 4 CENTS
NUMBER OF NICKELS?  9
 9 NICKELS = 45 CENTS
NUMBER OF DIMES?  3
 3 DIMES = 30 CENTS
NUMBER OF QUARTERS?  6
 6 QUARTERS = 150 CENTS
THE TOTAL VALUE WAS $ 2.29

READY.
```

Line 10 assigns the type (A$) and value (V) of the first coin. Line 20 causes a jump to the subroutine, which begins at line 200, where the number of coins is input. Line 210 prints information about the particular coin being considered, and line 240 adds its contribution to the previous total value of all coins up to this point. Line 250 returns the program to the line following the most recently used GOSUB statement. This entire process, beginning at line 200, repeats itself three more times, and then the dollar total is printed. What would happen if line 100 were deleted?

ON... GOTO

The GOTO statement allows a program to jump to a single specified line. The ON... GOTO statement allows jumps to one of several lines, depending on the value of a numeric variable at the time the statement is encountered. This statement takes the form:

$$ON \ <variable> \ GOTO \ <list \ of \ line \ numbers>$$

For example:

$$50 \ ON \ X \ GOTO \ 100, \ 120, \ 140, \ 160$$

If X = 1, the program jumps to line 100; if X = 2, it jumps to line 120 and so on. Note that X should not be less than one or greater than the number of line numbers in the list.

Program 5.2

This program simulates the random path taken by a mouse through the following maze:

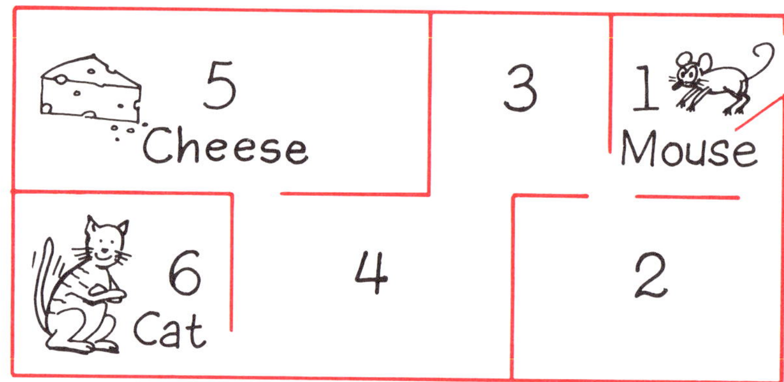

Once the mouse enters the maze, the door is shut. The mouse wanders about until it either finds the cheese or stumbles upon the cat.

```
100 PRINT 1,
110 X = INT(2*RND(0)+1)
120 ON X GOTO 200,300
200 PRINT 2,
210 X = INT(2*RND(0)+1)
220 ON X GOTO 100,300
300 PRINT 3,
310 X = INT(3*RND(0)+1)
320 ON X GOTO 100,200,400
400 PRINT 4,
410 X = INT(3*RND(0)+1)
420 ON X GOTO 300,500,600
500 PRINT 5
510 PRINT "THE MOUSE IS GORGING ITSELF!"
520 END
600 PRINT 6
610 PRINT "THE CAT HAS BEEN AWAKENED BY ITS LUNCH."

RUN
 1           3           1           3
 2           3           4           6
THE CAT HAS BEEN AWAKENED BY ITS LUNCH.

READY.
```

At line 100 the program prints a 1 to indicate that the mouse is in room #1. Line 110 randomly picks either the number 1 or the number 2. The ON . . . GOTO statement at line 120 sends program execution to line 200 if X = 1, and to 300 if X = 2; lines 200 and 300 correspond to rooms 2 and 3, respectively. Once the mouse is in one of the other rooms, the program prints the room number and decides where the mouse will go from there. Execution continues until the mouse finds itself either in room 5 or room 6.

The ON . . . GOSUB statement operates in much the same way as the ON . . . GOTO statement. If there are a number of subroutines in a program, they can be called using the ON . . . GOSUB statement:

$$50 \text{ ON X GOSUB } 300, \ 400, \ 500$$

If X = 1, the program jumps to the subroutine at line 300; if X = 2, to the subroutine at line 400; and if X = 3, to the subroutine at line 500. When the subroutine is completed, the RETURN statement directs the program back to the first statement after line 50.

Program 5.3

This program uses ON . . . GOSUB in delivering a movie review:

```
10 PRINT "1- STAR WARS"
20 PRINT "2- THE EMPIRE STIKES BACK"
30 PRINT "3- RETURN OF THE JEDI"
40 PRINT "CHOOSE THE MOVIE REVIEW BY NUMBER."
50 INPUT "1,2 OR 3";X
60 ON X GOSUB 200,300,400
70 PRINT
80 GOTO 40
200 PRINT "LUKE BATTLES THE EMPIRE"
210 PRINT "RESCUES THE PRINCESS AND"
220 PRINT "DESTROYS THE DREADED DEATHSTAR."
230 RETURN
300 PRINT "THE REBEL ALLIANCE IS TEMPORARILY"
310 PRINT "SETBACK AND HAN IS CAPTURED"
320 PRINT "AND FROZEN."
330 RETURN
400 PRINT "YOU'LL HAVE TO SEE IT TO"
410 PRINT "FIND OUT WHAT HAPPENS."
420 RETURN

RUN
1- STAR WARS
2- THE EMPIRE STIKES BACK
3- RETURN OF THE JEDI
CHOOSE THE MOVIE REVIEW BY NUMBER.
1,2 OR 3? 1
LUKE BATTLES THE EMPIRE
RESCUES THE PRINCESS AND
DESTROYS THE DREADED DEATHSTAR.

CHOOSE THE MOVIE REVIEW BY NUMBER.
1,2 OR 3?
```

Review

1. Write a program in which names are input and then printed. If DONALD is input, use a subroutine to underline the name.

```
RUN
NAME? MARY
MARY
NAME? SUE
SUE
NAME? DONALD
DONALD
------
NAME?
```

2. Write a program to draw five cards from a deck. The computer picks two random numbers, the first between 1 and 4, inclusive, and the second between 1 and 13, inclusive. An ON . . . GOTO statement should use the first number to pick each suit. The second represents the card's value within the suit.

```
RUN
CARD 1 IS THE   6 OF HEARTS
CARD 2 IS THE   2 OF SPADES
CARD 3 IS THE   3 OF CLUBS
CARD 4 IS THE   9 OF SPADES
CARD 5 IS THE   1 OF SPADES

READY.
```

3. Write a program using an ON . . . GOSUB statement that takes one of four different courses of action depending on the number entered (A).

```
If A = 0        Print "You are a zero"
   A = 1        Print "Danielle loves Michael"
   A = 2        Print "Michael loves Danielle"
   A = 3        Print "Who is Danielle?"
```

Planning a Program

Now that you are familiar with most of the BASIC commands it is important to spend time refining your programming techniques. The first step to this end is learning to plan your program.

The programmer's first concern in planning a program is to define precisely the problem to be solved. This requires the programmer to analyze the problem carefully and to develop a logical sequence of steps to solve the problem. The problem is first broken down into smaller units, each of which should be easier to solve. Just as the task of building a house is made manageable by breaking it down into a series of smaller tasks, so such subdivision of a problem can simplify programming. The solution to the total problem will be accomplished when the solutions to the smaller problems are pieced together in a logical sequence.

The plan used to solve a problem is called an algorithm. Each step in the algorithm should be clear, feasible and unambiguous. A useful technique to develop an algorithm is to determine how a problem could be solved using only pencil and paper. The same step by step sequence required to produce this non-computer solution can usually be translated directly into the sequence employed within a computer program.

Proper planning, as suggested above, will enable the programmer to avoid the common mistake of writing the program before the problem or its solution is understood. Premature "coding" (the term "code" is used to define the instructions which comprise a program) frequently results in a program which must be modified by adding or deleting lines of code until the desired output is achieved, with the consequence that the resulting program is usually a "mish-mash" of statements which do not flow logically from one to another. For example, when excessive GOTO and IF . . . THEN statements have been added to a program to make it work, the sequential flow from line to line, a sign of good programming, is often destroyed. Moreover, the code itself will lack clarity and will be less easily understood by other programmers. Therefore, one should plan a program as thoroughly as possible before approaching the computer. As the computer pioneer R. W. Hamming declared, "Typing is no substitute for thinking."

To demonstrate the use of an algorithm, we will design a program that will give a student a mathematics quiz. This quiz will consist of ten questions, each of which will be one of four types: addition, subtraction, multiplication or division. Two randomly chosen numbers between 1 and 10, inclusive, will be used in each problem, and the student will be given two chances to answer each question correctly. If the student answers a question correctly on the first attempt, then he or she will receive full credit (10 points), or if the second attempt is correct, then half credit (5 points) is awarded. The quiz might be similar to the following:

```
WHAT DOES 5*8 = ?  30
WRONG
WHAT DOES 5*8 = ?  40
CORRECT
WHAT DOES 5 − 12 = ?  7
WRONG
WHAT DOES 5 − 12 = ?  −3
WRONG
YOU HAVE HAD 2 TRIES; THE ANSWER IS −7
```

At the outset, a plan or algorithm must be outlined and the problem broken down into separate parts. For example:

(1) Print instructions
(2) Randomly select the type of problem
    (addition, subtraction, multiplication, division)
(3) Choose two random numbers between 1 and 10
    to be used in the problem
(4) Prompt the user for his or her answer
(5) Compare the student's answer to the correct answer
(6) Compute the score
(7) Repeat steps 2 through 6 ten times

Notice that no matter which type of problem (add., subt., mult., or div.) is chosen, the testing procedure remains the same. This means that we could place each type of problem in its own subroutine. Since we want a random selection of four types of problems, we could generate a random number from 1 to 4 and use it as the variable in an ON . . . GOSUB statement.

At this point it is useful to assign names to the variables we will use and then use these names in refining our algorithm. We will call the variable that represents the type of question (N), the two random numbers used in each question (A) and (B), the student's answer (ANSWER), and the loop variable (QUEST), the correct answer (C), and the score (SCR).

Because ten questions are to be asked, a FOR . . . NEXT loop will be used. The algorithm using variable names can now be further refined to read:

```
Print Instructions
FOR QUEST = 1 to 10
     Choose random number N from 1 to 4 inclusive
     Choose two random numbers (A,B) from 1 to 10 inclusive
     ON N GOSUB (add, sub., mult., div.)
     FOR GUESS = 1 to 2
          INPUT ANSWER
          Compare ANSWER to correct answer (C)
          Compute SCR
     NEXT GUESS
NEXT QUEST
PRINT SCR
END
Subroutines:
Addition
Subtraction
Multiplication
Division
```

The structure of the algorithm is now quite clear. First the student will be given instructions. The body of the program will consist of a main loop which is repeated ten times. Within the loop the computer will choose the type of question to ask and the numbers to be used in the question, ask for an answer, and then compute the score depending on the answer. The last step will print the final score.

Each of the four subroutines will ask one type of problem and compute the correct answer. We have attempted to put parts of the program common to each type of problem in the main body (within the QUEST loop) and only those parts which are unique to a specific type of problem in each subroutine. For example, the subroutine for addition will print the question and determine the correct answer:

```
PRINT "WHAT DOES"; A; "+"; B; "=";
C = A + B
```

This plan will work for each of the four subroutines, each of which will have a different PRINT statement and answer for the variable C.

In order to structure a program properly, observe the following rules :

1. Place REM statements at the beginning of a program to indicate what the program does and to define the variables used within the program. In addition, REM statements strategically placed throughout the program can be helpful in explaining how the program works.
2. Indent the lines within FOR ... NEXT loops to clarify where the loops begin and end and what portions of the program are contained within each loop.
3. Break a program down into separate modules or subroutines, where each performs a specific task. It is a good programming practice to separate each subroutine from the others by choosing appropriate line numbers. For example, if a program contains three subroutines, each of which is about 15 lines long, then number the lines of the first subroutine from 100 to 250, the second from 300 to 450, and the third from 500 to 650. In addition, each subroutine should be separated from the next by using blank REM statements, and each subroutine should start with a REM which explains its function.

Program 5.4

With these rules in mind, we are now ready to translate our plan into a program. Note the almost one to one correspondence between the program and the math quiz algorithm:

```
1 REM    N = TYPE OF QUESTION
3 REM    ANSWER = STUDENT'S ANSWER
4 REM    QUEST = QUESTION NUMBER
5 REM    GUESS = STUDENT'S ATTEMPT NUMBER
6 REM    SCR = STUDENT'S SCORE
10 PRINT "YOU WILL BE ASKED TEN QUESTIONS THAT"
20 PRINT "COULD BE OF 4 TYPES: ADDITION,"
30 PRINT "SUBTRACTION, MULTIPLICATION, OR"
40 PRINT "DIVISION. YOU WILL GET 2 TRIES TO"
50 PRINT "GET EACH CORRECT. YOUR SCORE WILL"
60 PRINT "BE BASED ON THE NUMBER OF GUESSES"
70 PRINT "YOU TAKE."
80 PRINT
100 FOR QUEST = 1 TO 10
110    N = INT(4*RND(0)+1)
120    A = INT(10*RND(0)+1)
130    B = INT(10*RND(0)+1)
140    ON N GOSUB 300,400,500,600
150    FOR GUESS = 1 TO 2
160       INPUT "YOUR ANSWER IS";ANSWER
170       IF ANSWER <> C THEN PRINT "WRONG": GOTO 210
180       PRINT "CORRECT"
190       IF GUESS = 1 THEN SCR = SCR+10: GOTO 230
200       SCR = SCR+5: GOTO 230
210    NEXT GUESS
220    PRINT "YOU'VE HAD 2 TRIES; THE ANSWER IS";C
230    PRINT
240 NEXT QUEST
250 PRINT "YOU HAVE SCORED";SCR;"%"
260 END
270 REM
280 REM
```

```
300 REM    ADDITION
310 PRINT "WHAT DOES";A;"+";B;"="
320 C = A+B
330 RETURN
340 REM
350 REM
400 REM    SUBTRACTION
410 PRINT "WHAT DOES";A;"-";B;"="
420 C = A-B
430 RETURN
440 REM
450 REM
500 REM    MULTIPLICATION
510 PRINT "WHAT DOES";A;"*";B;"="
520 C = A*B
530 RETURN
540 REM
550 REM
600 REM    DIVISION
610 PRINT "WHAT DOES";A;"/";B;"="
620 C = A/B
630 RETURN

RUN
YOU WILL BE ASKED TEN QUESTIONS THAT
COULD BE OF 4 TYPES: ADDITION,
SUBTRACTION, MULTIPLICATION, OR
DIVISION. YOU WILL GET 2 TRIES TO
GET EACH CORRECT. YOUR SCORE WILL
BE BASED ON THE NUMBER OF GUESSES
YOU TAKE.

WHAT DOES 2 + 9 =
YOUR ANSWER IS? 18
WRONG
YOUR ANSWER IS? 29
WRONG
YOU'VE HAD 2 TRIES; THE ANSWER IS 11

WHAT DOES 7 * 8 =
YOUR ANSWER IS? 78
WRONG
YOUR ANSWER IS? 56
CORRECT

WHAT DOES 3 / 2 =
YOUR ANSWER IS? 1.4
WRONG
YOUR ANSWER IS? 1.5
CORRECT
```

```
WHAT DOES 8 / 9 =
YOUR ANSWER IS? .9
WRONG
YOUR ANSWER IS? .888
WRONG
YOU'VE HAD 2 TRIES; THE ANSWER IS .888888889

WHAT DOES 4 - 7 =
YOUR ANSWER IS? -3
CORRECT

WHAT DOES 4 + 7 =
YOUR ANSWER IS? 11
CORRECT

WHAT DOES 3 - 5 =
YOUR ANSWER IS? -2
CORRECT

WHAT DOES 6 * 1 =
YOUR ANSWER IS? 7
WRONG
YOUR ANSWER IS? 6
CORRECT

WHAT DOES 6 * 7 =
YOUR ANSWER IS? 42
CORRECT

WHAT DOES 5 / 1 =
YOUR ANSWER IS? 5
CORRECT

YOU HAVE SCORED 65 %

READY.
```

This math quiz example illustrates that some problems cannot always be foreseen in planning a program. A good algorithm, however, can make correcting these problems substantially easier. In addition, a clearly structured and annotated program can eliminate any unnecessary confusion. The run of Program 5.4 illustrates that there is something wrong in the division subroutine. Although the student answered the division problem correctly each time, the computer did not always acknowledge that fact. The error occurs in the division at line 620, where a rounding error is introduced. At line 170 the student's response, ANSWER, is compared with the desired answer, C. Unfortunately, these variables are compared to ten decimal places of accuracy, and because the student responded by giving an answer to only three decimal places, the comparison failed. The problem might be corrected by rounding the correct answer, C, to 3 decimal places by the line

$$620 \ C = INT \ (1000*A/B + 0.5) \ /1000$$

but then a new rounding error is introduced by dividing by 1000. In order to get an accurate comparison to only 3 decimal places, it will be necessary to compare the integer values of ANSWER∗1000 with C which is multiplied by 1000 in lines 320, 420, 520, and 620.

$$170 \text{ IF INT (ANSWER}*1000 + 0.5) <> \text{INT } (C + 0.5)$$
$$\text{THEN PRINT ``WRONG'': GOTO 210}$$

This statement will correct the rounding problem without affecting the other operations. In addition, the instructions should be modified so that the student is asked to round his or her responses to 3 decimal places.

The following modifications can be made to Program 5.4 to account for the rounding error in the division problems:

```
70 PRINT "YOU TAKE. ROUND YOUR ANSWERS"
80 PRINT "TO 3 DECIMAL PLACES. GOOD LUCK!"
90 PRINT
170    IF INT(ANSWER*1000+0.5) <> INT(C+0.5)
          THEN PRINT "WRONG" : GOTO 210
220     PRINT "YOU'VE HAD 2 TRIES; THE ANSWER IS"; C/1000
320 C = (A + B) * 1000
420 C = (A - B) * 1000
520 C = (A * B) * 1000
620 C = INT(A / B * 1000 + 0.5)



RUN
YOU WILL BE ASKED TEN QUESTIONS THAT
COULD BE OF 4 TYPES: ADDITION,
SUBTRACTION, MULTIPLICATION, OR
DIVISION. YOU WILL GET 2 TRIES TO
GET EACH CORRECT. YOUR SCORE WILL
BE BASED ON THE NUMBER OF GUESSES
YOU TAKE. ROUND DIVISION PROBLEMS
TO 3 DECIMAL PLACES. GOOD LUCK

WHAT DOES 5 - 7 =
YOUR ANSWER IS? -2
CORRECT

           •

           •                              (A complete run is not shown)

           •
WHAT DOES 8 * 6 =
YOUR ANSWER IS? 44
WRONG
YOUR ANSWER IS? 48
CORRECT
```

```
WHAT DOES 4 / 9 =
YOUR ANSWER IS? .35
WRONG
YOUR ANSWER IS? .444
CORRECT

YOU HAVE SCORED 85 %

READY.
```

Debugging

Debugging is the process of locating errors or "bugs" in a program and then correcting them. Obviously, the best approach is to avoid bugs by carefully planning a program, but even the most carefully written programs will often contain errors. The rounding error encountered in Program 5.4 illustrates how even a well planned program can have unforeseen errors. Two other types of errors which will cause a program to fail are runtime and logic errors.

Runtime Errors

Runtime errors are detected by the computer when a program is run. These errors result from either syntactical and/or semantic errors. Syntactical errors are caused by typing an improper statement. For example,

```
10 REED X, Y
```

should be

```
10 READ X, Y
```

A semantic error is one that violates the computer's rules of operation. For example,

```
10 READ A$, B
20 DATA 35, SMITH
```

is a semantic violation since the computer attempts to assign the string "SMITH" to the numeric variable B. Another common runtime error is caused by using two different variables in defining a FOR . . . NEXT loop:

```
10 FOR X = 1 TO 10
20    PRINT X, X * 2, X * 3
30 NEXT W
```

Fortunately, the computer detects the runtime error and prints an appropriate error message.

Logic Errors

If the program does not violate any of the syntactical or semantic rules of BASIC, the computer will accept and run it even though the output may not reflect the programmer's true intent. In such a case the errors in the program may stem instead from the programmer's incorrect analysis of how to develop a logical sequence of statements to achieve the intended goal. These forms of errors—referred to as logic errors—are the most difficult to detect and correct.

Program 5.5

This program is supposed to print the areas of circles whose radii are integers varying from 1 to 100 except for those whose computed areas are integers (note line 30). The equation $A = \pi R^2$ is used with the value of π taken as 3.1:

```
10 FOR X = 1 TO 100
20    A = 3.1 * X^2
30    IF A = INT(A) THEN 10
40    PRINT A,
50 NEXT X
60 END

RUN
  3.1          12.4          27.9          49.6
  77.5         111.6         151.9         198.4
  251.1        3.1           12.4          27.9
  49.6         77.5          111.6         151.9
  198.4        251.1         3.1           12.4
  27.9
BREAK IN 40

READY.
```

Note that the printed areas go as high as 251.1 and then start to repeat. The program actually goes into an infinite loop, which means that it keeps running until the STOP key is struck.

A good way to detect the logic error in Program 5.5 is to place an extra PRINT statement in the program in order to print the loop variable X. This extra statement can later be removed when the error has been corrected:

```
25 PRINT "X ="; X,
```

```
RUN
X= 1         3.1          X= 2          12.4
X= 3         27.9         X= 4          49.6
X= 5         77.5         X= 6          111.6
X= 7         151.9        X= 8          198.4
X= 9         251.1        X= 10         X= 1
  3.1        X= 2           12.4        X= 3
  27.9       X= 4           49.6        X= 5
  77.5       X= 6           111.6       X= 7
  151.9      X= 8           198.4       X= 9
  251.1      X= 10        X= 1            3.1
X= 2           12.4        X= 3           27.9
BREAK IN 40
READY.
```

The output indicates that X reaches only 10 and then starts repeating rather than continuing on to 100 as it should. The problem is that line 30 should send the program to line 50 rather than to line 10, where it restarts the X loop at one.

In longer programs it is often useful to place additional print statements at a number of locations to check the value of variables and then remove them when the program is operating properly.

Another technique is to place a line in the program to indicate whether it is getting to a certain point as anticipated. For example:

50 PRINT "I'M AT LINE 50 NOW"

The line can be removed later when no longer needed.

Hand Tracing

It is almost impossible to guarantee that a program will run properly for all possible situations that it may encounter, but one technique that creates confidence in the validity of a program is called hand tracing. Using test data, the programmer solves calculations by hand and checks the results against those produced by the program. If the computer program produces identical answers for the same data, the programmer is then confident that the program works at least for the data that is being tested.

Program 5.6

This is a program which attempts to find the sum of the first N *odd* integers:

```
10 PRINT "NUMBER", "SUM"
20 S = 0
30 READ N
40 FOR K = 1 TO N
50    S = S + 2*K -1
60 NEXT K
70 PRINT N, S
80 GOTO 30
90 DATA 3, 8, 10
100 END

RUN
NUMBER      SUM
  3          9
  8          73
 10          173

?OUT OF DATA  ERROR IN 30
READY.
```

If the output of Program 5.6 is checked by hand for N = 3, S = 1 + 3 + 5 = 9 is a correct answer. In relying on this piece of test data alone, however, the programmer overlooks a serious program error. A major limitation of the test data technique is that the data chosen may bypass the bug. If Program 5.6 is further hand-tested with N = 8, S = 1 + 3 + 5 + 7 + 9 + 11 + 13 + 15 = 64, this result disagrees with the output above. The presence of a bug is now apparent.

The next problem is to locate the position of the error in the program. One effective way to do this, or even better, to avoid errors in the first place, is to "play computer" with the program. This method is commonly called *hand simulation* or *hand tracing*.

To find the bug in Program 5.6 by this method, the programmer makes a table displaying each variable in the program and then performs the numerical assignments of the variables as the program dictates, line-by-line:

Line	N	K	S	
20			0	
30	3			
40		1		
50			1	
60→40		2		
50			4	
60→40		3		
50			9	
60→70				(Print 3,9)
80→30	8			
40		1		
50			10	(Error! S should now be 1)

The error was caused by not resetting S to 0 before reading the new data N = 8. Hence, to correct the error, change line 80 to:

```
80 GOTO 20

RUN
NUMBER     SUM
  3          9
  8         64
 10        100

?OUT OF DATA  ERROR IN 30
READY.
```

STOP and CONT

Halting a program at certain points by using one or more STOP statements is a useful debugging technique. Upon interruption, the values of the program's variables may be examined. Typing CONT will continue program execution from the point at which it was interrupted.

Program 5.7

```
10 FOR X = 1 TO 100
20    A = 3*X^3 + 2*X^2 + 5
30    B = 7*X^2 + 2*X + 5
40     IF B > A THEN PRINT B;">";A
50 NEXT X
60 END
RUN
 14 > 10

READY.
```

When Program 5.7 is run, the computer prints one solution to the condition at line 40 and then gives the appearance of being at rest until it finally prints READY. Is there only one solution or is there a bug in the program? The values of A and B can be checked when $X = 50$ by adding the following line:

$$45 \text{ IF } X = 50 \text{ THEN STOP}$$

The values of A and B can then be examined when the program is halted by typing PRINT A,B. Typing CONT allows this program to continue to completion. Since A is much larger than B when $X = 50$, it is obvious that there will be no other solutions than the first one. Hence, there is no bug in the program:

```
RUN
 14 > 10

BREAK IN 45
READY.

PRINT A,B
 380005      17605

READY.

CONT

READY.
```

Review

4. Each of the following programs contains a 'bug'. Find it and correct it.

a)
```
10 INPUT A
20 FOR X=10 TO 1
30   C = A/X
40    PRINT INT(C)
50 NEXT X
```

b)
```
10 INPUT N
20 IF N < 0 THEN 10 : REM PREVENTS NEGATIVE INPUT
30 P = N*5
40 IF P < 0 THEN PRINT "THE PRODUCT IS NEGATIVE" : GOTO 60
50 PRINT "THE PRODUCT IS POSITIVE"
60 END
```

1. Have the computer produce the printout below. Use a subroutine to print out "PART" and the appropriate number:

```
RUN

PART 1
******************************
PART 2
!             !              !
PART 3
ABABABABABABABABABABABABABAB
READY.
```

2. Have the computer pick a random integer from 1 to 4 which will determine if the prize to be awarded will be a ball, balloon, toy car or candy bar.

3. Input an integer from 1 to 4. The integer should cause one of the following four phrases to be printed:

Avoid being a VICtim
Programming is COMmon sense
A little VICe is sometimes nice
A COMmon COMic COMuter COMmands his COMmodore

4. What is the exact output for the following program?

```
10 READ X
20 ON X GOTO 30,40,50,60,70,80,100
30 PRINT "MERRILY, ";: GOTO 10
40 PRINT "ROW, ";: GOTO 10
50 PRINT "YOUR BOAT": GOTO 10
60 PRINT "GENTLY DOWN THE STREAM": GOTO 10
70 PRINT "LIFE IS BUT A DREAM": GOTO 10
80 PRINT: GOTO 10
90 DATA 2,2,2,3,4,1,1,1,1,6,5,7
100 END
```

5. (a) Give the exact order in which the lines of the following program are executed:
(b) If line 80 is changed to:

$$80 \text{ DATA } 3, 0, 4, -5, -1, -8, 1, 5, 999$$

what will be the output?

```
10  READ X
20  IF X=999 THEN 90
30  ON SGN(X)+2 GOSUB 50,60,70
40  GOTO 10
50  N = N+1:  RETURN
60  Z = Z+1:  RETURN
70  P = P+1:  RETURN
80  DATA 6,-1,0,999
90  PRINT  "N=";N, "Z=";Z, "P=";P
100 END
```

6. (a) Give the exact order in which the lines of the following program are executed:
(b) If line 90 were changed to:

$$90 \text{ DATA, } 1, 8, -2, 5, -3, -6, 2, 4, -7, 0$$

what would the output be?

```
10  READ X
20  IF X=0 THEN 95
30  GOSUB 60
40  T = T+X
50  GOTO 10
60  IF X < 0 THEN 80
70  P = P+X
80  RETURN
90  DATA 5,2,-9,0,3,5
95  PRINT  "T=";T, "P=";P
100 END
```

7. Write a program which reads the dimensions of a triangle from a DATA statement and prints its area and perimeter if it is a right triangle. The program should call a subroutine to check whether the triangle is a right triangle or not. Begin by developing an algorithm for this problem.

8. Let X and Y be the coordinates of a point in a plane. Write a program which randomly picks X and Y, each as an integer from -5 and 5, inclusive. The user of the program is to guess X and Y, with the guesses being called X1 and Y1. A subroutine must be used to print the distance between the guessed point and the actual point after each guess. The user is to be given 3 guesses and, if unsuccessful, is then to be given the value of X as well as 2 more tries to guess Y. Begin by developing an algorithm for this problem.

9. Isolated in his ski-lodge in the Swiss Alps, Bjorn Rich often gets his mail late. As a result the statements from his Swiss bank account rarely arrive on time. To solve this problem, write

a program to assist Bjorn in keeping his account up to date. Have three subroutines which take care of deposits, withdrawals and the interest (5¾% compounded quarterly). Begin by developing an algorithm for this problem.

```
RUN
WITHDRAWAL(1),DEPOSIT(2),
CALCULATE INTEREST(3), OR EXIT(4)
1,2,3, OR 4? 2
HOW MUCH WOULD YOU LIKE TO DEPOSIT
? 500.75
YOUR BALANCE STANDS AT $ 500.75

WITHDRAWAL(1),DEPOSIT(2),
CALCULATE INTEREST(3), OR EXIT(4)
1,2,3, OR 4? 3
HOW MANY MONTHS SINCE LAST CALCULATION
? 5
YOUR BALANCE STANDS AT $ 507.95

WITHDRAWAL(1),DEPOSIT(2),
CALCULATE INTEREST(3), OR EXIT(4)
1,2,3, OR 4? 1
HOW MUCH WOULD YOU LIKE TO WITHDRAW
? 175.45
YOUR BALANCE STANDS AT $ 332.5

WITHDRAWAL(1),DEPOSIT(2),
CALCULATE INTEREST(3), OR EXIT(4)
1,2,3, OR 4? 3
HOW MANY MONTHS SINCE LAST CALCULATION
? 1
TOO SOON
YOUR BALANCE STANDS AT $ 332.5

WITHDRAWAL(1),DEPOSIT(2),
CALCULATE INTEREST(3), OR EXIT(4)
1,2,3, OR 4? 4

READY.
```

10. The area of any triangle may be found from Hero's formula

$$AREA = \sqrt{S(S-A)(S-B)(S-C)}$$

where A, B, and C are the length of each side of the triangle and S is the semiperimeter. S = (A+B+C)/2. Write a program that uses Hero's formula in a subroutine to calculate the area of a triangle.

11. Develop an algorithm to play the game Black Jack. The computer will act as dealer in this game. The object of the game is to get closer than your opponent to 21 without going over. Picture cards are worth ten, and aces are worth one or eleven. All other cards are worth their face value. The dealer and the player are each dealt two cards. The player then takes as many cards as he wants to get as close to but not exceed 21. When the player determines that he has enough cards, the dealer takes cards until his cards total at least 17 but not more than 21. The winner is the one who is closest to 21 without going over 21. In the event of a tie the dealer wins.

12. Develop an algorithm for playing the card game War on the computer. The computer will run through the game in a simulation. In this game two players are each given half a normal deck of cards. The top card of each players stack is revealed and the higher card takes the lower card. In the event of a tie each player puts in three cards face down and then reveals a fourth card to determine who will win all ten cards. Whoever runs out of cards first for any reason loses.

13. Each of the following programs contains an error. In each case identify and correct the error(s):

```
(a)  10  READ A,B,C,D
     20  E = A*B+C+D
     30  PRINT E
     40  DATA 2,3,4
     50  END

(b)  10  READ A,B
     20  DATA 1,2,3,4
     30  PRINT A/B
     40  GOTO 20
     50  END

(c)  10  READ A,B,C
     20  PRINT A*/B+C
     30  PRINT D/F=;D/F
     40  DATA 5,6,10
     50  END

(d)  10  READ F,G
     20  IF F>5 OR < 10 THEN 40
     30  GOTO 10
     40  PRINT F,G
     50  DATA 1,10,6,9,11,4
     60  END
```

```
(e) 10 FOR X=1 TO 8
    20    FOR Y=1 TO 3
    30       X = X+Y
    40    NEXT X
    50 NEXT Y
    60 PRINT X
    70 END

(f) 10 READ C,D,F
    20 DATA 3,6,9,4,7,10
    30 PRINT C+D+F
    40 GOTO 20
    50 END
```

14. Trace the following program by hand and determine its output:

```
10 READ N,A,B
20 FOR I=1 TO N
30    FOR J=2 TO N+1
40       A = 2*A+B
50       B = 2*B+A
60    NEXT J
70    PRINT A;B
80 NEXT I
90 DATA 3,-1,2
100 END
```

15. What output is produced by the following program? (Do not run the program.)

```
10 FOR X=1 TO 5 STEP 2
20    READ K1,K2
30    A = A+K1-K2
40    B = B-K1+K2
50 NEXT X
60 PRINT A,B
70 DATA 1,3,2,4,3,5
80 END
```

16. The following simple programs have errors in logic (i.e. the program runs, but the output is illogical). Find and correct the errors:

```
(a) 10 READ A,B,C
    20 PRINT A+B+C
    30 GOTO 20
    40 DATA 1,2,3,4,5,6
    50 END

(b) 10 FOR X=1 TO 10
    20    IF X>5 THEN 50
    30    PRINT X; "IS GREATER THAN 5"
    40    GOTO 60
    50    PRINT X; "IS LESS THAN 5
    60 NEXT X
    70 END
```

(c)
```
10 READ A,B,C
20 FOR X=1 TO 10
30    Y = (A*B)/(C-X)
40    IF Y<1 THEN 50
50    PRINT "Y<1";Y
60 NEXT X
70 DATA 20,10,5,5,10,20
80 END
```

17. Each of the following programs contains errors which will result in error messages being printed by the computer when the program is run. Find and correct the errors:

(a)
```
10 PRINT "WHAT IS THE FORMULA WEIGHT OF ELEMENT"
20 INPUT FORMULA WEIGHT
30 IF X > 20 THEN 50
40 X = X/2
50 PRINT X
999 END
```

(b)
```
15 FOR X=1 TO 2
25    FOR Y=1 TO 3
35       IF Y=X THEN A = A+1 : GOTO 50
45    NEXT Y
55    PRINT "X AND Y ARE EQUAL";A;"TIMES"
65   NEXT X
75 END
```

(c)
```
5 READ B,A,C
10 X1 = (B+(SQR(B^2-4*A*C)/2*A)
20 X2 = (B+(SQR(B^2-4*A*C)/2*A)
30 IF X1 > X2 THE 50
40 GOTO 5
50 PRINT "X1=";X1; "X2=";X2
60 GOTO 5
70 DATA 1,2,3,4,5,6
80 END
```

(d)
```
10 READ A,B,C
20 X = A * B + C
30 IF X > 200 THEN LINE 10
40 PRINT X
50 DATA 25,26,27,28,29,30
60 END
```

(e)
```
10 FOR X=1 TO 26
20    A$ = A$+X
30 NEXT X
40 PRINT A$
50 END
```

18. The following program is designed to arrange sets of numbers in descending order. If the second number is larger than the first, the computer interchanges the two values. (This occurs in lines 30 and 40.) Explain the output and correct the program to give the desired output:

```
10 READ A,B
20 IF A > B THEN 50
30 A = B
40 B = A
50 PRINT A,B
60 GOTO 10
70 DATA 10,20,20,10
80 END
RUN
 20          20
 20          10

?OUT OF DATA  ERROR IN 10
READY.
```

19. The area of a square that measures one inch on a side is equal to one square inch. If the computer takes various slices of this same square and sums the areas of the slices, the answer should be one square inch. In the following program 100, 500, 1000 and 1024 slices are used and the output printed below. Explain the results:

```
10 READ N
20 FOR X=1 TO N
30    Y = Y+1/N
40 NEXT X
50 PRINT Y;"SQ. INCHES FOR";N;"SLICES"
60 Y = 0
70 GOTO 10
80 DATA 100,500,1000,1024
90 END
RUN
 1 SQ. INCHES FOR 100 SLICES
 1.00000002 SQ. INCHES FOR 500 SLICES
 .999999975 SQ. INCHES FOR 1000 SLICES
 1 SQ. INCHES FOR 1024 SLICES

?OUT OF DATA  ERROR IN 10
READY.
```

20. Structure the following programs by adding spaces and REM statements and by indenting where appropriate and necessary:

```
(a)  10 FORX=1TO10
     20 B=RND(0)
     30 IFB>=.5THENPRINT"HEADS":GOTO50
     40 PRINT"TAILS"
     50 NEXTX
     60 END
```

(b)
```
1 DIMJ(8,8)
2 FORX=0TO7
3 PRINTTAB(X*4+5);X+1;
4 NEXTX
5 PRINT
6 FORX=0TO6
7 PRINTTAB(X*4+6);"--";
8 NEXTX
9 PRINTTAB(34);"--"
10 FORX=1TO8
11 FORY=1TO8
12 J(X,Y)=X+Y
13 IFF=0THENPRINTX;":";
14 PRINTTAB(F*4+5);J(X,Y);
15 F=F+1
16 IFF=8THENPRINT:F=0
17 NEXTY
18 NEXTX
19 END
```

PEEK
POKE
PEEK
POKE
PEEK
POKE
PEEK
POKE
PEEK
POKE
PEEK
POKE
PEEK
POKE
PEEK
POKE
PEEK
POKE
PEEK
POKE
PEEK
POKE
PEEK
POKE
PEEK
POKE

The Commodore-64 and VIC-20 computers have the ability to display a multitude of shapes and colors. Using the special color and graphic keys, which are unique to the Commodore computers, the programmer can create pictures and graphs.

Color

The Commodore-64 and the VIC-20 computers can print text (letters, numbers, and other symbols) in a variety of colors on the display screen. Along the top row of the keyboard, on the front side of the number keys (1-8), are eight color selections. These keys, when pressed simultaneously with the CTRL key, are used to change the color of the characters as they appear on the display screen. For example, by pressing and holding the CTRL key (in the same manner that the SHIFT key is operated) along with the 3 key, the programmer selects the color red. Notice that all subsequent text appears in red until another color is selected. The following key combinations allow 1 of 8 colors to be selected:

Combination	Color
CTRL-1	Black
CTRL-2	White
CTRL-3	Red
CTRL-4	Cyan
CTRL-5	Purple
CTRL-6	Green
CTRL-7	Blue
CTRL-8	Yellow

Unlike the VIC-20 the Commodore-64 can print text in an additional 8 colors. The programmer selects these 8 colors with the C= (Commodore) key instead of the CTRL key, again using the number keys 1 through 8. The following key combinations can be used to select one of the eight additional colors on the Commodore-64.

Combination	Color
C= -1	Orange
C= -2	Brown
C= -3	Light Red
C= -4	Dark Gray
C= -5	Gray
C= -6	Light Green
C= -7	Light Blue
C= -8	Light Gray

When any of the color key combinations are used, the color change takes place immediately *unless* the selection is made within quotation marks such as in a PRINT statement. When used within quotation marks, each color selection is displayed as a unique graphic code.

Keyboard	Color	Display	Keyboard	Color	Display
CTRL–1	Black		C=–1	Orange	
CTRL–2	White		C=–2	Brown	
CTRL–3	Red		C=–3	Light Red	
CTRL–4	Cyan		C=–4	Gray 1	
CTRL–5	Purple		C=–5	Gray 2	
CTRL–6	Green		C=–6	Light Green	
CTRL–7	Blue		C=–7	Light Blue	
CTRL–8	Yellow		C=–8	Gray 3	

For example, if the program line

$$10 \ PRINT \ ``C \ O \ L \ O \ R \ F \ U \ L"$$

$$\uparrow \ \uparrow \ \uparrow \ \uparrow \ \uparrow \ \uparrow \ \uparrow \ \uparrow$$

$$CTRL- \quad 1 \ 2 \ 3 \ 4 \ 5 \ 6 \ 7 \ 8$$

were typed, it would appear on the screen as:

```
10 PRINT "█C▧O▨L▚O▤R▣F▥U▦L"
RUN
COLORFUL

READY.
```

However, when line 10 is executed, each letter of the word COLORFUL will be in a different color. If line 10 is the last line in the program, then all subsequent output such as the "READY" prompt will appear in yellow since that was the last color selected. To get back to the normal display, simply press the RESTORE key while simultaneously holding the RUN/STOP key.

Reverse Mode

The RVS ON key (located on the 9 key) allows characters to be displayed in inverse or "reverse", much like a photographic negative. Normally, text appears in the "foreground" color, which is the color of the characters on the screen. The "background" color is the dominant color of the screen on which the characters themselves are displayed. It is possible to reverse the foreground and background colors for one or more characters by pressing CTRL-9. Then all subsequent characters typed will be in reverse until reverse mode is exited by pressing RVS OFF (CTRL-0) or until the end of a line is reached. Remember that the front of each number key indicates the action that takes place when it is used simultaneously with the CTRL key. For example:

$$REM \ THIS \ IS \ IN \ REVERSE, \ BUT \ THIS \ ISN'T$$

$$\qquad \uparrow \qquad\qquad\qquad\qquad \uparrow$$

$$\quad CTRL-9 \qquad\qquad\qquad CTRL-0$$

If the background color is blue and the foreground color is white, then normal output is white on blue. However, characters will appear blue on a white background when reverse mode is selected. It is important to note that the dominant background itself does not change, but rather each character printed appears with its own reversed background.

```
REM THIS IS IN REVERSE BUT THIS ISN'T
```

It is possible to combine normal and reverse text on a single line of output. For example:

```
REM THIS IS REVERSED EXCEPT THIS HERE
```

Reverse mode is automatically exited at the end of each line of output. If more than one line of reverse text is desired, then it is necessary to use RVS ON (CTRL-9) in each additional PRINT statement which starts a new line of output. When RVS ON or RVS OFF is used within quotation marks, a unique graphic code appears in the same manner as for the color key combinations.

Key	Action	Display
CTRL–9	Reverse On	R
CTRL–0	Reverse Off	■

For example, when the program line

```
20 PRINT "[R]REVERSE THIS,[■] BUT NOT THIS"
```

is executed, the following output is produced:

```
REVERSE THIS, BUT NOT THIS
```

Remember that reverse video mode is only active for a single line of output on the screen and reverses the background of only that line.

Program 6.1

This program illustrates how the reverse video mode is used.

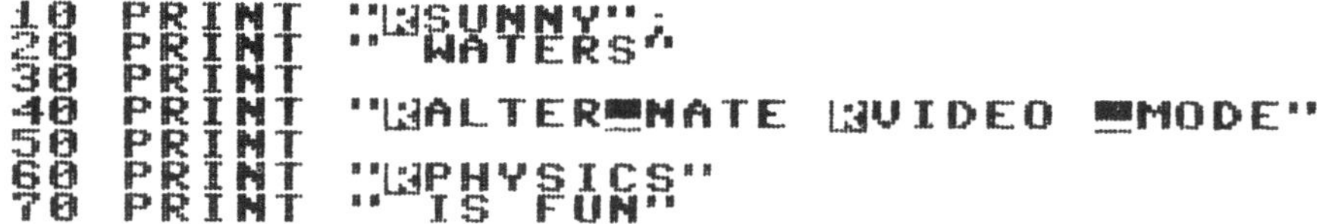

```
10 PRINT "[R]SUNNY";
20 PRINT " WATERS";
30 PRINT
40 PRINT "[R]ALTER[■]NATE [R]VIDEO [■]MODE"
50 PRINT
60 PRINT "[R]PHYSICS"
70 PRINT " IS FUN"
```

```
RUN
SUNNY WEATHERS
ALTERNATE VIDEO MODE
PHYSICS
   IS FUN
READY.
```

Examine the output produced by lines 60 and 70. The word PHYSICS appears in reverse, but " IS FUN" does not, even though reverse mode was not cancelled with a CTRL-0. Yet the output produced by line 10 and 20 is in reverse. Because there is a semicolon at the end of line 10, line 20 does not start a new line of output. If a semicolon were appended to the end of line 60 in Program 6.1, then the last three words would appear in reverse.

Program 6.2

This program illustrates how color and the inverse mode can be used to create a rainbow of colors:

```
10 FOR C = 1 TO 16
20    READ C$ : PRINT C$;
30    PRINT "                                        "
40 NEXT C
50 REM
100 REM COLOR CODE DATA
110 DATA "■","■","■","■","■","■","■","■"
120 DATA "■","■","■","■","■","■","■","■"
```

(A RAINBOW OF 16 COLORS APPEARS HERE)

Line 10 defines a loop which will be repeated 16 times. The variable C is used in a READ operation at line 20 to select one of 16 colors for each line of the rainbow. Note how RVS ON is used in line 30 to print a solid bar on the display for each color. Because reverse mode is automatically exited at the end of each line of output, RVS OFF is not needed.

Graphic Symbols

The Commodore-64 and the VIC-20 are equipped with 62 unique graphic symbols which can be used to create simple drawings and graphs. The symbols are easily accessed through SHIFT or C= (Commodore) keys. Notice that the front side of most of the keys is marked with two small blocks, each of which contains a special symbol:

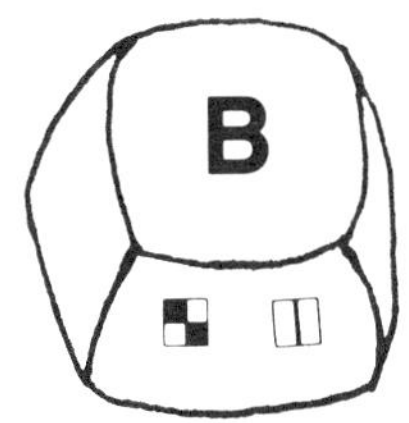

The symbol contained in the rightmost box is generated by striking the corresponding graphic symbol key while depressing the SHIFT key. For example, to produce the symbol ▢ (located on the B key), it is necessary to press SHIFT and B. The symbol on the left is produced by striking the desired symbol key while depressing the C= (Commodore) key. Thus, the symbol ▧ is produced by pressing C= and B. Remember that the C= key and SHIFT key are operated in the same manner; that is, one key is depressed while another key is typed.

The box in which each symbol is shown serves only as an outline. This allows symbols of various shapes and sizes to be compared easily.

Program 6.3

This program creates a large block, a diamond and a triangle:

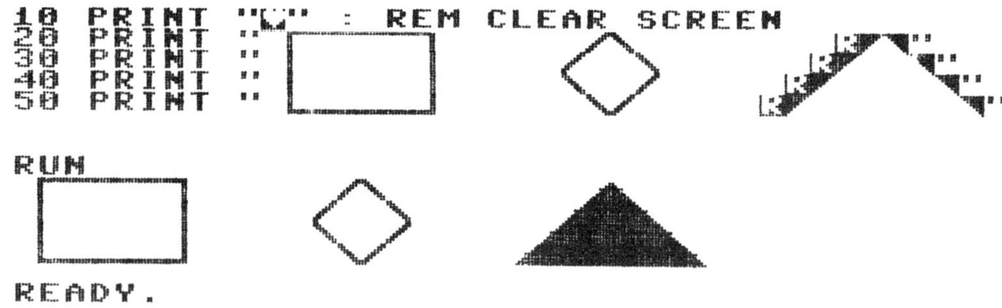

Program 6.4

This program produces a picture of E.T. Note how adjacent symbols touch one another on the screen. This is useful for creating complete figures:

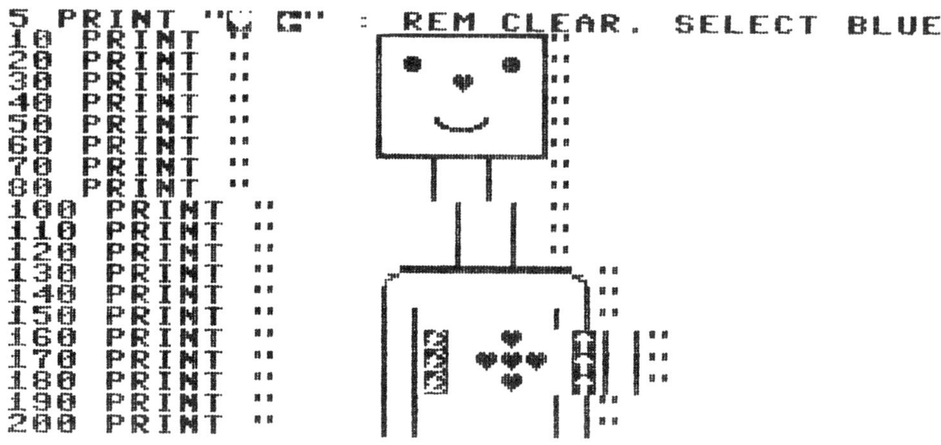

Cursor Movement

The Commodore-64 video display is capable of holding 25 lines of text, each line consisting of 40 characters. The VIC-20 is able to display only 23 lines of text of 22 characters each. The two keys, located in the lower right corner of the keyboard, can be used to move the cursor to any position on the display screen.

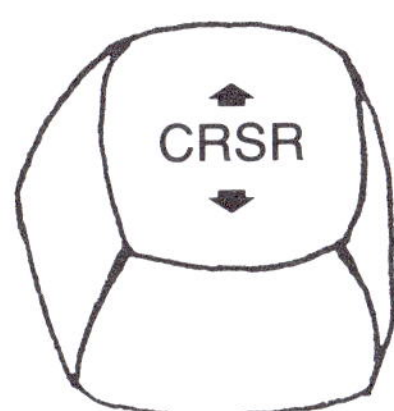

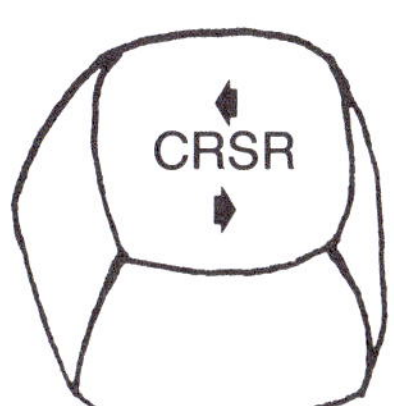

When the cursor keys are used within quotation marks (e.g., in a PRINT statement), a special graphic code is produced. The cursor movement takes place when the PRINT statement containing the code is executed. For example, the following line moves the cursor up 5 lines and then prints a name:

```
30 PRINT "     CAROL"
```

Note the graphic symbol produced when CRSR ← is pressed within the quotation marks. Other keys are also able to manipulate the display screen. The CLR/HOME key positions the cursor at the top left corner of the display (home), and when it is pressed simultaneously with the SHIFT key, the display is first cleared, then the cursor is repositioned at "home."

The following table shows the keys required to move the cursor and the unique graphic symbols that will appear when the key is used within quotation marks:

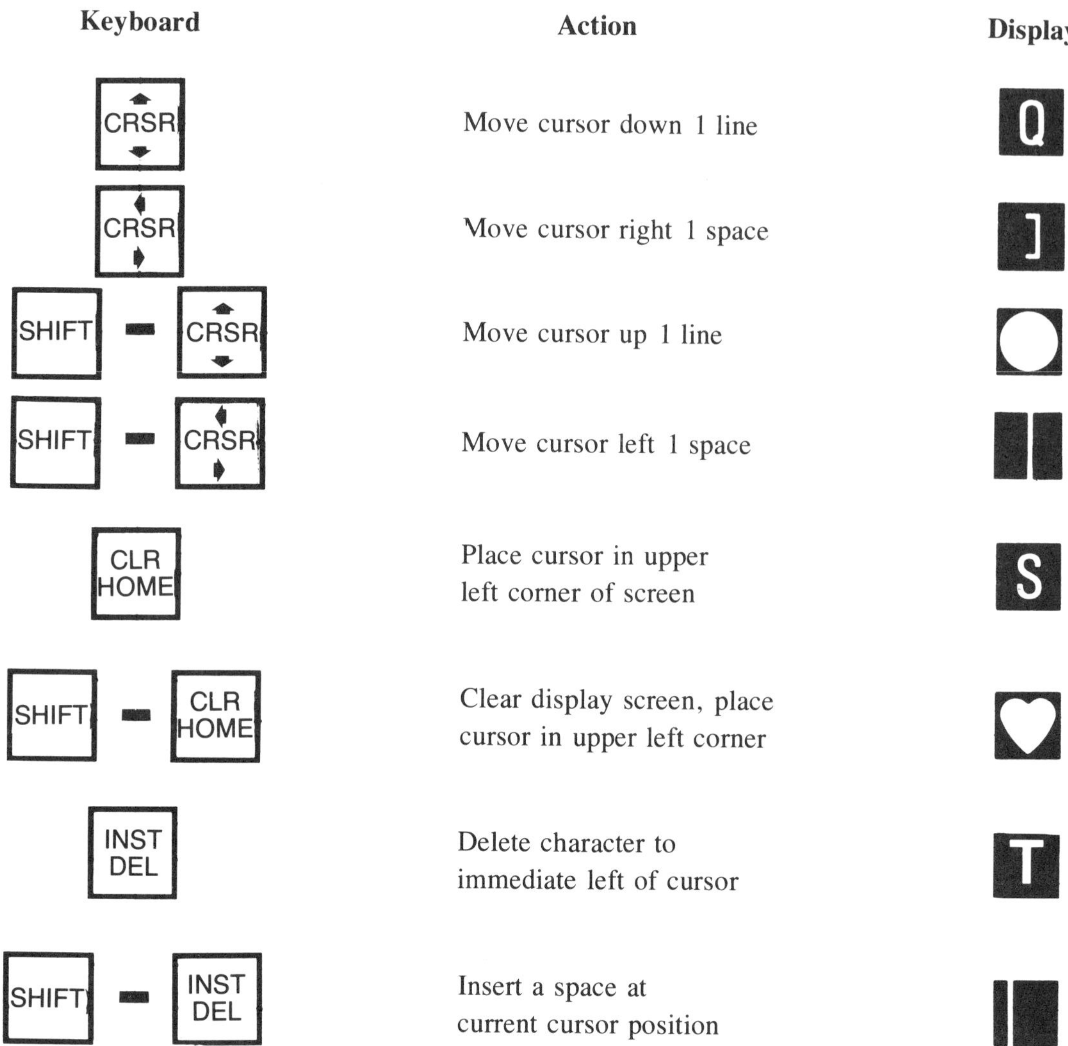

Keyboard	Action	Display
CRSR	Move cursor down 1 line	Q
CRSR	Move cursor right 1 space	]
SHIFT — CRSR	Move cursor up 1 line	○
SHIFT — CRSR	Move cursor left 1 space	▌▌
CLR HOME	Place cursor in upper left corner of screen	S
SHIFT — CLR HOME	Clear display screen, place cursor in upper left corner	♥
INST DEL	Delete character to immediate left of cursor	T
SHIFT — INST DEL	Insert a space at current cursor position	▌▌

Program 6.5

Bar graphs are useful for displaying and comparing groups of data. This program plots a bar graph of gross income for Tropical Waters Inc., a construction management company. Carefully examine the program, noting how color and cursor movement are used in creating the graph:

```
10 PRINT "◻ ◻"; TAB(9);"TROPICAL WATERS
INC."
15 PRINT TAB(13); "GROSS INCOME"
20 X0=0 : Y0=22 : GOSUB 500
30 REM FOUR YEARS OF DATA
40 FOR Y = 1 TO 4
50   READ YR$(Y),GR(Y) : REM YEAR,GROSS
60   PRINT "";YR$(Y),
70 NEXT Y : PRINT
80 REM
```

```
90 REM NOW PLOT BAR FOR EACH YEAR
100 PRINT "[Z]"; :REM COLOR
110 FOR Y = 1 TO 4
120    X0 = (Y-1)*10
130    FOR Y0 = 22-GR(Y) TO 21
140       GOSUB 500 : REM POSITION CURSOR
150          PRINT "[R]   [#]";
160       NEXT Y0
170 NEXT Y
180 PRINT "[#]"; : GOTO 2000
500 REM
501 REM POSITION CURSOR AT (X0,Y0)
510 PRINT "[S]"; :REM PUT CURSOR AT (0,0)
520 IF X0 = 0 THEN 560
530 FOR L = 0 TO X0-1
540    PRINT "[U]"; :REM MOVE CURSOR RIGHT
550 NEXT L
560 IF Y0 = 0 THEN RETURN
570 FOR L = 0 TO Y0-1
580    PRINT "[U]"; : REM MOVE CURSOR DOWN
590 NEXT L
600 RETURN
1000 DATA 1981,7, 1982,16
1010 DATA 1983,11, 1984,20
2000 END

RUN
```

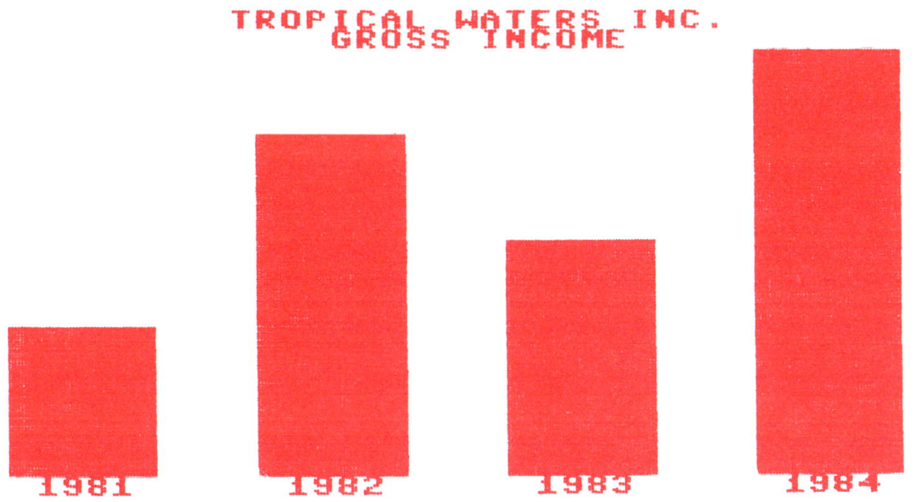

Lines 10 and 15 clear the screen and print a header; lines 20 and 70 label each bar in the graph. The four bars are plotted by lines 100 through 170. Note that a subroutine, beginning at line 500, is used to position the cursor at the desired point on the display screen. Although this program is written for the 40-column display of the Commodore-64, it can easily be rewritten for the VIC-20. The following changes to Program 6.5 will allow it to run on the VIC-20:

```
10  PRINT "[CLR] TROPICAL WATERS INC."
15  PRINT "     GROSS INCOME"
20  X0=0 : Y0=21 : GOSUB 500
60     PRINT " ";YR$(Y);
120    X0 = (Y-1)*5+2
130    FOR Y0 = 21-GR(Y) TO 20
150       PRINT "[R]  [#]";
180 PRINT "[#]"; : GOTO 2000
```

Review

1. Write a program that will print N squares, where N is entered from the keyboard.

```
RUN
? 2

□

□

READY.
```

2. What is the output of the following program?

```
10 PRINT " COMPUTERS ARE FUN"
20 PRINT "PROGRAMMING IS ";
30 PRINT "VERY"
```

PEEK and POKE

The PEEK function is used to retrieve the contents of a particular location in the computer's memory. The general format for PEEK is:

$$N = PEEK\ (<address>)$$

The contents of the memory address specified are assigned to the variable N. Note that a value between 0 and 225, inclusive, is returned by PEEK. PEEK can also be used in a PRINT statement. For example:

```
PRINT PEEK(1023)
 165

READY.
```

As can be seen, the contents of memory location 1023 are currently 165.

The POKE statement is used to change the contents of a single memory location. The format for POKE is:

$$POKE\ <address>,\ <value>$$

The "value" specified, a number which must be between 0 and 255, is placed into the computer's memory at the location specified by "address." The statement

$$POKE\ 1023,223$$

changes the contents of location 1023 from 165 to 223. A subsequent PEEK confirms the value contained at 1023 to be 223:

```
PRINT PEEK(1023)
 223

READY.
```

Proper care should be exercised when using the POKE statement. Incorrect use can drastically impair the proper operation of the computer. Should a problem occur, simply press the RUN/STOP and RESTORE keys simultaneously to reset the computer to normal operation. In some situations it may be necessary to turn the computer off and then on again. However, it is very important to realize that by doing this everything stored in the computer's memory will be lost.

Peeking and Poking on the Commodore-64

The following table lists some of the more important memory locations on the Commodore-64 which can be examined and modified. A more complete memory table can be found in the Commodore-64 Programmer's Reference Guide. This table does NOT apply to the VIC-20 computer. Refer to the next section in this chapter for information on peeking and poking on the VIC-20.

COMMODORE-64 MEMORY TABLE

Address	Description
199	Reverse Mode active (0 = no, 1 = yes)
209-210	Current screen line address
211	Cursor horizontal position on screen (0-39)
214	Cursor vertical position on screen (0-24)
646	Current foreground color
53272	Video interface memory control register
	(21 = Normal character set)
	(23 = Lower case character set)
53280	Current border color
53281	Current background color

Memory locations 211 and 214 contain the current coordinates of the cursor on the display screen. Consider the display as a 40x25 grid containing 1,000 character positions. The upper left corner of the screen is (0,0); the lower left, (0,24); the upper right, (39,0); and the lower right, (39,24). The line

$$40 \ X = PEEK(211) : Y = PEEK(214)$$

returns the current cursor position (X,Y), X being the horizontal position of the cursor (0-39), and Y the vertical position (0-24).

The horizontal position of the cursor can be changed by the statement

$$POKE \ 211, X$$

in which X is the desired column number (0-39). The vertical position can be changed by the following statements, assuming Y contains a value between 0 and 39, representing the desired row number:

```
POKE 214, Y
POKE 209, (( 1024 + 40 * Y) AND 255)
POKE 210, INT (( 1024 + 40 * Y) / 256)
```

The program segment

```
50 POKE 211,29
60 POKE 214,8
70 T = 1024 + 40 * 8
80 POKE 209, (T AND 255)
90 POKE 210, INT (T / 256)
```

will place the cursor at (19,8), as shown in the grid below: A subsequent PRINT statement will cause output to begin at that location on the screen.

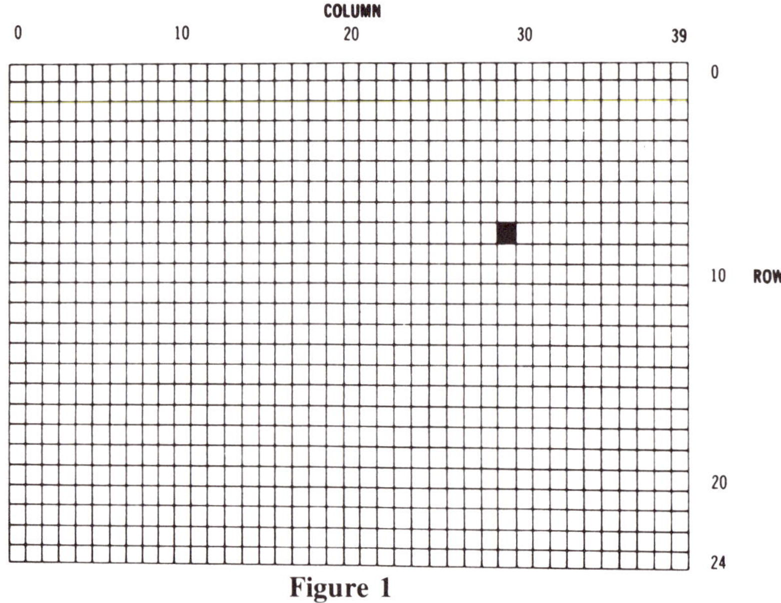

Figure 1

Note that the horizontal (column) position varies from 0 to 39 whereas the vertical (row) position varies from 0 to 24.

Memory location 646 contains the color code for the foreground color; 53280, the color code for the border color; and 53281, the color code for the current background color. Refer to the Color Table below for a list of screen colors and their associated color codes.

COMMODORE-64
COLOR CODE TABLE

0	Black	8	Orange
1	White	9	Brown
2	Red	10	Light Red
3	Cyan	11	Dark Gray
4	Purple	12	Gray
5	Green	13	Light Green
6	Blue	14	Light Blue
7	Yellow	15	Light Gray

For example, to find the current background color of the display, simply type:

```
PRINT PEEK(53281) AND 15
 6

READY.
```

In this case, the color code returned is 6; therefore, the background color is blue. To change the background color to red, use:

POKE 53281,2

Be sure that the foreground color (that of the cursor) differs from the background color; otherwise, output will not be visible because characters will be the same color as their background. The border color can also be changed by a POKE statement. For example, the statement

POKE 53280,8

changes the border color to orange.

The foreground color, the color of the characters, can be changed by a PRINT statement (using a CTRL or c= key with a number key, discussed earlier in this chapter) or by a POKE statement. The statement

POKE 646,1

changes the foreground color to white. Then all subsequent output will appear in white until a new color is selected.

Program 6.6

This program simulates an explosion on the Commodore-64 by drawing the word "BOOM!" on the display screen and then rapidly changing the background and border colors by using POKE:

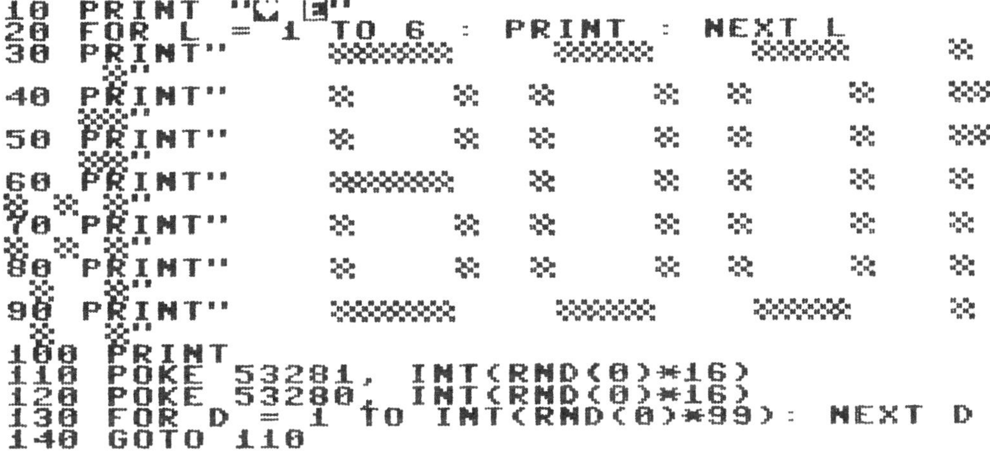

Note that the letter M wraps around to a new line in lines 30 through 90 because of the limited screen width. Line 110 selects a random background color, whereas line 120 picks a random border color. The inconsistent flash of the explosion is created by the randomly timed delay loop at line 130.

Peeking and Poking on the VIC-20

The following table lists some of the more important memory locations on the VIC-20 which can be examined and modified. A more complete memory table can be found in the VIC-20 Programmer's Reference Guide. This table does NOT apply to the Commodore-64 computer.

VIC-20 MEMORY TABLE

Address	Description
199	Reverse Mode active (0 = no, 1 = yes)
209-210	Current screen line address
211	Cursor horizontal position on screen (0-23)
214	Cursor vertical position on screen (0-22)
646	Current foreground color
36869	Video interface memory control register
	(240 = Normal character set)
	(242 = Lower case character set)
36879	Current border color and border colors (see text)

Memory locations 211 and 214 contain the current coordinates of the cursor on the display screen. Consider the display as a 22x23 grid containing 506 character positions. The upper left corner of the screen is (0,0); the lower left, (0,22); the upper right, (21,0); and the lower right, (21,22). The line

$$40 \ X = PEEK(211) : Y = PEEK(214)$$

returns the current cursor position (X,Y), X being the horizontal position of the cursor (0-21), and Y the vertical position (0-22).

The horizontal position of the cursor can be changed by the statement

POKE 211, X

in which X is the desired column number (0-21). The vertical position can be changed by the following statements, assuming Y contains a value between 0 and 22, representing the desired row number:

POKE 214, Y
POKE 209, ((7680 + 22 * Y) AND 255)
POKE 210, INT ((7680 + 22 * Y) / 256)

The program segment

50 POKE 211,29
60 POKE 214,8
70 T = 7680 + 22 * 8
80 POKE 209, (T AND 255)
90 POKE 210, INT (T / 256)

will place the cursor at (19,8), as shown in the grid below:

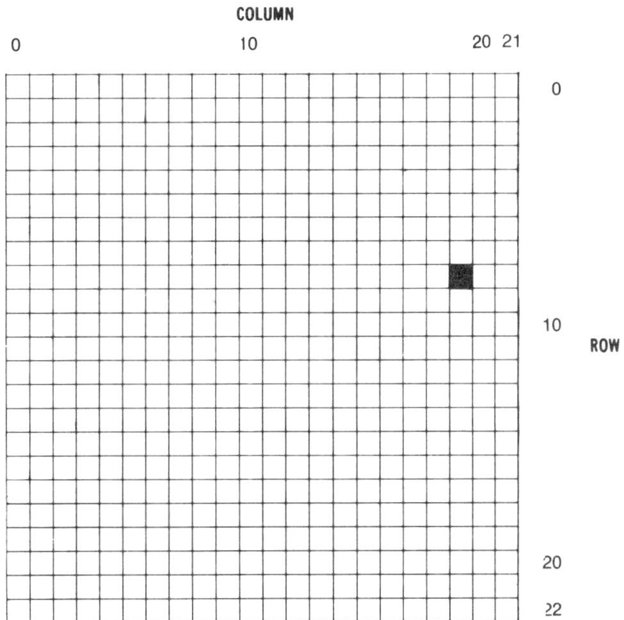

Note that the horizontal (column) position varies from 0 to 21 whereas the vertical (row) position varies from 0 to 22.

Memory locations 646 and 36879 contain data relevant to screen colors. Refer to the Color Code Table below for a list of screen colors and their associated color codes.

VIC-20
COLOR CODE TABLE

0	Black		8	Orange
1	White		9	Pink
2	Red		10	Light Red
3	Cyan		11	Light Cyan
4	Purple		12	Light Purple
5	Green		13	Light Green
6	Blue		14	Light Blue
7	Yellow		15	Light Yellow

Memory location 36879 deserves special attention because it is used to store three pieces of information, namely the background and the border colors, and the screen mode. The following statement assigns the variable B a value between 0 and 7 which corresponds to the current border color.

$$B = PEEK\ (36879)\ AND\ 7$$

On the VIC-20 the border color may only be 1 of 8 colors whereas the background color can be 1 of 16. The variable K is assigned a value corresponding to the background color in the following statement:

$$K = (PEEK(36879)\ AND\ 240)\ /\ 16$$

For example, to find the color code of the current background color, simply type:

In this case the color code is 1; therefore, the background color is white.

In addition to the background and border colors, location 36879 also contains data relevant to reverse text mode. The following statement determines whether reverse or normal mode is the current display mode on the VIC-20:

$$Z = (PEEK\ (36879)\ AND\ 8)\ /\ 8$$

If Z is 0, the reverse mode is in effect; if Z is 1, then normal mode is in effect.

To change either the background color or border colors or the current text mode, it is necessary to specify all three. If the variable X contains the border color (0-7), and the variable T contains the background color (0-15), and variable R contains the desired text mode (0-1), then the statement

$$POKE\ 36879,\ T*16 + R*8 + X$$

will select the colors and mode as specified by the three variables. For example, to select normal text mode, a light blue background, and a red border, use the statement:

POKE 36879, 14* 16 + 1*8 + 2

or

POKE 36879, 234

Be sure that the foreground color (the color of the cursor) differs from the background color; otherwise, output will not be visible because characters will be the same color as their background.

The foreground color, the color of the characters, can be changed by either a PRINT statement (using a CTRL or ⊂ key with a number key, discussed earlier in this chapter) or by a POKE statement. The statement

POKE 646, 1

changes the foreground color to white. Then all subsequent output will appear in white until a new color is selected.

Program 6.7

This program draws a milk truck and moves it across the screen using a FOR . . . NEXT loop and PRINT TAB:

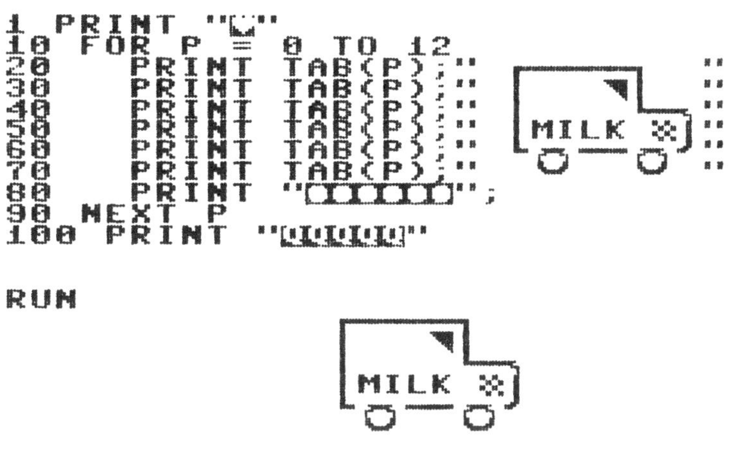

Line 80 repositions the cursor using CRSR◆ so that output begins at the same screen location each time the loop is executed. Line 100 moves the cursor down 6 lines (5 CRSR◆ and 1 RETURN) so that READY appears below the truck.

Lower Case Mode

The Commodore computers are capable of generating both upper and lower case characters. Normally, the computer only displays upper case output along with a variety of graphic symbols. When the SHIFT key is depressed in combination with a letter key, a graphic symbol is produced. In lower case mode, lower case characters can be typed and the SHIFT key is then used to generate upper case characters. Unfortunately, in this mode many of the graphic symbols are sacrificed.

Lower case mode is entered by pressing the C= and SHIFT keys simultaneously. Note that the change is immediate and affects all characters on the display screen. In lower case mode, the line

```
20 PRINT " ──┌\√┬─┬─-64 ┌ ┗ X ┏ ⁿ ● ◆ ♥"
```

will appear as

```
20 print " COMMODORE-64 ┌ ┗ U ▨ ▨ Q Z S"
```

Pressing SHIFT- C= a second time causes lower case mode to be exited. Again, the change is immediate. Normal and lower case mode may be selected from within a program via the POKE statement, as indicated in the following table:

	To Select Lower Case Mode	To Select Normal Mode
Commodore-64	POKE 53272,23	POKE 53272,21
VIC-20	POKE 36869,242	POKE 36869,240

Review

3. Write a program that will allow two numbers, A and B, to be entered. The background color of the screen should then be set to A, and the border color set to B.

4. Modify the answer to Review question 3 so that a third number can be entered as C. If C is 1, then use a POKE statement to select lower case mode; otherwise select normal mode.

Commodore-64 Screen Memory

Certain sections of memory contain information about the computer's display screen. Memory locations 1024-2023 contain values which correspond to a character code for the characters displayed on the screen, and memory locations 55296-56295 contain values which correspond to a color code for the color of each character displayed. The display screen may be thought of as a 40x25 grid containing 1000 character positions, as shown in figure 6-1. It is possible to use PEEK and POKE to examine and change the contents of the screen. The statement

$$L = PEEK(1024 + X + 40 * Y)$$

will assign L the character code for the character position (X,Y) on the screen. The list of possible character codes is shown in the character code table. For example,

```
PRINT PEEK(1024 + 39 + 40*24)
 1

READY.
```

indicates that position (39,24) contains the letter "A" in normal mode or the letter "a" in lower case mode. The statement

$$C = PEEK(55296 + X + 40*Y) \text{ AND } 15$$

will assign C the color code for the color of the character in position (X,Y). The list of color codes is shown in the Commodore-64 color code table in this chapter. For example,

```
PRINT PEEK(55296 + 39 + 40*24) AND 15
 6

READY.
```

indicates that the color at position (39,24) is 6, that is, blue.

Character Code Table

SET 1	SET 2	CODE	SET 1	SET 2	CODE	SET 1	SET 2	CODE	SET 1	SET 2	CODE
@		0	SPACE		32			64	SPACE		96
A	a	1	!		33		A	65			97
B	b	2	"		34		B	66			98
C	c	3	#		35		C	67			99
D	d	4	$		36		D	68			100
E	e	5	%		37		E	69			101
F	f	6	&		38		F	70			102
G	g	7	'		39		G	71			103
H	h	8	(		40		H	72			104
I	i	9	)		41		I	73			105
J	j	10	*		42		J	74			106
K	k	11	+		43		K	75			107
L	l	12	,		44		L	76			108
M	m	13	−		45		M	77			109
N	n	14	.		46		N	78			110
O	o	15	/		47		O	79			111
P	p	16	0		48		P	80			112
Q	q	17	1		49		Q	81			113
R	r	18	2		50		R	82			114
S	s	19	3		51		S	83			115
T	t	20	4		52		T	84			116
U	u	21	5		53		U	85			117
V	v	22	6		54		V	86			118
W	w	23	7		55		W	87			119
X	x	24	8		56		X	88			120
Y	y	25	9		57		Y	89			121
Z	z	26	:		58		Z	90			122
[		27	;		59			91			123
£		28	<		60			92			124
]		29	=		61			93			125
↑		30	>		62			94			126
←		31	?		63			95			127

Codes 128-255 are reverse images of codes 0-127.

The statement

$$\text{POKE } 1024 + X + 40*Y, \text{ <character code>}$$

is used to place a character on the screen at position (X,Y). For example,

$$\text{POKE } 1024 + 20 + 40*12,2$$

will place the letter "B" at position (20,12), which is about the middle of the screen. Note that the character will be invisible if its color is the same as the background color. Therefore, it may be necessary to change the color of the character in order to see it, using the following statement:

$$\text{POKE } 55296 + X + 40*Y, \text{ <color code>}$$

The statement

$$\text{POKE } 55296 + 20 + 40*12,0$$

will change the color of the character at position (20,12) to black.

Program 6.8

This program demonstrates how to examine and change the Commodore-64 screen memory by printing a gray, white and red dart board on the screen. It then takes ten random shots at the board and computes a score, with the gray area worth 0 points, white 1 point, and red 10 points:

```
10 POKE 646,0 : REM FOREGROUND COLOR=BLACK
20 POKE 53280,6 : REM BORDER COLOR=BLUE
30 POKE 53281,15 : REM BACKGROUND COLOR=WHITE
40 PRINT ""
50 REM
100 FOR X=8 TO 31
110   FOR Y = 6 TO 18
120     POKE 1024+X+40*Y,160
130     POKE 55296+X+40*Y,1
140   NEXT Y
150 NEXT X
160 REM
170 FOR X = 16 TO 22
180   FOR Y = 10 TO 14
190     POKE 1024+X+40*Y,160
200     POKE 55296+X+40*Y,2
210   NEXT Y
220 NEXT X
230 REM
240 REM
```

```
300 REM NOW TAKE RANDOM SHOTS
310 FOR I = 1 TO 10
320   X = INT(40*RND(0))
330   Y = INT(25*RND(0))
340   C = PEEK(55296+X+40*Y) AND 15
350   POKE 1024+X+40*Y,42
360   POKE 55296+X+40*Y,0
370   IF C=1 THEN S = S + 1
380   IF C=2 THEN S = S + 10
390 NEXT I
400 REM
410 PRINT "YOU SCORED";S;"POINTS."
```

Lines 20-30 set up the screen with a gray background and a blue border. Lines 120-130, which plot a space in reverse mode in white, are placed in a nested loop to plot the white area of the dart board. Similarly, line 200 is placed in a nested loop to plot the red portion of the dart board. The loop contained in lines 310-390 causes ten random shots to be taken at the board. Lines 320-330 pick the random X and Y coordinate, and line 340 checks the color at that coordinate. Next, a star ("*") is plotted in black by lines 350 and 360 to indicate the coordinate hit, and lines 370-380 update the score according to the color found. Note that if a spot is hit twice, its point value will be counted only once.

VIC-20 Screen Memory

Certain sections of memory contain information about the computer's display screen. Memory locations 7680-8185 contain values which correspond to a character code for the characters displayed on the screen, and memory locations 38400-38905 contain values which correspond to a color code for the color of each character displayed. The display screen may be thought of as a 22x23 grid containing 506 character positions, as shown in figure 6-3. It is possible to use PEEK and POKE to examine and change the contents of the screen. The statement

$$L = PEEK(7680 + X + 22*Y)$$

will assign L the character code for the character position (X,Y) on the screen. The list of possible character codes is shown in the character code table. For example,

```
PRINT PEEK(7680 + 21 + 22*23)
 1

READY.
```

indicates that position (21,23) contains the letter "A" in normal mode or the letter "a" in lower case mode. The statement

$$C = PEEK(38400 + X + 22*Y) \text{ AND } 15$$

will assign C the color code for the color of the character in position (X,Y). The list of color codes is shown in the VIC-20 color code table in this chapter. For example,

```
PRINT PEEK(38400 + 21 + 22*23) AND 15
 6

READY.
```

indicates that the color at position (21,23) is 6, that is, blue.

The statement

$$POKE\ 7680 + X + 22*Y, <character\ code>$$

is used to place a character on the screen at position (X,Y). For example,

$$POKE\ 7680 + 11 + 22*12,2$$

will place the letter "B" at position (11,12), which is about the middle of the screen. Note that the character will be invisible if its color is the same as the background color. Therefore, it may be necessary to change the color of the character in order to see it, using the following statement:

$$POKE\ 38400 + X + 22*Y, <color\ code>$$

The statement

$$POKE\ 38400 + 11 + 22*12,0$$

will change the color of the character at position (11,12) to black.

Program 6.9

This program demonstrates how to examine and to change the VIC-20 screen memory by printing a white, yellow and red dart board on the screen. It then takes ten random shots at the board and computes a score, with the white area worth 0 points, yellow 1 point, and red 10 points:

```
10 POKE 646,0 : REM FOREGROUND COLOR=BLACK
20 POKE 36879,1*16+1*8+6 : REM BACKGROUND=WHITE, BORDER=BLUE
30 PRINT "⬛": REM CLEAR SCREEN
40 REM
100 FOR X = 5 TO 16
110    FOR Y = 6 TO 16
120       POKE 7680+X+22*Y,160
130       POKE 38400+X+22*Y,7 : REM YELLOW AREA
140    NEXT Y
150 NEXT X
160 REM
200 FOR X = 9 TO 12
210    FOR Y = 9 TO 12
220       POKE 38400+X+22*Y,2 : REM RED AREA
230    NEXT Y
240 NEXT X
250 REM
300 REM NOW TAKE TEN RANDOM SHOTS
310 FOR I = 1 TO 10
320    X = INT(22*RND(0))
330    Y = INT(23*RND(0))
340    C = (PEEK(38400+X+22*Y) AND 15)
350    POKE 7680+X+22*Y,42 : REM 42="*", FOR SHOT TAKEN
360    POKE 38400+X+22*Y,0 : REM SHOW "*" IN BLACK
370    IF C=7 THEN S = S + 1 : REM YELLOW = 1 POINT
380    IF C=2 THEN S = S + 10 : REM RED = 10 POINTS
390 NEXT I
410 PRINT "YOU SCORED";S;"POINTS."
```

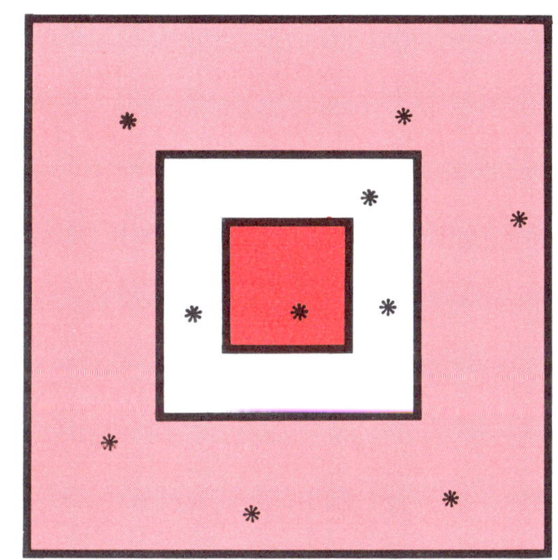

Lines 20 sets up the screen for normal text mode with a white background and a blue
border. Lines 120-130, which plot a space in reverse mode in yellow, are placed in a nested
loop to plot the yellow area of the dart board. Similarly, line 220 is placed in a nested loop to plot
the red portion of the dart board. The loop contained in lines 310-390 causes ten random shots
to be taken at the board. Lines 320-330 pick the random X and Y coordinate, and line 340
checks the color at that coordinate. Next, a star ("*") is plotted in black by lines 350 and 360 to
indicate the coordinate hit, and lines 370-380 update the score according to the color found.
Note that if a spot is hit twice, its point value will be counted only once.

Joysticks

A joystick is an alternate device for interfacing with the computer. Typically found on most arcade game machines, the joystick is used on the computer in a similar fashion.

Joysticks can be used in a variety of ways. Typical game applications include moving a figure around on the screen or firing a missile. The joystick has four internal direction switches which represent up, down, left and right and which are activated by moving the stick. If two of the switches are activated simultaneously, then a diagonal direction is indicated. For example, the down switch and the left switch would be activated when the stick is moved to the lower left. The joystick also has a fire button, which operates independently of the stick. A different set of commands is required to use the joystick on the Commodore-64 than on the VIC-20. Each will be explained separately.

Commodore-64 Joysticks

Two joysticks may be connected to the Commodore-64, both of which are used similarly. Joystick 1 is plugged into Control-Port 1 and joystick 2 is plugged into Control-Port 2.

The following statements are used to determine which direction the sticks are presently being moved:

$$J1 = 15 - (PEEK(56321) \text{ AND } 15) \qquad \text{for joystick 1}$$
$$J2 = 15 - (PEEK(56320) \text{ AND } 15) \qquad \text{for joystick 2}$$

The value of the variables J1 and J2 will indicate one of the following:

Value	Direction Indicated
0	Joystick CENTERED
1	UP
2	DOWN
4	LEFT
5	UP and LEFT
6	DOWN and LEFT
8	RIGHT
9	UP and RIGHT
10	DOWN and RIGHT

To determine if the fire button is being pressed the following statements are used:

$$F1 = PEEK(56321) \text{ AND } 16 \qquad \text{for joystick 1}$$
$$F2 = PEEK(56320) \text{ AND } 16 \qquad \text{for joystick 2}$$

If either the variables F1 or F2 equal 0, then the respective fire button is being pressed; otherwise, if the button is not being pressed, the value returned is 16.

Program 6.10

Each time the fire button on joystick 1 is pressed, this program prints the stick's direction. The loop at line 70 delays execution of the program to allow the user sufficient time to release the fire button before the computer checks at line 40 to see if the button is being pressed:

```
10 FOR I = Ø TO 1Ø
20   READ J$(I)
30 NEXT I
40 IF (PEEK(56321) AND 16)=16 THEN 40
50 J1 = 15-(PEEK(56321) AND 15)
60 PRINT "THE JOYSTICK IS ";J$(J1)
70 FOR J = 1 TO 200 : NEXT J : REM DELAY LOOP
80 GOTO 40
100 DATA CENTERED,UP,DOWN,,LEFT,UP AND LEFT
110 DATA DOWN AND LEFT,,RIGHT,UP AND RIGHT,DOWN AND RIGHT

RUN
THE JOYSTICK IS CENTERED
THE JOYSTICK IS UP
THE JOYSTICK IS RIGHT
THE JOYSTICK IS LEFT
THE JOYSTICK IS LEFT
THE JOYSTICK IS UP AND RIGHT
THE JOYSTICK IS DOWN AND RIGHT
THE JOYSTICK IS DOWN
THE JOYSTICK IS UP AND LEFT
THE JOYSTICK IS DOWN AND LEFT

BREAK IN 40
READY.
```

Review

5. Write a program for the Commodore-64 that will place the symbol ● in one of nine locations on the display screen, depending upon the movement of the joystick. For example, if the joystick is moved down and right, the ● should appear at coordinates (39,24), which is the lower right hand corner of the screen. If the joystick is centered, the ● should appear in the middle of the screen.

VIC-20 Joystick

Only one joystick can be connected to the VIC-20. The following initialization statement must be used in a program before the joystick can be used:

$$POKE\ 37139,0$$

After this statement has been used the following statement determines the status of the fire button:

$$F = PEEK(37137)\ AND\ 32$$

This will set F to 0 if the fire button is being pressed; otherwise F will equal 32.

To determine the direction in which the joystick is being moved, an additional initialization statement is needed:

$$POKE\ 37154,127$$

After the above is executed, the statement

$$J = 15 - ((PEEK(37137)\ AND\ 28) / 4 + (PEEK(37152)\ AND\ 128) / 16)$$

will assign to the variable J a value which indicates the direction of the joystick. These values are the same as those given in figure 6-6 for the Commodore-64.

Because the statements used to make the joystick operative render the keyboard inoperative, it is necessary to use the following statement to restore the use of the keyboard and disengage the joystick:

$$POKE\ 37154,255$$

Program 6.11

This program prints the direction of the joystick each time the fire button is pressed. The loop at line 130 delays execution of the program to allow the user sufficient time to release the fire button before the computer checks at line 80 to see if the fire button is being pressed:

```
10 REM INITIALIZE
20 POKE 37139,0
30 REM
40 FOR I = 0 TO 10
50    READ J$(I)
60 NEXT I
70 REM
80 IF (PEEK(37137) AND 32)=32 THEN 80
90 POKE 37154,127
100 J = 15-((PEEK(37137) AND 28)/4 + (PEEK(37152) AND 128)/16)
110 POKE 37154,255 : REM RESET FOR KEYBOARD INPUT
120 PRINT "THE JOYSTICK IS ";J$(J)
130 FOR J = 1 TO 200 : NEXT J
140 GOTO 80
200 DATA CENTERED,UP,DOWN,,LEFT,UP AND LEFT
210 DATA DOWN AND LEFT,,RIGHT,UP AND RIGHT,DOWN AND RIGHT
RUN
THE JOYSTICK IS RIGHT
THE JOYSTICK IS LEFT
THE JOYSTICK IS UP AND LEFT
THE JOYSTICK IS DOWN AND RIGHT
THE JOYSTICK IS DOWN AND LEFT
THE JOYSTICK IS DOWN
THE JOYSTICK IS UP
THE JOYSTICK IS UP AND RIGHT
THE JOYSTICK IS CENTERED
THE JOYSTICK IS DOWN

BREAK IN 80
READY.
```

6. Write a program for the VIC-20 that will place the symbol ● in one of nine locations on the display screen, depending upon the movement of the joystick. For example, if the joystick is moved down and right, the ● should appear at coordinates (21,22), which is the lower right hand corner of the screen. If the joystick is centered, the ● should appear in the middle of the screen.

Sound on the Commodore-64

The Commodore-64 computer, using its built-in sound generator, is capable of producing a wide range of sounds. Six locations in the computer's memory are used to control the volume and pitch of the sound:

Memory Location	Purpose	Poke Range
54272	Least significant digits of tone code	0-255
54273	Most significant digits of tone code	0-255
54276	Sound control Register	0, 17, 33, 129
54277	Sound ATTACK and DECAY cycle control	0-255
54278	Sound SUSTAIN and RELEASE cycle control	0-255
54296	Peak volume control	0-15

The tone code can be any value between 0 and 65535, inclusive, with 0 the lowest note and 65535 the highest. The following program segment will set the tone registers (locations 54272 and 54273):

```
50 T = 16457 : REM TONE TO PLAY
60 POKE 54272, T – INT (T / 256) * 256 : REM LOW DIGITS
70 POKE 542573, INT (T / 256) : REM HIGH DIGITS
```

The sound generator is capable of producing notes over a range of 8 musical octaves. The following table can be used to find the tone code of a particular sound, given the octave and note:

OCTAVE

NOTE	1	2	3	4	5	6	7	8
C	268	536	1072	2145	4291	8583	17167	34334
C#	284	568	1136	2273	4547	9094	18188	36376
D	301	602	1204	2408	4817	9634	19269	38539
D#	318	637	1275	2551	5103	10207	20415	40830
E	337	675	1351	2703	5407	10814	21629	43258
F	358	716	1432	2864	5728	11457	22915	45830
F#	379	758	1517	3034	6069	12139	24278	48556
G	401	803	1607	3215	6430	12860	25721	51443
G#	425	851	1703	3406	6812	13625	27251	54502
A	451	902	1804	3608	7217	14435	28871	57743
A#	477	955	1911	3823	7647	15294	30588	61176
B	506	1012	2025	4050	8101	16203	32407	64814

For example, to produce the note F# in the sixth octave, use the tone code 12139. Remember that two POKE statements are used when setting the tone code.

```
100 C = 12139 : REM F#, SIXTH OCTAVE
110 POKE 54272, C - INT (C / 256) * 256
120 POKE 54273, INT (C / 256)
```

Before any sound can be heard, several additional steps must be taken. First, the volume level must be set by poking a value between 0 and 15 into memory location 54296, the volume control register. For example, the statement:

```
POKE 54296,8
```

sets the volume level to about half of the loudest setting, which is 15.

The second step is to select the desired ATTACK, DECAY, SUSTAIN, and RELEASE rates of the sound to be played. When a musical tone is played, for instance on a piano, its volume changes continuously. The ATTACK is the rate at which the volume level rises from zero to maximum or peak value. After peak volume has been reached, the sound begins to subside. The rate at which this happens is called the DECAY. The sound will diminish until it hits the SUSTAIN level, which is the proportion of the peak volume that will be maintained after the DECAY cycle. The RELEASE is the rate at which the sound volume falls from the SUSTAIN level to zero. Graphically, the sound appears as follows:

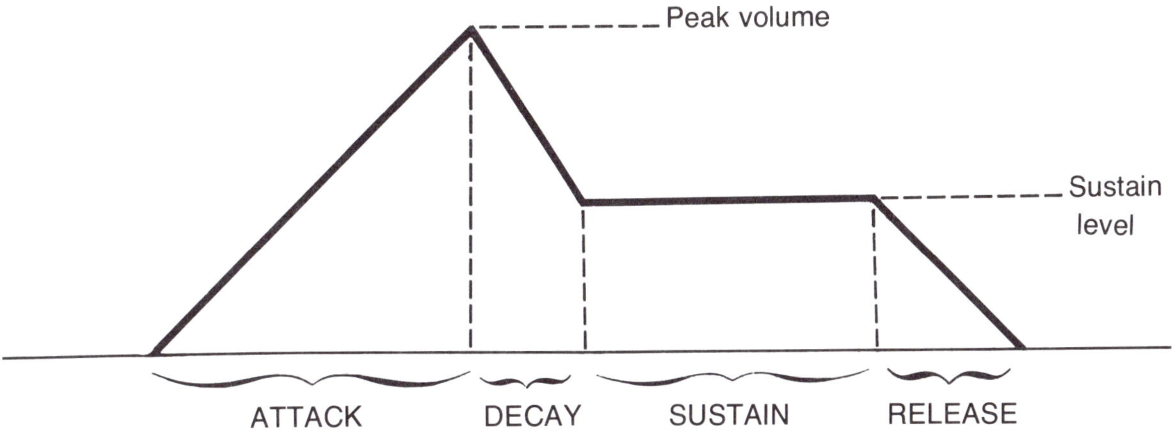

The ATTACK and DECAY rates, each of which is between 0 and 15, are set by poking memory location 54277. For example:

```
80 A = 12 : REM ATTACK RATE
90 D = 5  : REM DECAY RATE
100 POKE 54277, A * 16 + D
```

Since both the ATTACK and DECAY share the same memory location, it is necessary to multiply the ATTACK by 16. Remember that neither the ATTACK nor the DECAY rates can exceed 15, which is the slowest rate of change.

The third step is to set the SUSTAIN level and RELEASE rate, each of which must also be between 0 and 15. Similar to ATTACK and DECAY, SUSTAIN and RELEASE share a single memory location. These values can be set by poking location 54278 as follows:

```
100 S = 8 : REM SUSTAIN 50% VOLUME
120 R = 2 : REM RELEASE QUICKLY
130 POKE 54278, S * 16 + R
```

Remember to multiply the SUSTAIN level by 16 and add it to the RELEASE rate in poking location 54278. The slowest RELEASE rate is obtained by using 15, while the fastest is 0.

The fourth step is to select the wave form of the sound to be heard. The following table is a summary of available wave forms:

Poke Value	Action	Wave Form
0	Disable Sound	
17	Select Triangle Wave	
33	Select Sawtooth Wave	
129	Select Random Wave (Static Sound)	

As soon as the wave form is selected and location 54276 is poked, the sound will begin to play. The ATTACK cycle is started, followed by the DECAY cycle, until the SUSTAIN level is reached. The sound will continue to play at the sustain level until the sound control register is again poked with the statement:

POKE 54276, (K AND 254)

The variable K represents the value used in the first POKE done on memory location 54276, which started the sound to play. This second use of the POKE statement starts the RELEASE cycle, causing the sound to fade out. Optionally, the sound may be immediately cut off by poking zero into the sound control register (location 54276). Be sure to provide an ample delay before beginning the RELEASE cycle to allow the ATTACK, DECAY and SUSTAIN cycles to occur properly.

Program 6.12

This program plays the note G# from the 7th octave. The RELEASE cycle is not begun until the user presses the spacebar.

```
10 K = 33 : REM SAWTOOTH WAVE
20 F = 27251 : REM G#, OCTAVE 7
30 A = 12 : REM ATTACK RATE = SLOW
40 D = 8  : REM DECAY RATE = MEDIUM
50 S = 4  : REM SUSTAIN 25% VOLUME
60 R = 4  : REM RELEASE RATE = FAST
70 POKE 54272, F-INT(F/256)*256 : REM TONE
80 POKE 54273, INT(F/256)
90 POKE 54296, 12 : REM SET VOLUME
100 POKE 54277, A*16 + D
110 POKE 54278, S*16 + R
120 POKE 54276, K : REM START NOTE
130 GET A$ : IF A$ <> " " THEN 130
140 POKE 54276, (K AND 254) : REM RELEASE
150 FOR D = 1 TO 1500 : NEXT D
160 POKE 54276, 0 : REM DISABLE SOUND
170 END
```

A delay is created by line 130 which allows the tone to play for a few seconds. If line 160 were omitted, the sound would continue to play, even after the program finished its run.

Review

7. Write a program that will play the note D# in the third octave followed by the note A in the seventh octave.

Sound on the VIC-20

The VIC-20 computer is capable of producing a variety of sounds using its 4 built-in sound generators. Five locations in the computer's memory, called "registers", are used to control the volume and pitch of the sounds. There are 3 tone generators, which are each capable of generating an independent sound. In addition, there is a separate noise generator, which produces a static sound. By combining the static noise generator with the tone generators, interesting sound effects can be created. The following table lists the five memory locations relevant to sound control:

Memory Location	Purpose	Poke Range
36874	Generate a tone in the 1st, 2nd, or 3rd octave	128-254
36875	Generate a tone in the 2nd, 3rd, or 4th octave	128-254
36876	Generate a rone in the 3rd, 4th, or 5th octave	128-254
36877	Produce static noise	128-254
36878	Volume control (for all 4 sound generators)	0-15

Note that each tone generator is capable of producing a sound in a three octave range, yet all three cover only a five octave range. The tone generators are staggered so that the octaves of each overlap.

The following musical notes can be played by poking appropriate values into any of the three tone generators:

MUSICAL NOTE	POKE VALUE	MUSICAL NOTE	POKE VALUE	MUSICAL NOTE	POKE VALUE
C	135	C	195	C	225
C#	143	C#	199	C#	227
D	147	D	201	D	228
D#	151	D#	203	D#	229
E	159	E	207	E	231
F	163	F	209	F	232
F#	167	F#	212	F#	233
G	175	G	215	G	235
G#	179	G#	217	G#	236
A	183	A	219	A	237
A#	187	A#	221	A#	238
B	191	B	223	B	239

For example, to play F# in the fifth octave, the statement

POKE 36876, 233

can be used. The note will continue to play until the tone generator is turned off by the statement:

POKE 36876, 0

Note that each tone generator must be turned off individually. If the tone generator located at 36874 is used, then the statement

POKE 36874, 0

will turn that tone generator off.

Before any sound can be heard, it is necessary to set the volume by poking register 36878 with a value from 0 to 15, where 15 is the loudest setting. For example,

POKE 36878, 8

sets the volume output to about half. The sound from all four generators is controlled by this single setting. The sound can be turned off by the statement:

POKE 36878, 0

One of the best features of the VIC-20 sound generators is that up to four different sounds can be played simultaneously. To play C# in the third octave and G# in the fifth, the following program segment is used:

```
50 POKE 36878, 12  : REM SET VOLUME
60 POKE 36875, 199 : REM C#, OCTAVE 3
70 POKE 36876, 235 : REM G, OCTAVE 5
```

The sound is turned off by the statements:

```
200 POKE 36875, 0 : REM GENERATOR 2 OFF
210 POKE 36876, 0 : REM GENERATOR 3 OFF
```

or

```
200 POKE 36878, 0 : REM NO VOLUME
```

Program 6.13

This program creates an acceleration sound effect by staggering the notes played by each tone generator and the static sound generator:

```
1 REM S - SOUND LOOP
2 REM A - ADDRESS LOOP
10 POKE 36878,15
20 FOR S = 128 TO 254
30 POKE 36874,S
40 POKE 36875,S-32
50 POKE 36876,S-64
60 POKE 36877,S-96
70 NEXT S
100 REM
110 REM TURN OFF SOUND
120 FOR A = 36874 TO 36878
130 POKE A,0
140 NEXT A
150 GOTO 10
```

Note that the S loop (lines 20-70) runs from 128 to 254, but the second tone generator creates no sound until S–32 exceeds 127. Likewise, the third generator creates no sound until S–64 exceeds 127, and the static generator doesn't produce sound until S–96 exceeds 127. Remember that a sound generator does not produce sound until the value of the POKE statement is between 128 and 255.

Review

8. Write a program that will play F# from the first octave followed by the note A# from the fifth octave.

Program 6.14

This program plays a simplified space game. The enemy, an "@", starts at the top left hand corner of the screen and begins walking. When an edge of the screen is reached, she moves one row closer to the player and reverses direction. The player, which is represented by a "⊥", must destroy the alien before it reaches the row in front of the player. To do this the player may move left or right with either the joystick or the comma (,) and period (.) keys on the keyboard. The player must shoot the alien with an arrow (↑) by using the joystick's fire button or the space bar. If the player hits the alien with the arrow, the alien is destroyed and a smoke ring appears; otherwise, if the alien reaches the player, the player is destroyed.

```
1 REM D = INVADER'S DIRECTION; 1=RIGHT, -1=LEFT
2 REM XI,YI = INVADER'S POSITION
3 REM XP = X COORDINATE OF PLAYER
4 REM XA,YA = ARROW'S POSITION
5 REM X,Y = EXPLOSION COORDINATES
6 REM F = FIRING STATUS; 1=SHOT IS BEING FIRED, OTHERWISE F=0
7 REM XM,YM = X AND Y MAXIMUM COORDINATES RESPECTIVELY
8 REM COLR,SCRN = START OF COLOR AND SCREEN MEMORY RESPECTIVELY
9 REM
10 PRINT "⌂" : REM CLEAR SCREEN
20 POKE 53280,7 : POKE 53281,1 : POKE 646,0
30 REM
40 POKE 54296,3 : POKE 54277,9 : POKE 54278,0 : REM SOUND INIT
100 D=1 : XI=0 : YI=0 : XP=20 : XA=20 : YA=22 : F=0
110 XM=40 : YM=23 : COLR=55296 : SCRN=1024
120 REM CHECK FOR GAME COMPLETION CONDITIONS
130 IF YA=YI AND (XA<XI+2 AND XA>XI-2) THEN X=XI:Y=YI:GOTO 800
140 IF YI=YM-2 THEN X=XP : Y=YM-1 : W=1 : GOTO 800
150 POKE 54276,32 : C = 3215 : REM SOME SOUND
160 POKE 54272,C-INT(C/256)*256 : POKE 54273,INT(C/256)
170 POKE 54276,33
180 REM
190 REM
200 REM PLAYER UPDATE
210 POKE SCRN+XP+YM*XM,32 : REM REMOVE OLD PLAYER
215 GET D$ : J=(15-PEEK(56321) AND 15)
220 IF (D$=" " OR (PEEK(56321) AND 16)=0) THEN F=1
230 IF (D$="." OR J=8) AND XP<(XM-2) THEN XP=XP+1
```

```
240 IF (D$="," OR J=4) AND XP>1 THEN XP=XP-1
250 POKE SCRN+XP+XM*YM,113 : POKE COLR+XP+XM*YM,14
260 REM
270 REM
300 REM ARROW UPDATE
310 POKE SCRN+XA+XM*YA,32 : REM REMOVE OLD ARROW
320 IF F=1 THEN YA=YA-1 : IF YA<0 THEN YA=YM-1 : XA=XP : F=0
330 IF F=0 THEN XA=XP
340 POKE SCRN+XA+XM*YA,30 : POKE COLR+XA+XM*YA,2
350 REM
360 REM
400 REM INVADER UPDATE
410 POKE 54276,32 : C=3608 : REM SOUND
420 POKE 54272,C-INT(C/256)*256 : POKE 54273,INT(C/256)
430 POKE 54276,33
440 POKE SCRN+XI+XM*YI,32 : REM BLANK OUT OLD INVADER
450 XI=XI+D : IF XI>(XM-1) THEN XI=XM-1 : D=-1 : YI=YI+1
460 IF XI<0 THEN XI=0 : D=1 : YI=YI+1
470 POKE SCRN+XI+XM*YI,0 : POKE COLR+XI+XM*YI,0
480 REM
490 REM
500 GOTO 130
510 REM
800 REM EXPLOSION SEQUENCE
810 POKE 54296,15 : POKE 54276,129 : C=8000
820 POKE 54272,C-INT(C/256)*256 : POKE 54273,INT(C/256)
830 POKE SCRN+X+XM*Y,73 : POKE COLR+X+XM*Y,0
840 POKE SCRN+X-1+XM*Y,85 : POKE COLR+X-1+XM*Y,0
850 POKE SCRN+X-1+XM*(Y+1),74 : POKE COLR+X-1+XM*(Y+1),0
860 POKE SCRN+X+XM*(Y+1),75 : POKE COLR+X+XM*(Y+1),0
870 FOR D = 1 TO 750 : NEXT D : POKE 54276,128 : POKE 54296,0
880 IF W=0 THEN PRINT "YOU WIN!"
890 IF W=1 THEN PRINT "YOU LOSE."
900 END
```

Lines 10-20 clear the screen, set the background to white, and the border to blue. Lines 100-110 initialize the needed variables.

The section at 200-250 tests to see what the player wants to do. First the player's old position is blanked out, then line 215 gets a character from the keyboard and the joystick direction value. The conditions in line 220 check to see if a shot is to be fired, while lines 230-240 check to see if the player wishes to move either right or left. Finally, line 250 redraws the player on the screen.

The block from 300-340 moves the arrow on the screen. After line 310 erases the arrow, line 320 calculates the arrow's next position only if it is being fired. Otherwise line 330 keeps the arrow positioned immediately above the player. The arrow is redrawn in its new position by line 340.

Lines 410-430, in combination with lines 150-170, produce the sound of the moving alien, whereas lines 440-470 move the alien. The old position in blanked out by line 440, then lines 450-460 calculate the invader's next position. The invader's X coordinate is either increased or decreased by 1, depending on the direction she is moving. However, if an edge of the screen is reached the invader's Y position is increased by 1, and the direction of movement is changed.

This is repeated until either the alien is hit, which is checked for at line 130, or the invader reaches row 21. When one of these conditions is found to be true, the variables X and Y are set to the coordinates of where the explosion is to occur. Then program control is passed to line 800, where the explosion sound is produced and the explosion is drawn.

Note that this program will only work on the Commodore-64. To run this program on the VIC-20 the following lines must be changed:

```
20 POKE 36879, 7*16+8+1 : POKE 646,0
40 POKE 36878,3 : POKE 37139,0
100 D=1 : XI=0 : YI=0 : XP=10 : XA=20 : YA=20 : F=0
110 XM=22 : YM=21 : COLR=38400 : SCRN=7680
150 POKE 36875,142
215 GET D$ : POKE 37154,127
217 J = 15-((PEEK(37137) AND 28)/4 + (PEEK(37152) AND 128) / 16)
220 IF (D$=" " OR (PEEK(37137) AND 32)=0) THEN F=1
245 POKE 37154,255
410 POKE 36875,225
810 FOR I = 135 TO 239
815    POKE 36875,I
820 NEXT I : POKE 36878,0
```

Also, lines 160, 170, 420, 430 and 870 must be deleted.

EXERCISES

1. Have the computer draw a solid red rectangle with its upper left corner at (4,8), a length of 16 columns and a height of 10 rows.

2. Using graphic characters, draw a black vertical line and a black horizontal line which intersect at (5,17).

3. Place a flashing red notice on the text screen which advertises Uncle Bill's Whamburgers for 79¢. The screen should have a blue background and a green border.

4. Using graphics, have the computer produce the following logo:

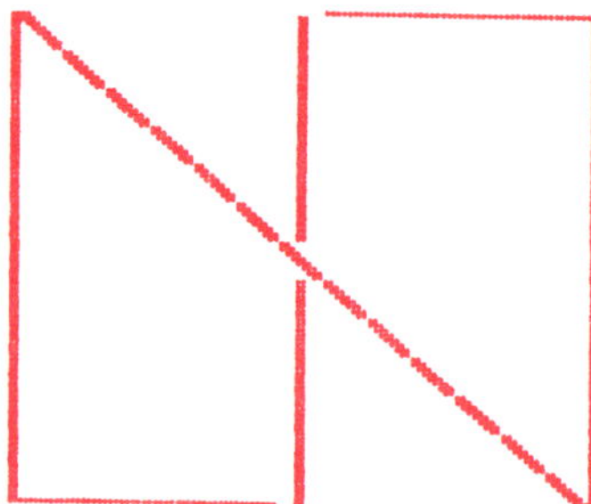

5. Have the computer completely fill the left half of the screen with randomly colored points.
(a) Using the PEEK function, duplicate the left portion of the screen on the right side of the screen.
(b) Rewrite part (a) so that the right portion of the screen is a mirror image of the left portion.

6. Write a program that will play the game called Bomb in a Box. There are six boxes and only one box contains a bomb. The player and the computer alternately pick a box number, and if the box chosen contains the bomb, the bomb explodes. The player chooses first, and then the computer chooses from the remaining boxes, using a random number. Use the sound generator to simulate a click of the lid of an empty box being opened or an appropriate sound for the explosion of the bomb. If the computer loses, have the screen and the cursor turn black.

7. Have the computer generate 100 random integers between 1 and 10, inclusive. Plot a properly labeled bar graph showing the number of occurrences of each number.

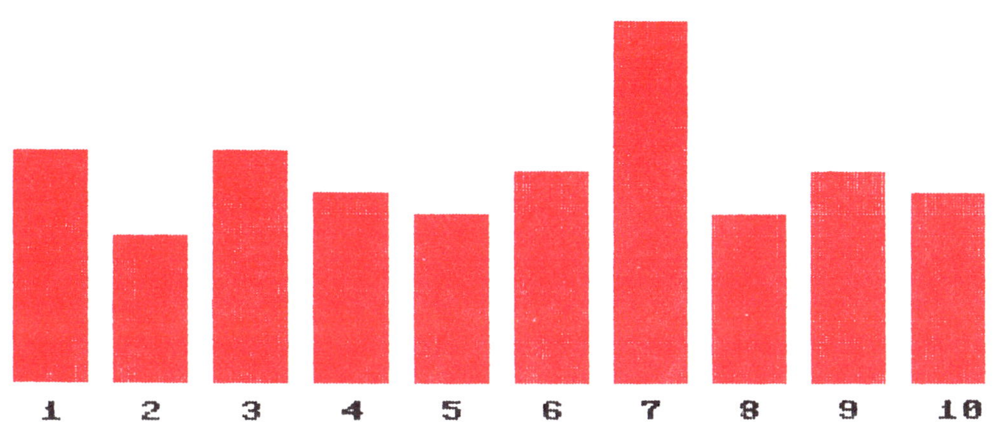

8. Write a program to produce a bar graph for Cheryl's Shoe Shop. The data given below represents the number of pairs of shoes sold a day by each of the five employees over the course of a week. Make a bar graph showing the average number of shoes sold per day for each employee.

Name	Pairs of shoes sold per day for a week
Howard	7, 10, 10, 10, 8, 9, 7
Jason	11, 20, 18, 15, 27, 20, 20
Josh	17, 20, 12, 18, 10, 15, 22
Jared	21, 25, 17, 16, 20, 14, 22
Jess	17, 11, 8, 10, 14, 21, 13

9. Turn the Commodore into an organ. Pressing a key on the keyboard should cause certain notes to play continuously until another key is depressed. Use the following table of keys and fifth octave notes:

key	Z	S	X	D	C	V	G	B	H	N	J	M	,
note	C	C#	D	D#	E	F	F#	G#	A	A#	B	C	

If a key other than one in the table is pressed, all sound should stop until a key in the table is pressed. Your program should make sure a moment of silence is heard if the same note is played more than once in a row.

10. A programmer can make computer animation by flashing pictures on a screen in quick succession.
(a) Write a program that will make an arrow similar to the one shown below:

(b) Make the arrow appear to move across the screen by continuously redrawing it a space to the right each time, using the TAB function.

11. (a) Write a program that will make a stick figure run in place on the screen. The runner is made of five different pictures flashed on the screen in sequence. The five different pictures, given below in sequence, are made from the special graphic characters on the keyboard:

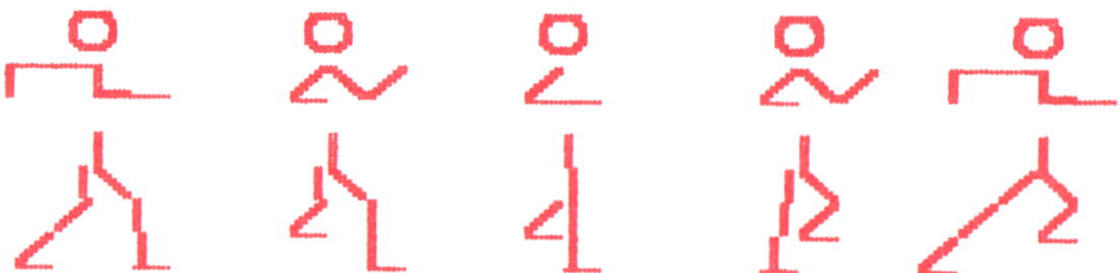

(b) Make the runner appear to move across the screen by redrawing the runner a space or two to the right after the last picture.

12. Write a program to simulate the roll of a single die which shows a picture of the die on the screen. The die should be rerolled with each press of any key.

13. A seven segment display is used to represent a number on a digital clock. The seven segments are arranged as shown below in figure-a (numbered zero through six), and when certain segments are lit, they form the figure of a numeral:

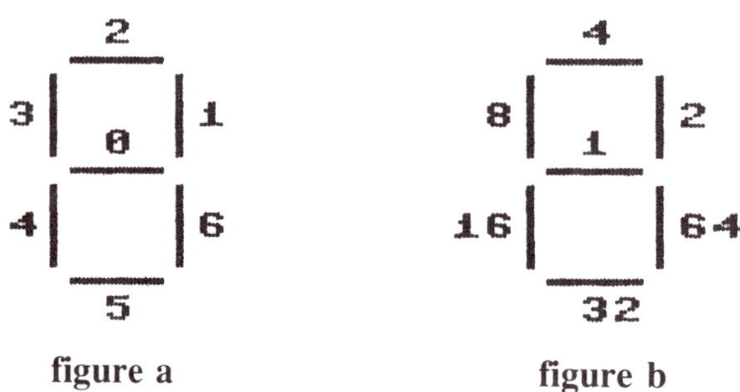

figure a   figure b

For example, if a figure five is to be represented, then segments 0, 2, 3, 5 and 6 would be lit. If each segment is assigned a value of a power of two as shown in figure-b, it is possible to encode the form of a numeral as the sum of the values of the segments that must be lit to represent that numeral. For example, the encoded information of a figure five would be the sum of segments 0, 2, 3, 5 and 6 or $1 + 4 + 8 + 32 + 64 = 109$. to decode a number like

109, successively divide it by two. If the result of the first division is not an integer, then the segment numbered zero should be lit. Then take the INT of the result and again divide by two. If on this second pass the result is again not an integer, then the segment numbered one should be lit. Again take the INT of the result. Continue this process of dividing by two and checking the result seven times (once for each segment). Use POKE to place the bars on the screen as three connecting horizontal or vertical graphic characters.

(a) Write a program to produce one seven segment display as described above, and program the computer to display slowly the sequence from zero to nine.

(b) Modify part (a) of this problem to incorporate a second seven segment display and have the computer count slowly to ninety-nine.

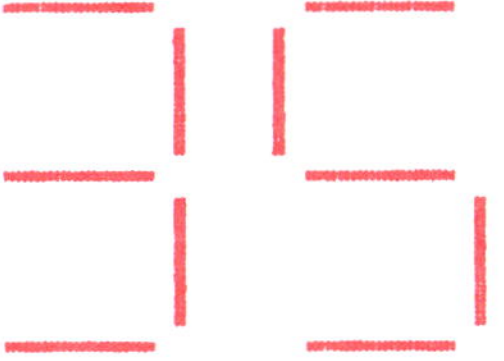

MATHEMATICAL FUNCTIONS

SQR
SGN
ABS
SIN
COS
TAB
ATN
LOG
EXP
DEF
SQR
SGN
ABS
SIN
COS
TAB
ATN
LOG
EXP
DEF
SQR
SGN
ABS
SIN
COS
TAB
ATN
LOG

This chapter covers the various mathematical functions that the computer can perform. The extent to which they can be useful to an individual depends on his or her mathematical background. Generally speaking, the functions presented here are primarily employed by mathematicians, scientists and engineers.

SQR

The SQR function calculates the positive square root of a number:

$$10 \text{ PRINT SQR}(14)$$

The square root of a number N is defined as that value which, when multiplied by itself, gives N. For instance, the square root of 36 is 6 because $6 \times 6 = 36$.

Program 7.1

This program illustrates the square root function:

```
10 FOR X = 1 TO 4
20   PRINT "THE SQUARE ROOT OF"; X; "IS"; SQR(X)
30 NEXT X

RUN
THE SQUARE ROOT OF 1 IS 1
THE SQUARE ROOT OF 2 IS 1.41421356
THE SQUARE ROOT OF 3 IS 1.73205081
THE SQUARE ROOT OF 4 IS 2

READY.
```

In the expression SQR(X), SQR is the function name and X is called the argument. With the SQR function, the argument may be any mathematical expression with a non-negative value. For example, SQR(3∗X + 5) is perfectly acceptable provided that the expression 3∗X + 5 produces a non-negative value.

Note that the argument of a function must be enclosed in parentheses. In its evaluation of a mathematical function, the computer first evaluates the argument and then the function. Some functions have a limitation on the value of the argument. Such limitations will be indicated as the functions are introduced.

SGN and ABS

In some situations it may be necessary to know if a variable is positive or negative. The SGN function has only three possible values: 1, 0 and −1.

$$
\begin{aligned}
\text{SGN}(X) &= 1 & &\text{if } X>0 \\
\text{SGN}(X) &= 0 & &\text{if } X=0 \\
\text{SGN}(X) &= -1 & &\text{if } X<0
\end{aligned}
$$

Program 7.2

This program finds the SGN (signum) of the numbers from 6 to −6, incrementing by −1.2:

```
10 FOR  X = 6 TO -6 STEP -1.2
20   A = SGN(X)
30    PRINT "SGN("; X; ") ="; A
40 NEXT X

RUN
SGN( 6 ) = 1
SGN( 4.8 ) = 1
SGN( 3.6 ) = 1
SGN( 2.4 ) = 1
SGN( 1.2 ) = 1
SGN( Ø ) = Ø
SGN(-1.2 ) =-1
SGN(-2.4 ) =-1
SGN(-3.6 ) =-1
SGN(-4.8 ) =-1

READY.
```

Note that X does not reach −6. This is due to the rounding error.

The ABS function can be used to find the absolute value of a number. The ABS function yields values according to the rule:

$$ABS(X) = X \qquad \text{if } X{>}{=}0$$
$$ABS(X) = -1*X \qquad \text{if } X{<}0$$

Program 7.3

This program illustrates the use of the ABS function:

```
10 FOR  X = 6 TO -6 STEP -1.2
20   A = ABS(X)
30    PRINT A;
40 NEXT X

RUN
 6  4.8  3.6  2.4  1.2  Ø  1.2  2.4  3.6  4.8
READY.
```

Again, X does not reach −6 due to the rounding error.

Review

1. What is X when

$$X = SQR (ABS(SGN(-9+9/3)-6)+9)?$$

2. Write a program to calculate the distance between any 2 points in a Cartesian coordinate system. Hint: use the formula:

$$D = \sqrt{(X1 - X2)^2 + (Y1 - Y2)^2}$$

```
RUN
FIRST COORDINATE (X1,Y1)? 1,1
SECOND COORDINATE (X2,Y2)? 4,5
DISTANCE IS 5

READY.
```

Trigonometric Functions: SIN, COS, TAN

The computer is able to find the values of several trigonometric functions. The functions SIN(X), COS(X) or TAN(X) will produce the value of the sine, cosine or tangent of the angle X, where X is measured in radians. To convert an angle from degrees to radians, multiply it by π and then divide the result by 180 (180 degrees equals π radians). On the computer π = 3.14159265.

Program 7.4

The following program illustrates these functions:

```
10 INPUT "VALUE";A
20 X = A * π / 180
30 PRINT A; "DEGREES EQUALS"; X; "RADIANS."
40 PRINT "SIN(";A;") =";SIN(X)
50 PRINT "COS(";A;") =";COS(X)
60 PRINT "TAN(";A;") =";TAN(X)
70 PRINT
80 GOTO 10

RUN
VALUE 30
 30 DEGREES EQUALS .523598776 RADIANS.
SIN( 30 ) = .5
COS( 30 ) = .866025404
TAN( 30 ) = .577350269

VALUE 45
 45 DEGREES EQUALS .785398163 RADIANS.
SIN( 45 ) = .707106781
COS( 45 ) = .707106782
TAN( 45 ) = .999999999

VALUE?
```

(Note the rounding error that occurs in the output.)

The only inverse trigonometric function supplied by the computer is the principal arctangent function ATN. The function ATN(X) is used to find the angle whose tanget is X. The value produced by the ATN function is in radians. Thus, the arctangent of 1 is π/4 radians = .785398163. To convert an angle from radians to degrees, multiply it by 180 and then divide the result by π. The ATN function, just like the principal arctangent function in mathematics, gives values only between − π/2 and π/2 radians. There is no limitation on the value that the argument may assume.

Program 7.5

This program finds the angle whose tangent is entered and prints the result in degrees:

```
10 INPUT "ENTER A TANGENT VALUE"; T
20 R = ATN(T)
30 D = R * 180 / π
40 PRINT "THE ANGLE WHOSE TANGENT IS";T;"IS";D;"DEGREES."
50 PRINT : GOTO 10

RUN
ENTER A TANGENT VALUE? 1
THE ANGLE WHOSE TANGENT IS 1 IS 45 DEGREES.

ENTER A TANGENT VALUE? 0
THE ANGLE WHOSE TANGENT IS 0 IS 0 DEGREES.

ENTER A TANGENT VALUE? .57735
THE ANGLE WHOSE TANGENT IS .57735 IS 29.9999884 DEGREES.

ENTER A TANGENT VALUE?
```

To find the principal arcsine of a number, the programmer must use the following identity:

$$\text{ARCSINE }(X) = \text{ARCTAN} \frac{X}{\sqrt{1 - X^2}}$$

Therefore, to find the principal angle whose sine is X, the expression ATN(X/SQR(1 − X↑2)) is used. This angle will be measured in radians and will be between −π/2 and π/2. The value of X, however, must be between −1 and 1, not inclusive.

To find the arc cosine of X, use the expression ATN(SQR(1−X↑2)/X). This gives the angle, which is between −π/2 and π/2 whose cosine is X. In this expression, X must be between −1 and 1, inclusive, not not equal to 0.

Program 7.6

This program finds the arcsine and arc cosine of X in both radians and degrees:

```
10  INPUT "VALUE";X
20  S = ATN(X / SQR(1 - X^2))
30  S1 = S * 180 / π
40  C = ATN(SQR(1 - X^2) / X)
50  C1 = C * 180 / π
60  PRINT "THE ANGLE WHOSE SIN IS";X;"IS";S;"RADIANS"
70  PRINT "THE ANGLE WHOSE COSINE IS";X;"IS";C;"RADIANS."
80  PRINT "THE ANGLE WHOSE SIN IS";X;"IS";S1;"DEGREES."
90  PRINT "THE ANGLE WHOSE COSINE IS";X;"IS";C1;"DEGREES."
100 PRINT : GOTO 10

RUN
VALUE? .5
THE ANGLE WHOSE SIN IS .5 IS .523598776 RADIANS
THE ANGLE WHOSE COSINE IS .5 IS 1.04719755 RADIANS.
THE ANGLE WHOSE SIN IS .5 IS 30 DEGREES.
THE ANGLE WHOSE COSINE IS .5 IS 60 DEGREES.

VALUE? .877
THE ANGLE WHOSE SIN IS .877 IS 1.06958255 RADIANS
THE ANGLE WHOSE COSINE IS .877 IS .501213777 RADIANS.
THE ANGLE WHOSE SIN IS .877 IS 61.282566 DEGREES.
THE ANGLE WHOSE COSINE IS .877 IS 28.7174341 DEGREES.

VALUE?
```

Logarithms and the Exponential Function: LOG, EXP

The LOG function can be used to find natural logarithms, that is, logarithms to the base e. To find the natural logarithm of X, LOG(X) is used. Do not confuse the natural logarithm with the common logarithm usually studied in a second year algebra course. The common logarithm, that is, logarithm to base 10, can be found from the natural logarithm by using the formula:

$$\log_{10}(X) = \frac{\ln(X)}{\ln(10)}$$

In the above ln(X) designates the natural logarithm of X. Therefore, to find $\log_{10}(X)$, simply use LOG(X)/LOG(10). The argument in the LOG function must always be positive.

The function EXP(X) is used to find values of the exponential function e^x, where e = 2.71828. This number is the same as the base of the natural logarithm function.

Program 7.7

This program illustrates the use of the above functions:

```
10  INPUT "ENTER X"; X
20  PRINT "LN(X) ="; LOG(X)
30  IF X < 87 THEN PRINT "E RAISED TO X ="; EXP(X)
40  T = LOG(X) / LOG(10)
50  PRINT "THE COMMON LOGARITHM OF";X;"IS";T
60  PRINT : GOTO 10

RUN
ENTER X? 1
LN(X) = 0
E RAISED TO X = 2.71828183
THE COMMON LOGARITHM OF 1 IS 0

ENTER X? .01
LN(X) =-4.60517019
E RAISED TO X = 1.01005017
THE COMMON LOGARITHM OF .01 IS-2

ENTER X? 10000
LN(X) = 9.21034038
THE COMMON LOGARITHM OF 10000 IS 4

ENTER X? .525
LN(X) =-.644357016
E RAISED TO X = 1.69045885
THE COMMON LOGARITHM OF .525 IS-.279840697

ENTER X?
```

Line 30 is necessary to avoid the memory overflow that occurs when X is larger than 88.

DEF

Several standard functions, such as SQR, ABS and LOG, have already been introduced in this chapter. In addition, the programmer can define other functions by using a DEF statement. The major advantage of DEF lies in the fact that the expression for the function need only be written once, even though the function can be evaluated at more than one location within the program. The form of a DEF statement is:

$$DEF \quad FN < function\ name> (<variable\ name>) = <expression>$$

The function name may be any acceptable numeric variable name (e.g., FNA, FNF, FNG3). The variable name (i.e., the argument) following the function name must always appear within parentheses and may be any appropriate numeric variable. In the following example,

$$10\ DEF\ FNP(X) = X{\uparrow}2 - 2*X - 1$$

P is the function name, X is the variable name, and $X^2 - 2X - 1$ is the expression used to compute the function's value. For instance, when X = 5, FNP(X) = 14 because $5\uparrow2 - 2*5 - 1 = 14$.

Program 7.8

The following program evaluates the polynomial function FNP(X) several times:

```
10 DEF FNP(X) = X^2 - 2*X - 1
20 PRINT " X","FNP(X)"
30 FOR A = 1 TO 5
40    PRINT A,FNP(A)
50 NEXT A
60 INPUT X
70 PRINT "THE RESULT OF FNP(";X;") IS";FNP(X)

RUN
 X                FNP(X)
 1                 -2
 2                 -1
 3                  2
 4                  7
 5                 14
? -10
THE RESULT OF FNP(-10 ) IS 119

READY.
```

When the function is evaluated at line 40, the variable in parentheses is A. When it is evaluated at line 70, the variable is X. The name of the variable in parentheses may be the same as or different from the variable name used in the DEF statement. Note also that if the DEF statement were not used, the formula on line 10 would have to appear twice (lines 40 and 70). Though the function is defined only once, it may be evaluated anywhere within the program, providing program economy.

Another advantage of the DEF statement is that it can be easily retyped to define a different function. This is illustrated by re-running Program 7.8 with line 10 changed to:

```
10 DEF FNP(X) = X^3 - 5*X^2 + 1
RUN
 X                FNP(X)
 1                 -3
 2                -11
 3                -17
 4                -15
 5                  1
? -10
THE RESULT OF FNP(-10 ) IS-1499

READY.
```

Review

3. Write a program that will produce the following output. Two user defined functions should be
   used: one to convert degrees to radians, the other to convert radians to degrees:

```
RUN
DEGREES? 30
THAT IS .523598775 RADIANS.

RADIANS? .785375
THAT IS 44.9986729 DEGREES.

READY.
```

1. When a number is input, have the computer generate the following output. Be sure to account for a negative input:

```
RUN
? -1
NO NEGATIVE NUMBERS ALLOWED.
? 4
N = 4        SQUARE ROOTS = + OR - 2
?
```

2. Write a program which prints the integers from 121 to 144, inclusive, and their respective square roots. Label each column of the output.

3. Write a program that will print COS(X) and SIN(X+90°), where X varies from 0 to 360 degrees in increments of 10 degrees.

4. Input a number N. If N is zero, print 0. Otherwise, print ABS(N)/N. What does the program do?

5. Input a number N and print the product of SGN(N) and N. What does this program do?

6. Input a number N, square it and print the square root of the result. What should the program produce?

7. Print a table consisting of 2 columns with headings showing each angle in radians and degrees. The angles in radians are to be 0, .25, .5, .75, ..., 3.0. Remember that $180° = \pi$ radians.

8. Input an angle in degrees and convert it to a fraction of a revolution (1 rev. = 360°) and to radians.

9. Input an angle in degrees. Of the three functions sine, cosine, and tangent, print the value of the one which has the greatest value.

10. For angles from 0° to 180° (at intervals of 10°) print the angle in degrees, the sine, the cosine, and the sum of their squares in columns with headings. What patterns emerge?

11. Input two numbers (A,B). Print the quantity F(B)−F(A), given that $F(X) = 9X^3 - 7X^2 + 4X - 1$.

12. Input a number N. Print the values of F(N) and F(F(N)), where $F(X) = 20 * SQR (ABS(X)) - 10 * SGN(X) + 5 * INT(X)$.

13. Print a table (with headings) of X, the natural logarithm of X and the exponential function of X for X = 1 to 15.

14. Print a table (with headings) of X, the logarithm of X to the base 10, and 10 raised to the power X for X = 1 to 15.

15. What is the exact output for the following program? Check by running the program:

```
10 READ A,B,C,D
20 PRINT SQR(A),INT(B),SQR(INT(C)),INT(SQR(D))
30 DATA 25,-3.4,9.7,24
```

16. Print the square root of the integers from 50 to 60, inclusive.

17. What is the exact output for the following program? Check by running the program:

```
10 DEF FNF(N) = 3*N - 6
20 FOR X = -4 TO 6 STEP 2
30    IF FNF(X)>0 THEN PRINT "FNF(";X;") IS POSITIVE"
40    IF FNF(X)=0 THEN PRINT "FNF(";X;") IS ZERO"
50    IF FNF(X)<0 THEN PRINT "FNF(";X;") IS NEGATIVE"
60 NEXT X
```

18. Input a number and print the square root, sign, log and sine of the number. For example:

```
RUN
? 16
SQR( 16 ) = 4
SGN( 16 ) = 1
LOG( 16 ) = 2.77258872
SIN( 16 ) =-.287903315

READY.
```

19. What is the exact output for the following program? Check by running the program:

```
10 FOR X = -3 TO 4
20    READ A
30    PRINT SGN(X) * ABS(X)
40 NEXT X
50 DATA 3,-5,1,6,-2,4,-9,5
```

20. Using three user-defined functions, have the computer evaluate the following for the integers from -10 to 10:

$$X^2 + 3X + 2$$
$$LOG(X^2 + 1) - X$$
$$ATN(SIN(X))$$

21. Write a program to convert from polar to rectangular coordinates (i.e., from (r, θ) to (X, Y)).

22. If two functions, f and g, are inverse to each other, the following relations hold:
$f(g(x)) = x$ and $g(f(x)) = x$.

(a) Tabulate the values of the following quantities for $X = -5$ to 10: X, EXP(X), LOG(EXP(X)).
(b) Print a table for $X = 1$ to 151 of X, LOG(X), EXP(LOG(X)), using STEP 10.
(c) Do EXP and LOG appear to be inverse to each other?

23. Produce your own sequence of random numbers without using the RND function. To do this, let X vary from 1 to 100 in steps of 1. Obtain SIN(X) and multiply this by 1000, calling the absolute value of the product Y. Divide INT(Y) by 16, and let the remainder R serve as your random number. Hint: the remainder of $A \div B$ is $A/B - INT(A/B)$.

24. Six year old Dennis the Menace has decided to invest 50¢ in the Last Chew Bubble Gum Company. Starting with the 11th year, he withdraws 5¢ at the beginning of each year. His money earns 8% interest compounded continually. The formula for interest compounded continually is $P = P_0 e^{it}$, where t is the elapsed time in years, P_0 is the initial deposit, P is the amount at time t, and i is the interest rate. In this case the formula would be $P = P_0 e^{.08t}$. How much is Dennis's deposit worth after 50 years?

25. Use the SIN function to generate the following:

```
RUN
                        SHAZAM!
                          SHAZAM!
                            SHAZAM!
                              SHAZAM!
                                SHAZAM!
                                  SHAZAM!
                                   SHAZAM!
                                    SHAZAM!
                                    SHAZAM!
                                    SHAZAM!
                                   SHAZAM!
                                  SHAZAM!
                                SHAZAM!
                               SHAZAM!
                             SHAZAM!
                           SHAZAM!
                         SHAZAM!
                       SHAZAM!
                      SHAZAM!
                    SHAZAM!
                   SHAZAM!
                 SHAZAM!
                SHAZAM!
               SHAZAM!
               SHAZAM!
               SHAZAM!
               SHAZAM!
                SHAZAM!
                 SHAZAM!
                  SHAZAM!
                   SHAZAM!
                     SHAZAM!
                      SHAZAM!

READY.
```

26. Write a program that will solve a triangle (computer the unknown sides and angles) for the
    following situations:
    (a) given two sides and the included angle,
    (b) given two angles and any side,
    (c) given three sides.

STRING FUNCTIONS AND DATA TYPES

8

ASC
CHR$
LEFT$
LEN
MID$
RIGHT$
STR$
VAL
ASC
CHR$
LEFT$
LEN
MID$
RIGHT$
STR$
VAL
ASC
CHR$
LEFT$
LEN
MID$
RIGHT$
STR$
VAL
ASC
CHR$
LEFT$
LEN

Modern computers have resulted from the union of the binary system with the principles of electricity. The binary number system uses only two digits, 0 and 1, and can therefore be represented by the two states of an electric circuit, off or on. This concept has made digital computers possible because they operate by reducing all data to a binary code. How different types of data can be reduced to a binary system is explained in this chapter.

Binary Code

The most familiar number system, the decimal system, uses ten digits: 0, 1, 2, 3, 4, 5, 6, 7, 8, 9 and is therefore considered to be base ten. In contrast, the binary system, which uses only the digits 0 and 1, is base two.

In the base ten system, columns are used to represent powers of ten with the first column left of the decimal point representing 10^0, the second 10^1, the third 10^2 and so on. For example, in the numeral 458, 8 represents 8×10^0, 5 represents 5×10^1 and 4 represents 4×10^2. The numeral itself represents the sum: $4 \times 10^2 + 5 \times 10^1 + 8 \times 10^0$.

The base two system works identically *except the columns represent powers of two* instead of ten. For example, in the numeral 101, the 1 on the right represents 1×2^0, the 0 represents 0×2^1 and the 1 on the left represents 1×2^2. The numeral itself represents the sum $1 \times 2^2 + 0 \times 2^1 + 1 \times 2^0$, which is known as five in the base ten system.

Base Two		**Base Ten**
$11 = 1 \times 2^1 + 1 \times 2^0$		$= \quad 3$
$1011 = 1 \times 2^3 + 0 \times 2^2 + 1 \times 2^1 + 1 \times 2^0$		$= \quad 11$
$11001 = 1 \times 2^4 + 1 \times 2^3 + 0 \times 2^2 + 0 \times 2^1 + 1 \times 2^0$		$= \quad 25$

To convert a number from base ten to base two, we must find which powers of two add up to the number. Since $13 = 8 + 4 + 1$, the base two representation for 13 is 1101 ($1 \times 8 + 1 \times 4 + 0 \times 2 + 1 \times 1$).

Base Ten		**Base Two**
$6 = 4 + 2 = 1 \times 2^2 + 1 \times 2^1 + 0 \times 2^0$		$= \quad 110$
$29 = 16 + 8 + 4 + 1 = 1 \times 2^4 + 1 \times 2^3 + 1 \times 2^2 + 0 \times 2^1 + 1 \times 2^0$		$= \quad 11101$
$52 = 32 + 16 + 4 = 1 \times 2^5 + 1 \times 2^4 + 0 \times 2^3 + 1 \times 2^2 + 0 \times 2^1 + 0 \times 2^0$		$= \quad 110100$

Computer Memory and Processing

The computer is composed of a solid-state electronic memory, which stores information, and a central processing unit (CPU), which performs calculations, makes decisions and moves information.

Because electricity has two states, ON and OFF, it is ideal for expressing binary numbers. A circuit (called a "flip-flop") when on stands for a "1" and when off stands for a "0". Designing computers to contain millions of simple flip-flop circuits allows huge quantities of information to be stored.

A single binary digit (0 or 1) is called a "bit", and eight of these bits constitute a "byte". Single characters require one byte and integers two bytes of memory for storage. The memory stores both instructions for the CPU and data as binary digits.

The power of a computer is vastly increased when it is capable of storing letters and special characters as well as numbers. In order to do this, a code has been established to translate letters and special characters into numbers, which can then be stored in a binary form. This code has been standardized by the computer industry as the American Standard Code for Information Interchange (ASCII). In this code each letter of the alphabet, both upper case and lower case, each symbol, and each control function used by the computer is represented by a number. For example, the name JIM is translated by the computer into ASCII numbers 74,73,77. In turn these numbers are then stored by the computer in binary form:

$$J = 74 = 01001010$$
$$I = 73 = 01001001$$
$$M = 77 = 01001101$$

In order for the computer to store a name such as JIM, or any piece of non-numeric information, it must be entered in the form of a string, converted character by character to ASCII numbers, and then stored in memory as binary numbers. On the following page is a table of the ASCII character codes available on the computer.

ASCII Code Table

ASCII Value	Character	ASCII Value	Character	ASCII Value	Character	ASCII Value	Character
0		50	2	100		150	(light red)
1		51	3	101		151	(dark gray)
2		52	4	102		152	(medium gray)
3		53	5	103		153	(light green)
4		54	6	104		154	(light blue)
5	(white)	55	7	105		155	(light gray)
6		56	8	106		156	(purple)
7		57	9	107		157	(cursor left)
8	(disables C= SHIFT)	58	:	108		158	(yellow)
9	(enables C= SHIFT)	59	;	109		159	(cyan)
10		60	<	110		160	(space)
11		61	=	111		161	
12		62	>	112		162	
13	(carriage return)	63	?	113		163	
14	(switch to lower case)	64	@	114		164	
15		65	A	115		165	
16		66	B	116		166	
17	(cursor down)	67	C	117		167	
18	(reverse on)	68	D	118		168	
19	(home)	69	E	119		169	
20	(delete)	70	F	120		170	
21		71	G	121		171	
22		72	H	122		172	
23		73	I	123		173	
24		74	J	124		174	
25		75	K	125		175	
26		76	L	126		176	
27		77	M	127		177	
28	(red)	78	N	128		178	
29	(cursor right)	79	O	129	(orange)	179	
30	(green)	80	P	130		180	
31	(blue)	81	Q	131		181	
32	(space)	82	R	132		182	
33		83	S	133	f1	183	
34	"	84	T	134	f3	184	
35	#	85	U	135	f5	185	
36	$	86	V	136	f7	186	
37	%	87	W	137	f2	187	
38	&	88	X	138	f4	188	
39	'	89	Y	139	f6	189	
40	(	90	Z	140	f8	190	
41	)	91	[	141	(SHIFT-RETURN)	191	
42	*	92	£	142	(switch to upper case)	192-223	Same as 96-127
43	+	93	]	143		224-254	Same as 160-190
44	,	94	↑	144	(black)	255	Same as 126
45	−	95	←	145	(cursor up)		
46	.	96		146	(reverse off)		
47	/	97	♠	147	(clear screen)		
48	0	98		148	(insert)		
49	1	99		149	(brown)		

Data Types

When information is entered into the computer, it can take one of three forms: ASCII characters, integers or floating point numbers. An integer is a number without decimal places, while a floating point number has either a decimal point or an implied decimal point and decimal places. For example, the number 29 could be either integer or floating point, but 29.73 is definitely floating point. Floating point numbers are internally accurate to ten significant figures but rounded to nine when printed.

Storage of an integer requires 16 bits, a floating point number 32 bits, and an ASCII character 8 bits. Because of storage requirements it is important to distinguish among the several forms. When files are presented in Chapter 9, the significance of this factor in planning efficient storage of data will become apparent.

The three data types employ different symbols to inform the computer as to which is being used. Strings of ASCII characters employ the familiar symbol ($) for string variable names (e.g. G$, B3$). Integers, which have the disadvantage of being restricted to the range −32768 to 32767, are denoted by a percent sign (%). B% and Z% are variable names for integers. While integers have a severe range limitation, they are processed fastest by the computer. Variables and constants not specifically declared otherwise are assumed to be floating point (e.g., R, L).

Program 8.1

This program demonstrates the difference between floating point and integer arithmetic:

```
10 A%=4/3
20 PRINT A%
30 A=4/3
40 PRINT A
50 END
RUN
 1
 1.33333333

READY.
```

The computer approximates the fraction 4/3 as 1.33333333 and assigns this value to the floating point variable A at line 30. However, as A% can only have integer values, the computer truncates all the numbers after the decimal point and assigns it the value of 1.

Review

1. What are the minimum number of bits required to store the following data in the computer?

   (a) 6 167
   (b) APRIL 1, 1963
   (c) 42864
   (d) 35.78

Earlier in this chapter the ASCII code was described as a method by which the computer converts information in the form of strings into numbers. Commands exist to convert strings into ASCII values and vice versa:

Function	Operation
X = ASC(P$)	Converts only the first character of the string P$ to its ASCII code number.
P$ = CHR$(X)	Assigns the character with the ASCII code number of X to P$, which now contains only one character.

Program 8.2

This program demonstrates the use of the ASCII character conversions:

```
1 REM   C$ = CHARACTER INPUT
2 REM   A = ASCII VALUE OF C$
3 REM   K$ = NEW STRING
4 REM   Y$ = INDICATOR
5 REM
6 REM
10 K$=""
20 INPUT "ENTER ANY CHARACTER";C$
30 A=ASC(C$)
40 PRINT "THE ASCII VALUE OF '";C$;"'";
50 PRINT "IS:";A
60 PRINT "'";CHR$(A);"' REPEATED 17";
70 PRINT " TIMES LOOKS LIKE THIS:"
80 FOR X=1 TO 17
90    K$=K$+CHR$(A)
100 NEXT X
110 PRINT K$
120 PRINT "WOULD YOU LIKE TO RUN THIS";
130 INPUT " AGAIN";Y$
140 IF ASC(Y$)=89 THEN 10
150 END

RUN
ENTER ANY CHARACTER? R
THE ASCII VALUE OF 'R'IS: 82
'R' REPEATED 17 TIMES LOOKS LIKE THIS:
RRRRRRRRRRRRRRRRR
WOULD YOU LIKE TO RUN THIS AGAIN? N

READY.
```

2. Write a program that will allow the user to input a letter. Have the computer print that letter's ASCII code and then print the letter that comes two letters after it in the alphabet. If Y or Z is the letter input, then A or B should be returned respectively.

```
RUN
INPUT A LETTER? R
THE ASCII OF 'R' IS 82
TWO LETTERS AFTER 'R' IS 'T'

READY.
```

String Manipulation Functions

Strings can be manipulated with the following functions:

Function	Operation
L$ = LEFT$(A$,N)	Assigns L$ a substring of the string A$ from the leftmost character up to and including the Nth character.
L = LEN(A$)	Assigns L a value equal to the number of characters in the string A$, including blank spaces.
M$ = MID$(A$,N)	Assigns M$ a substring of the string A$ from the Nth character to the rightmost character of the string.
M$ = MID$(A$,N1,N2)	Assigns M$ a substring of the string A$, starting with the character N1 and being N2 characters long.
R$ = RIGHT$(A$,N)	Assigns R$ a substring of the string A$ consisting of the rightmost N characters.
S$ = STR$(X)	Converts X into a string of numeric characters and assigns it to S$.
V = VAL(A$)	Converts the first set of numeric characters in the string A$ into a numeric value that is assigned to V. Non-numeric characters are ignored.

Program 8.3

This program will input a string and manipulate it to show the use of string functions:

```
10  INPUT T$
20  PRINT
30  PRINT "'";T$;"' BACKWARDS IS:  ";
40  FOR X=LEN(T$) TO 1 STEP -1
50    PRINT MID$(T$,X,1);
60  NEXT X
70  PRINT
80  PRINT "THE VALUE OF '";T$;"' IS:";VAL(T$)
90  PRINT "'";T$;"' HALVED AND FLIPPED IS:"
100 PRINT RIGHT$(T$,LEN(T$)/2);LEFT$(T$,LEN(T$)/2)
110 PRINT "'";VAL(T$);"' BACKWARDS IS:  ";
120 FOR X=LEN(STR$(VAL(T$))) TO 1 STEP -1
130   PRINT MID$(STR$(VAL(T$)),X,1);
140 NEXT X

RUN
? 145RTLMJDQ

'145RTLMJDQ' BACKWARDS IS: QDJMLTR541
THE VALUE OF '145RTLMJDQ' IS: 145
'145RTLMJDQ' HALVED AND FLIPPED IS:
LMJDQ145RT
' 145 ' BACKWARDS IS: 541
READY.
```

Program 8.4

This program plays the game Hangman with the user. The computer picks a random word from the DATA statements and allows the user to guess letters which may be contained in the word. If the letter guessed is in the word, the computer shows the user the position in which it appears. If the letter guessed is not in the word, it is counted as a mistake. Play continues until the user guesses all the letters in the word or makes 6 mistakes.

```
10  FOR I=0 TO INT(10*RND(0))
20    READ W$
30  NEXT I
40  PRINT "O.K.  I'M THINKING OF A WORD."
50  PRINT : F=1
60  FOR I=1 TO LEN(W$)
70    D$=D$+"?"
80  NEXT I
90  PRINT D$
100 PRINT "YOU HAVE";M;"MISTAKES."
110 INPUT "LETTER";L$
120 REM
```

```
200 REM   PRINT CURRENT WORD STATUS
210 FOR I=1 TO LEN(W$)
220    IF MID$(W$,I,1)<>L$ THEN 240
230       D$=LEFT$(D$,I-1)+L$+RIGHT$(D$,LEN(D$)-I) : F=0
240 NEXT I
250 IF D$=W$ THEN 400
260 M=M+F : F=1
270 IF M=6 THEN 500
300 GOTO 90
310 REM
400 PRINT "YOU GOT IT!!" : END
410 REM
500 PRINT "YOU HAVE TOO MANY MISTAKES."
510 PRINT "THE WORD WAS ";W$;"."
520 REM
600 REM DATA SECTION
610 DATA COMMODORE,COMPUTER,KEYBOARD,MONITOR
620 DATA HUTT,JEDI,EWOK,CARBONITE,SABER,FALCON

RUN
O.K. I'M THINKING OF A WORD.

????
YOU HAVE 0 MISTAKES.
LETTER? H
H???
YOU HAVE 0 MISTAKES.
LETTER? O
H???
YOU HAVE 1 MISTAKES.
LETTER? T
H?TT
YOU HAVE 1 MISTAKES.
LETTER? U
YOU GOT IT!!

READY.
```

Function Keys

Both the Commodore-64 and VIC-20 computers have a set of function keys on the right hand side of the keyboard. In order to tell which key is being pressed, a GET must be used in conjunction with the ASC function. The table below shows the ASCII codes that correspond with the function keys:

Key	ASCII
F1	133
F2	137
F3	134
F4	138
F5	135
F6	139
F7	136
F8	140

The odd-numbered keys are activated by pressing the appropriately numbered key, even-numbered keys by pressing SHIFT and the appropriately numbered key. The function keys are useful in allowing a user to direct program flow to one of up to eight options.

Program 8.5

This program uses the function keys to send the flow of the program to one of eight subroutines. The technique demonstrated is useful when employed in programs in which selections must be made:

```
10 FOR X=1 TO 8
20    READ K(X)
30 NEXT X
40 PRINT "PRESS ONE OF THE FUNCTION KEYS"
50 GET G$ : IF G$="" THEN 50
60 X=ASC(G$)-132
70 ON K(X) GOSUB 100,200,300,400,500,600,700,800
80 END
90 REM
100 PRINT "YOU PRESSED F1"
110 RETURN
120 REM
200 PRINT "YOU PRESSED F2"
210 RETURN
220 REM
300 PRINT "YOU PRESSED F3"
310 RETURN
320 REM
400 PRINT "YOU PRESSED F4"
410 RETURN
420 REM
500 PRINT "YOU PRESSED F5"
510 RETURN
520 REM
600 PRINT "YOU PRESSED F6"
610 RETURN
620 REM
700 PRINT "YOU PRESSED F7"
710 RETURN
720 REM
800 PRINT "YOU PRESSED F8"
810 RETURN
820 REM
830 DATA 1,3,5,7,2,4,6,8

RUN
PRESS ONE OF THE FUNCTION KEYS
YOU PRESSED F3

READY.
```

The loop (lines 10-30) reads the data at line 830. This technique is required since the ASCII values of the function keys are not sequential. Note how line 60 is now able to produce a value for X of from 1 through 8, depending upon which key has been pressed at line 50.

1. Enter a string A$ and use a loop to print the ASCII number of each of its characters.

2. Input three letters, add their ASCII numbers, find the INT of one third of their sum and print the character corresponding to the result. Is there any meaning to this process?

3. Using properly selected ASCII numbers on a DATA line, print the sentence "ASCII DID THIS!"

4. Using ASCII numbers 45 and 46 and the PRINT TAB statement, print the following figure:

5. Enter the string THREE!@#$%STRING!@#$%FUNCTIONS. Use LEFT$, MID$, and RIGHT$ to print the phrase "THREE STRING FUNCTIONS".

6. Enter a string A$ of any length. Print the length of A$ and the ASCII number of its first and last characters.

7. Write a program where you input a name and then have the computer print the ASCII number of the letter which appears most often in the name.

8. Let A$ = "2598." Have the computer apply VAL to those parts of A$ whose sum is 123.

9. Enter the words "QUEEN," "LENGTH" and "REMEMBER." Print each word with all E's removed.

10. Use the computer or a hand calculator to find the binary equivalents of the decimal values given below:

89, 74, 80, 107, 255, 129, 28, 39, 29, 24, 43

11. Use the computer or a hand calculator to find the decimal equivalents for the binary values given below:

1011, 10100, 1111, 1110, 1010011, 110011, 1011100,
1101111, 11000000, 10000111

12. Input a string A$ which consists of the digits 0 to 9, inclusive, each to be used only once (e.g., 1956472038). Use string functions to obtain from A$ two numbers N1 and N2, N1 being the number represented by the first three digits of A$ and N2 the number represented by the last three digits. Print the sum of N1 and N2.

13. Let A$ consist of the first twelve letters of the alphabet. Using A$, construct the right triangle shown at the right:

```
RUN
A
AB
ABC
ABCD
ABCDE
ABCDEF
ABCDEFG
ABCDEFGH
ABCDEFGHI
ABCDEFGHIJ
ABCDEFGHIJK
ABCDEFGHIJKL

READY.
```

14. As a young boy Franklin Roosevelt signed his letters to his mother backwards: TLEVESOOR NILKNARF. Write a program that accepts a person's name and prints it backwards.

15. Using the ASCII chart given in the text, determine the output for the following program. Check by running the program:

```
10 FOR A=1 TO 4
20    READ A$
30    PRINT ASC(A$)
40 NEXT A
50 DATA "W","H","7","625"
60 END
```

16. The output of the following program is Foxy Moxie's message to Jimmy Band. What is the message? Check by running the program:

```
10 FOR W = 1 TO 6
20    READ A$,B$,C$
30    PRINT LEFT$(A$,1);MID$(B$,2,2);RIGHT$(C$,1)
40 NEXT W
50 END
```

```
60 REM DATA SECTION
70 DATA FDO,NOXP,LUY
80 DATA SSS,HAYE,RRS
90 DATA HYF,OELR,EVP
100 DATA WER,LILO,VEL
110 DATA CIS,TOMH,EIE
120 DATA SRS,WOOI,SHN
```

17. Choose fifteen random integers from 65 to 90, inclusive, to serve as ASCII code numbers. Convert these fifteen integers to the fifteen characters for which they stand and print the results.

18. Write a program which produces a sentence containing twenty nonsense words. Each word can contain from two to five letters. Use random numbers and the ASCII code to produce the words.

```
RUN
ET          IN          RWCEB       IDL
TLH         QNDYU       LWRIR       AWMM
UVSI        CNLQY       SXNV        FR
DO          PGL         XYKV        TQSGR
LJSRL       DX          QRLNL       QCOCU

READY.
```

19. Using random numbers and the ASCII code numbers from 32 to 126, inclusive, have the computer generate a string of 100 characters, allowing repetitions. Tabulate how many characters are letters, numbers or miscellaneous characters. Print the results.

20. Using string functions, write a program to play a word guessing game. Ask the player to guess a secret word. Search through each guess to see if the guess contains any correct letters. If any letter is correct, have the computer print the ones that are. If the entire word is guessed, type "YOU GUESSED IT!!"

```
RUN
GUESS A WORD? HANGMAN
'A' IS IN THE WORD
'A' IS IN THE WORD
GUESS A WORD? DATAPHONE
'A' IS IN THE WORD
'A' IS IN THE WORD
'E' IS IN THE WORD
GUESS A WORD? TERMINAL
'E' IS IN THE WORD
'R' IS IN THE WORD
'A' IS IN THE WORD
'L' IS IN THE WORD
GUESS A WORD? SCRABBLE
YOU GUESSED IT!!

READY.
```

21. You are a spy who will use the computer to produce a secret code.
(a) Input a short message and have the computer type back what appears to be nonsense words. To produce the coded words, convert each letter of the original message into its corresponding ASCII code number, add two to each number and convert to characters to produce the message. Keep all spaces between the words in their original places and understand that the letters Y and Z are to be converted to A and B.

(b) Write a program that will decode the following message:

22. When the following program is run, the output is:

$$A = 1500 \qquad B = 999.9764$$

Explain in a clear, brief manner why the value of B is not exactly 1000, and why the value of A is exactly 1500.

```
10 FOR X=1 TO 3000
20    A=A+1/2
30    B=B+1/3
40 NEXT X
50 PRINT "A =";A,"B =";B
60 END
```

23. Create bizarre "sentences" by having the computer print the words in a real sentence in reverse order. Your program should NOT reverse the order of the letters in each word.

24. Write a program which prints a triangle made up of parts of the word "triangle." The triangle should be obtuse, and the program should ask for its height (A), how far to indent the bottom edge (B), and where the bottom edge ends (C).

```
RUN
A,B, AND C? 10,10,20
 T
  RI
   IAN
    ANGL
     NGLET
      GLETRI
       LETRIAN
        ETRIANGL
         TRIANGLET
          RIANGLETRI

READY.
```

25. Enter a positive integer N$ as it would be expressed in binary form. That is, enter a string of ones and zeros. Have the computer print the equivalent of N$ as it is expressed in the decimal system.

8-14

FILES

OPEN
CLOSE
PRINT#
INPUT#
STATUS
OPEN
CLOSE
PRINT#
INPUT#
STATUS
OPEN
CLOSE
PRINT#
INPUT#
STATUS
OPEN
CLOSE
PRINT#
INPUT#
STATUS
OPEN
CLOSE
PRINT#
INPUT#
STATUS
OPEN
CLOSE
PRINT#

So far we have discussed only two methods for saving data in the computer. Variables could be assigned a constant value (e.g., A = 5) or the data could be placed in DATA statements that are read by the computer when the program is run. There are two drawbacks to these methods. First, if it becomes necessary to update the data, program lines have to be retyped, thus altering the program and increasing the chance for errors. Second, since the data is an integral part of a program, it cannot be accessed by other programs. The solution to these problems is to store the data in a file. Since files are separate from programs, they can be updated without changing any part of a program. Also, a single data file can be accessed by many programs, allowing more flexible use of the data. Files and programs should not be confused. A program is a set of instructions that tell the computer what do do; a file is a set of data used by a program.

The first part of this chapter will explain how to use data files stored on cassette tapes; the second part will cover files stored on diskettes. Before proceeding to learn the use of files stored on cassette tapes or diskettes, the programmer should read either Appendix B to become familiar with the operation of the cassette unit or Appendix C to become familiar with the disk drive.

Several conventions are used in this chapter. Writing to a file means transferring data from the computer's memory to a file stored on a tape or diskette. Reading from a file means transferring data from a file to the computer's memory. Whenever the general format for a new command or statement is presented, part of the definition will be enclosed in angle brackets (< . . . >). The brackets are not part of the statement. They indicate the parts of the statement that can change and require information to be supplied by the programmer. For example, <variable> means that an appropriate variable such as D1 or R$ is needed.

Cassette Files

The computer stores files on tape sequentially, one data item after another. Therefore, these files are best suited to situations in which the data will be recalled in the same order as it was originally stored.

OPEN

The OPEN statement establishes a line of communication between a program and a file. The OPEN statement must specify the name of the file, a file number, a device number and the mode of access desired. A file name is used by the computer to identify each file and program stored on a tape. Therefore, each file and program on a tape must have a different name. The file number must be an integer from 1 to 255, which is used throughout a program to identify a specific file. The device number specifies the device the file is to be stored on. For the cassette unit, the device number is 1. The three modes of access are:

    0: The computer will read data from a previously created file.
    1: The computer will write data to a new file.
    2: The computer will write data to a new file and place an end of tape marker after the end of the file.

Mode 2 is useful when the file is to be placed near the end of the tape because in searching for a file or program that is not on the tape the computer will end its search and print the message ?DEVICE NOT PRESENT ERROR only if an end of tape marker is found. Otherwise, the computer will continue its search even after the tape has run out.

The general format for the OPEN statement is:

$$\text{OPEN } <file\#>, <device\#>, <mode>, ``<file\ name>''$$

The file name must be enclosed in quotation marks. For example,

$$10 \text{ OPEN } 35,1,1,``\text{PAYROLL FILE}''$$

will instruct the computer to prepare to write to a new file called PAYROLL FILE (using file number 35) on the cassette (device 1). Since the mode is specified as 1, the computer will not place an end of tape marker after the end of the file. When the computer is instructed to use mode 1 or mode 2 to open a file, it will print the message PRESS RECORD & PLAY ON TAPE and then wait for the buttons to be pressed before opening the file. When the computer is instructed to open a file using mode 0, it will print the message PRESS PLAY ON TAPE and then wait for the button to be pressed before attempting to open the file.

CLOSE

Any file previously opened must be closed. This procedure is necessary in order to break the line of communication between a program in the computer's memory and a file. The format for a CLOSE statement is:

$$\text{CLOSE } <file\#>$$

For example,

$$100 \text{ CLOSE } 35$$

will close the file previously opened with the file number 35.

Closing a file ensures that all of its information will be properly retained. A tape with open files on it should not be removed from the cassette unit, nor should the tape be advanced or rewound before the files have been closed. Removing a tape prematurely may result in the loss of data.

PRINT#

After the OPEN statement establishes a line of communication between a program and a file, the PRINT# command is used to place data in the file. Its form is:

$$\text{PRINT\# } <file\#>, <variable>;``,'';<variable> \ldots$$

Information contained in the variables in the PRINT# statement will be placed in the file specified by the file number. If the contents of more than one variable are to be placed in a file by a single PRINT# statement, commas within quotation marks must be placed between each variable. The commas are stored in the file and act as markers so that the computer can distinguish each item of data when reading the file. For example,

$$PRINT\#5, A\$;",";C;",";Q\$$$

transfers the contents of a string (A$), floating point variable (C) and string (Q$) to the file, separating each with a comma.

Program 9.1

This program, named CREATE, opens a file on the tape named WORK FILE. In it are stored the names of four employees, their hourly wages and the number of hours they have worked. Note the structure of line 60, in which the name (N$), wage (W) and hours worked (H) for each employee are written to the file:

```
1 REM     N$ = EMPLOYEE NAME
2 REM     W = WAGE
3 REM     H = HOURS WORKED
4 REM
5 REM
10 OPEN 1,1,1,"WORK FILE"
20 FOR X=1 TO 4
30    INPUT "NAME";N$
40    INPUT "WAGE";W
50    INPUT "HOURS WORKED";H
60    PRINT#1,N$;",";W;",";H
70    PRINT
80 NEXT X
90 CLOSE 1
100 END

RUN
PRESS RECORD & PLAY ON TAPE
OK
NAME? GWEN WALDEN
WAGE? 4.45
HOURS WORKED? 39

NAME? SANDY BECKERMAN
WAGE? 4.75
HOURS WORKED? 42

NAME? RUBEN STECK
WAGE? 5.10
HOURS WORKED? 36.75

NAME? RUTH OBRE
WAGE? 4.95
HOURS WORKED? 27.5


READY.
```

Review

1. Write a program named CALENDAR that will create a file named MONTH FILE and store the names of the months of the year in it.

INPUT#

The INPUT# statement is used to read information from a file and transfer it to the computer's memory. Its format is similar to that of the PRINT# statement:

$$INPUT\# <file\#>,<variable>,<variable> \ldots$$

The commas between the variable names in the INPUT# statement are not enclosed in quotation marks. The order in which the variables are listed in the INPUT# statement must be the same as the order used originally in the PRINT# statement that created the file. For example, a program that reads the data from WORK FILE created by Program 9.1 would have to input the data in the order N$, W, H:

$$INPUT\#2, N\$, W, H$$

After a file has been closed, the same file number need not be used to access it at a later time.

Program 9.2

This program, named HOURS, will open the file WORK FILE created by Program 9.1 and print the names and hours worked for the four employees:

```
1 REM    N$ = EMPLOYEE NAME
2 REM    W = WAGE
3 REM    H = HOURS WORKED
4 REM
5 REM
10 OPEN 2,1,0,"WORK FILE"
20 PRINT "NAME";TAB(20);"HOURS WORKED"
30 FOR X=1 TO 4
40   INPUT#2,N$,W,H
50   PRINT N$;TAB(20);H
60 NEXT X
70 CLOSE 2
80 END
RUN

PRESS PLAY ON TAPE
OK
NAME                HOURS WORKED
GWEN WALDEN           39
SANDY BECKERMAN       42
RUBEN STECK          36.75
RUTH OBRE            27.5

READY.
```

Line 10 specifies the access mode as 0 because the program will input data from the file to the computer.

The data in WORK FILE appears as follows:

GWEN WALDEN, 4.45 , 39
SANDY BECKERMAN, 4.75 , 42
RUBEN STECK, 5.1 , 36.75
RUTH OBRE, 4.95 , 27.5

The variable W is read in the input line but is not printed. The computer has an internal pointer that indicates the next item of information that is to be transferred from the file by the INPUT# statement. When the INPUT# statement is executed, the pointer is moved across the data line as each item is read. To ensure that the data in the file is read in the correct sequence, it is important that all of the necessary variables be included in the INPUT# statement, even if some of them are not used by the program.

Review

2. Write a program named RETRIEVE that will retrieve the name of every other month of the year from MONTH FILE created in Review problem 1.

```
RUN

PRESS PLAY ON TAPE
OK
ODD MONTHS OF THE YEAR -
JANUARY
MARCH
MAY
JULY
SEPTEMBER
NOVEMBER

READY.
```

Updating Cassette Files

Commodore Basic does not have provisions for adding or removing data in already existing files. When an OPEN command is executed with either mode 1 or 2 specified, the computer opens a new file and prepares to write to it starting at the beginning of the file. Any old file with the same name is ignored. To add information to an old file, the programmer must first read the entire file into memory. A new file must then be opened and the old and new data written to the new file. To delete data from a file, the programmer must read the entire file into memory and then write the data to be retained into a new file.

Program 9.3

This program, named ADD, will update WORK FILE, created by Program 9.1, so that it includes information on two new employees just hired:

```
1 REM     N$,N$() = EMPLOYEE NAME
2 REM     W,W() = WAGE
3 REM     H,H() = HOURS WORKED
4 REM
5 REM
100 REM    READ OLD FILE
110 REM
120 DIM N$(4),W(4),H(4)
130 OPEN 1,1,0,"WORK FILE"
140 FOR X=1 TO 4
150    INPUT#1,N$(X),W(X),H(X)
160 NEXT X
170 CLOSE 1
180 REM
200 REM    DISPLAY PROMPT & WAIT
210 REM
220 PRINT "REWIND TAPE TO BEGINNING";
230 PRINT " OF FILE"
240 PRINT "STRIKE ANY KEY WHEN READY"
250 PRINT
260 GET G$ : IF G$="" THEN 260
270 REM
300 REM    MAKE NEW FILE
310 REM
320 OPEN 1,1,1,"WORK FILE"
330 FOR X=1 TO 4
340    PRINT#1,N$(X);",";W(X);",";H(X)
350 NEXT X
360 FOR X=1 TO 2
370    INPUT "NAME";N$
380    INPUT "WAGE";W
390    INPUT "HOURS WORKED";H
400    PRINT#1,N$;",";W;",";H
410    PRINT
420 NEXT X
430 CLOSE 1
440 END

RUN

PRESS PLAY ON TAPE
OK
REWIND TAPE TO BEGINNING OF FILE
STRIKE ANY KEY WHEN READY

PRESS RECORD & PLAY ON TAPE
OK
NAME? ROBERT LYNCH
WAGE? 4.60
HOURS WORKED? 44.25

NAME? ERMA MCCONNELL
WAGE? 4.80
HOURS WORKED? 41.5


READY.
```

Two aspects of Program 9.3 should be noted. First, the contents of each line of data from the old file are saved in memory by placing them in appropriately dimensioned subscripted variables. Second, a GET statement is used with an IF . . . THEN statement at line 260 to cause the computer to wait until the user strikes a key. This allows the user as much time as needed to rewind the tape. The tape is rewound so that the new file can be written over the old file thus saving space on the tape.

After the FOR . . . NEXT loop in Program 9.2 is changed, the program can be re-run to show that the new data is now in WORK FILE:

```
RUN

PRESS PLAY ON TAPE
OK
NAME                    HOURS WORKED
GWEN WALDEN              39
SANDY BECKERMAN         42
RUBEN STECK             36.75
RUTH OBRE               27.5
ROBERT LYNCH            44.25
ERMA MCCONNELL          41.5

READY.
```

Program 9.4

 When an employee retires, this program, named REMOVE, will remove the employee's name from WORK FILE. All of the data is read sequentially from WORK FILE and the data that is to be kept is written to a new WORK FILE:

```
1 REM    N$() = EMPLOYEE NAME
2 REM    W() = WAGE
3 REM    H() = HOURS WORKED
4 REM    R$ = RETIRED EMPLOYEE'S NAME
5 REM
6 REM
100 REM    READ OLD FILE
110 REM
120 DIM N$(6),W(6),H(6)
130 OPEN 1,1,0,"WORK FILE"
140 FOR X=1 TO 6
150    INPUT#1,N$(X),W(X),H(X)
160 NEXT X
170 CLOSE 1
180 REM
190 REM
200 REM    FIND OUT WHO RETIRED,
210 REM    DISPLAY PROMPT AND WAIT
220 REM
230 INPUT "WHO HAS RETIRED";R$
240 PRINT "REWIND TAPE TO BEGINNING";
250 PRINT " OF FILE"
260 PRINT "STRIKE ANY KEY WHEN READY"
270 PRINT
```

```
280 GET G$ : IF G$="" THEN 280
290 REM
300 REM
400 REM    MAKE NEW FILE
410 REM
420 OPEN 1,1,1,"WORK FILE"
430 FOR X=1 TO 6
440   IF N$(X)=R$ THEN 460
450    PRINT#1,N$(X);",";W(X);",";H(X)
460 NEXT X
470 CLOSE 1
480 PRINT "THE INFORMATION ON ";R$
490 PRINT "HAS BEEN REMOVED"
500 END

RUN

PRESS PLAY ON TAPE
OK
WHO HAS RETIRED? ERMA MCCONNELL
REWIND TAPE TO BEGINNING OF FILE
STRIKE ANY KEY WHEN READY

PRESS RECORD & PLAY ON TAPE
OK
THE INFORMATION ON ERMA MCCONNELL
HAS BEEN REMOVED

READY.
```

Programs 9.3 and 9.4 work well in this limited example, but the technique they use is not always practical. Both programs use a FOR ... NEXT loop to prevent the program from attempting to read past the end of the file. However, this method could only be used because the length of WORK FILE was known in both cases. To read a file of unknown length, the programmer must employ a loop containing a GOTO statement to ensure that the entire file is read. The file will then be read sequentially until the computer comes to the file's end. When the computer tries to read past the end of the file, however, an error will occur. This may result in files left open and lost data. To prevent this error, the system variable STATUS is used.

STATUS

The computer sets the value of the variable STATUS every time it attempts to read from or write to a file. When the computer has read the last item of data from a file, it automatically sets the value of STATUS:

```
50 INPUT#3,R$
60 IF (STATUS AND 64) = 64 THEN CLOSE 3 : END
```

In the program fragment above, the computer checks the value of STATUS at line 60. If at line 50 the input statement has read the last item of data in the file, the value of STATUS will be set so that the statement (STATUS AND 64) = 64 will be true. In this event the IF ... THEN statement at line 60 will cause the computer to close the file and stop execution of the program.

Program 9.5

This program, named REMOVE2, is a revision of Program 9.4, which allows WORK FILE
to have up to one hundred employees in it:

```
1 REM    N$() = EMPLOYEE NAME
2 REM    W() = WAGE
3 REM    H() = HOURS WORKED
4 REM    R$ = RETIRED EMPLOYEE'S NAME
5 REM    T = FLAG TO TEST FOR DATA
6 REM    OL = OLD FILE LENGTH
7 REM
8 REM
100 REM    FIND OUT WHO RETIRED
110 REM    AND READ OLD FILE
120 REM
130 DIM N$(100),W(100),H(100)
140 INPUT "WHO HAS RETIRED";R$
150 OPEN 1,1,0,"WORK FILE"
160 T=0
170 IF (STATUS AND 64)=64 THEN 220
180    OL=OL+1
190    INPUT#1,N$(OL),W(OL),H(OL)
200    IF N$(OL)=R$ THEN T=1
210 GOTO 170
220 CLOSE 1
230 IF T=1 THEN 300
240 PRINT "THERE IS NO ";R$;" ON"
250 PRINT "THE PAYROLL"
260 GOTO 500
270 REM
280 REM
300 REM    DISPLAY PROMPT AND WAIT
310 REM
320 PRINT "REWIND TAPE TO BEGINNING";
330 PRINT " OF FILE"
340 PRINT
350 GET G$ : IF G$="" THEN 350
360 REM
370 REM
400 REM    MAKE NEW FILE
410 REM
420 OPEN 1,1,1,"WORK FILE"
430 FOR X=1 TO OL
440    IF N$(X)=R$ THEN 460
450    PRINT#1,N$(X);",";W(X);",";H(X)
460 NEXT X
470 CLOSE 1
480 PRINT "THE INFORMATION ON ";R$
490 PRINT "HAS BEEN REMOVED"
500 END
```

```
RUN
WHO HAS RETIRED? JEANNETTE MCDONALD

PRESS PLAY ON TAPE
OK
THERE IS NO JEANNETTE MCDONALD ON
THE PAYROLL

READY.
```

Program 9.5 demonstrates two major improvements over Program 9.4. First, the program informs the user if a name has been entered that is not in the file, using the variable T as an indicator. If the name is in the file, T becomes 1; if not, T remains 0. Second, the STATUS variable and a GOTO loop are used to read the file. This technique is recommended for reading most files. The programmer must dimension the arrays used to a sufficient size to ensure that they hold the entire file, keeping in mind that the amount of memory available in the computer places a restriction on the size of files it can hold. If the size of the file exceeds the amount of memory available, it will be necessary to break the file down into several smaller files and work with each individually.

Demonstration Programs

The following programs illustrate applications for the material covered in this part of the chapter. They consist of a series of examples concerning the record keeping process of a sporting goods manufacturer.

Program 9.6

This program, named ACME, will produce a file named SALES FILE that contains the sales record of all salespeople working for the Acme Sporting Goods Company. Each salesperson sells bats, balls and helmets:

```
1 REM     N$ = NAME OF SALESPERSON
2 REM     B1 = BATS SOLD
3 REM     B2 - BALLS SOLD
4 REM     H = HELMETS SOLD
5 REM
100 OPEN 1,1,1,"SALES FILE"
120 PRINT "ENTER STOP FOR THE NAME";
130 PRINT " WHEN FINISHED"
140 PRINT
150   INPUT "SALESPERSON";N$
160   IF N$="STOP" THEN 220
170   INPUT "BATS SOLD";B1
180   INPUT "BALLS SOLD";B2
190   INPUT "HELMETS SOLD";H
200   PRINT#1,N$;",";B1;",";B2;",";H
210 GOTO 140
220 CLOSE 1
230 PRINT "THE INFORMATION IS IN";
240 PRINT " THE FILE"
250 END
```

```
RUN
PRESS RECORD & PLAY ON TAPE
OK
ENTER STOP FOR THE NAME WHEN FINISHED

SALESPERSON? LESTER WATERS
BATS SOLD? 4
BALLS SOLD? 10
HELMETS SOLD? 5

SALESPERSON? DONALD MIKAN
BATS SOLD? 29
BALLS SOLD? 34
HELMETS SOLD? 52

SALESPERSON? ELI HUROWITZ
BATS SOLD? 45
BALLS SOLD? 17
HELMETS SOLD? 39

SALESPERSON? STOP
THE INFORMATION IS IN THE FILE

READY.
```

Program 9.7

This program, named ACME2, will update the sales records for an individual salesperson:

```
1 REM     N$() = NAME OF SALESPERSON
2 REM     B1() = BATS SOLD
3 REM     B2() = BALLS SOLD
4 REM     H() = HELMETS SOLD
5 REM     C$ = PERSON WHOSE SALES CHANGED
6 REM     L = FILE LENGTH
7 REM     T = FLAG TO TEST FOR DATA
8 REM
9 REM
100 REM    FIND OUT WHOSE SALES CHANGED
110 REM    AND READ OLD FILE
120 REM
130 DIM N$(100),B1(100),B2(100),H(100)
140 OPEN 1,1,0,"SALES FILE"
150 INPUT "WHOSE SALES CHANGED";C$
160 T=0
170 IF (STATUS AND 64)=64 THEN 220
180    L=L+1
190    INPUT#1,N$(L),B1(L),B2(L),H(L)
200    IF N$(L)=C$ THEN T=-1 : GOSUB 300
210 GOTO 170
220 CLOSE 1
230 IF T=-1 THEN 400
240 PRINT "THERE IS NO ";C$
250 PRINT "ON THE PAYROLL"
260 GOTO 590
```

```
270 REM
280 REM
300 REM     INPUT NEW SALES DATA
310 REM
320 PRINT "INPUT NEW SALES"
330 INPUT "BATS";B1(L)
340 INPUT "BALLS";B2(L)
350 INPUT "HELMETS";H(L)
360 RETURN
370 REM
380 REM
400 REM     DISPLAY PROMPT & WAIT
410 REM
420 PRINT "REWIND TAPE TO BEGINNING";
430 PRINT " OF FILE"
440 PRINT "STRIKE ANY KEY WHEN READY"
450 GET G$ : IF G$="" THEN 450
460 REM
470 REM
500 REM     MAKE NEW FILE
510 REM
520 OPEN 1,1,1,"SALES FILE"
530 FOR X=1 TO L
540    PRINT#1,N$(X);",";B1(X);",";B2(X);",";H(X)
550 NEXT X
560 CLOSE 1
570 PRINT C$;"'S RECORDS HAVE"
580 PRINT "BEEN UPDATED"
590 END

RUN

PRESS PLAY ON TAPE
OK
WHOSE SALES HAVE CHANGED? DONALD MIKAN
INPUT NEW SALES
BATS? 32
BALLS? 37
HELMETS? 54
REWIND TAPE TO BEGINNING OF FILE
STRIKE ANY KEY WHEN READY
PRESS RECORD & PLAY ON TAPE
OK
DONALD MIKAN'S RECORDS HAVE
BEEN UPDATED

READY.
```

Program 9.8

This program, named ACME3, will write a personalized letter of congratulations to all salespersons who have sold 75 units or more:

```
1 REM    N$ = NAME OF SALESPERSON
2 REM    B1 = BATS SOLD
3 REM    B2 = BALLS SOLD
4 REM    H = HELMETS SOLD
5 REM    T = FLAG TO COUNT BONUSES
6 REM
100 REM    READ FILE
110 REM
120 OPEN 1,1,0,"SALES FILE"
130 T=0
140 IF (STATUS AND 64)=64 THEN 400
150    INPUT#1,N$,B1,B2,H
160    IF B1+B2+H >= 75 THEN GOSUB 200
170 GOTO 140
200 REM    PRINT LETTER
210 REM
220 PRINT
230 PRINT "DEAR ";N$;","
240 PRINT "     CONGRATULATIONS, YOU"
250 PRINT "ARE ONE OF OUR TOP SALES"
260 PRINT "PERSONS.  YOUR BONUS IS IN"
270 PRINT "THE MAIL."
280 PRINT : PRINT TAB(20);"YOUR BOSS"
290 PRINT
300 T=T+1
400 REM    PRINT TALLY
410 REM
420 IF T=0 THEN 460
430 PRINT T;"SALESPERSON(S) WILL GET";
440 PRINT " A BONUS"
450 GOTO 480
460 PRINT "NO ONE SOLD ENOUGH. GIVE'M";
470 PRINT " A PEP TALK."
480 CLOSE 1
490 END
RUN

PRESS PLAY ON TAPE
OK

DEAR DONALD MIKAN,
     CONGRATULATIONS, YOU
ARE ONE OF OUR TOP SALES
PERSONS.  YOUR BONUS IS IN
THE MAIL.

                    YOUR BOSS

 1 SALESPERSON(S) WILL GET A BONUS

READY.
```

Diskette Files

The programs that access diskette files are similar to the programs that access cassette files. Diskette files are stored sequentially, as are cassette files. The next part of this chapter will explain the differences between the use of diskette files and cassette files. It is assumed that the programmer has already read the section on cassette files.

OPEN

The only statement relating to files that has a different syntax for cassette and diskette files is the OPEN statement. The general format for the OPEN statement for diskette files is:

$$\text{OPEN} < \text{file\#} >, < \text{device\#} >, < \text{channel\#} >, \text{``} < \text{file name} >, \text{S}, < \text{mode} > \text{''}$$

The file number must be an integer from 1 to 255, which is used throughout a program to identify the file. The device number specifies the device on which the file is to be stored. For single drive systems this is usually 8. (The examples in this book are written for single drive systems.) The channel number must be an integer from 2 to 14, which is used to specify a channel of communication between the computer and the disk drive. To reduce confusion, a file is usually opened with the same file number and channel number. The file name, the S, and the mode of access must be enclosed within a single set of quotation marks.

The three modes of access are:
- W: WRITE. The computer will transfer data from memory to the file.
- R: READ. The computer will transfer data from the file to memory.
- A: APPEND. The computer will transfer data from memory and append it to the file. Previously stored data will be added to, not lost.

For example,

$$\text{OPEN 7, 8, 7, ``ADDRESSES,S,W''}$$

will instruct the computer to prepare to write to a file named ADDRESSES on the diskette (device #8), using the file and channel numbers 7.

Program 9.1 can be changed to store WORK FILE on a diskette simply by changing line 10 to

$$\text{10 OPEN 2, 8, 2, ``WORK FILE,S,W''}$$

To examine the contents of the diskette version of WORK FILE, the programmer changes line 10 of Program 9.2 to

$$\text{10 OPEN 2, 8, 2, ``WORK FILE,S,R''}$$

Updating Diskette Files

The procedures for updating diskette files are different from the procedures for updating cassette files. Specifying the (A)ppend mode allows the user to add new information directly to the end of an existing file on a diskette.

Program 9.9

This program, named ADD, is a modified version of Program 9.3. It will add information on two new employees to the diskette version of WORK FILE:

```
1 REM    N$ = EMPLOYEE NAME
2 REM    W = WAGE
3 REM    H = HOURS WORKED
4 REM
5 REM
10 OPEN 2,8,2,"WORK FILE,S,A"
20 FOR X=1 TO 2
30    INPUT "NAME";N$
40    INPUT "WAGE";W
50    INPUT "HOURS WORKED";H
60    PRINT#2,N$;",";W;",",H
70    PRINT
80 NEXT X
90 CLOSE 2
100 END

RUN
NAME? ROBERT LYNCH
WAGE? 4.60
HOURS WORKED? 44.25

NAME? ERMA MCCONNELL
WAGE? 4.80
HOURS WORKED? 41.5


READY.
```

There is no single command that will remove or alter outdated information in a diskette file. To change such a file, the programmer must transfer information to be kept to a new file along with the new or corrected information. After the transfer, the old file can be deleted and the new file given an appropriate name.

Program 9.10

This program, named RETIRE, will remove from the diskette version of WORK FILE the name of an employee who has retired. It should be examined very closely and compared to program to Program 9.5:

```
1 REM    N$ = EMPLOYEE NAME
2 REM    W = WAGE
3 REM    H = HOURS WORKED
4 REM    R$ = RETIRED EMPLOYEE'S NAME
5 REM
6 REM
10 INPUT "WHO HAS RETIRED";R$
20 OPEN 2,8,2,"WORK FILE,S,R"
30 OPEN 3,8,3,"TEMPORARY,S,W"
```

```
40 IF (S AND 64)=64 THEN 100
50   INPUT#2,N$,W,H
60   S=STATUS
70    IF N$=R$ THEN 40
80    PRINT#3,N$;",";W;",";H
90 GOTO 40
100 CLOSE 2 : CLOSE 3
110 OPEN 15,8,15
120 PRINT#15,"S:WORK FILE"
130 PRINT#15,"R:WORK FILE=TEMPORARY"
140 CLOSE 15
150 END

RUN
WHO HAS RETIRED? ERMA MCCONNELL

READY.
```

All of the data is read sequentially from WORK FILE, and the information to be retained is placed in the file TEMPORARY. After the program has finished building the new file TEMPORARY, the old WORK FILE is deleted and TEMPORARY is renamed as WORK FILE (lines 110-140). The value of STATUS is saved in S immediately after the INPUT# statement is executed because the computer will set the value of STATUS to 0 after executing the PRINT# statement at line 80. If the test at the top of the loop (line 40) were to check the value of STATUS instead of S, the test would always fail and the computer would repeat the loop indefinitely.

Bubble Sort

Sometimes it is desirable to sort data that has been originally placed in a file in random order. A list of names might be sorted into alphabetical order, or a list of numbers might be sorted into ascending or descending order. One of the most fundamental and easiest sorting techniques is known as a bubble sort. In a bubble sort the computer starts at the bottom of the list, then proceeds sequentially to the top, comparing each item in the list with the one above it. If the two elements are not in the proper order, they are interchanged. In this way the name that comes first alphabetically in the list is "bubbled" to the top of the list. For example, given the initial list

Lester
Don
Bruce
Rob
Eli

the computer would start by comparing the names Rob and Eli. Because Eli comes alphabetically before Rob, the computer would switch the names and the list would become:

Lester
Don
Bruce
Eli
Rob

Next, Bruce and Eli are compared. Because Bruce comes before Eli, no change is made. Then Don and Bruce are compared and interchanged, so the list becomes:

Lester

Bruce

Don

Eli

Rob

Bruce and Lester are then compared and interchanged. The order of the names in the list now becomes:

Bruce

Lester

Don

Eli

Rob

Bruce, the name that comes first alphabetically in the list, is now at the top of the list. Now the computer starts over at the bottom of the list, and the name that comes next alphabetically is "bubbled" up to its proper position. After the procedure has been repeated enough times, the order of the list becomes:

Bruce

Don

Eli

Lester

Rob

Program 9.11

This program uses a bubble sort to sort a list of first names into alphabetical order:

```
100 REM   NAME INPUT SECTION
110 REM
120 INPUT "HOW MANY NAMES TO SORT";N
130 DIM N$(N)
140 PRINT "ENTER NAMES"
150 FOR X=1 TO N
160    INPUT N$(X)
170 NEXT X
180 REM
190 REM
200 REM   BUBBLE SORT
210 REM
220 FOR T=1 TO N-1
230    FOR I=N TO T+1 STEP -1
240       IF N$(I)>N$(I-1) THEN 260
250       T$=N$(I):N$(I)=N$(I-1):N$(I-1)=T$
260    NEXT I
270 NEXT T
```

```
280 REM
290 REM
300 REM   NAME OUTPUT SECTION
310 REM
320 PRINT
330 FOR X=1 TO N
340 PRINT N$(X)
350 NEXT X
360 END

RUN
HOW MANY NAMES TO SORT? 5
ENTER NAMES
? ELI
? DON
? ROB
? LESTER
? BRUCE

BRUCE
DON
ELI
LESTER
ROB

READY.
```

The loop between lines 230 and 260 causes the computer to scan the list from the bottom (the Nth item) to the top. Each successive pair of items is compared at line 240, and they are interchanged at line 250 if they are out of order. The loop between lines 220 and 270 causes the computer to scan the list N-1 times. For a bubble sort to work properly, a list with N items must be scanned N-1 times. In addition this loop also controls how far the computer scans up the list on each pass. On the first pass all the items in the list are checked. On the second pass the item that comes first alphabetically is already at the top of the list, so the list is only scanned up to the second item. This upper bound is pushed down on each pass through the list until it is at the second to last item on the list (N-1), after which the sort is complete. By changing the variables used, the programmer may use this technique to sort a list of numbers also. To sort a list of names into reverse alphabetical order or a list of numbers into descending order, all that need be done is to change the direction of the inequality in the comparison. The integration of this sorting technique with programs that manipulate files is left as an exercise for the reader.

The first five problems can be answered using either cassette or diskette files. The next five should be answered using diskette files.

1. Store 50 random numbers between 0 and 20 in a file. Use a second program to retrieve the numbers, add them and print the sum.

2. Store in a file the names and prices of five different desserts served at MADGE'S DINER. With a second program add two additional desserts. Have a third program retrieve and print the information.

3. (a) Establish a file name SEQ FILE which contains the members of the following sequence: 1001, 1002, 1003, ...1128.
   (b) Write a program to retrieve any member of the sequence from SEQ FILE and print it when its place in the sequence (i.e. third number, eighth number, etc.) is entered.

4. Store ten different first names of friends in a file. A second program is to print all the names in the file which begin with the letters D, E, F, G and H or a message if none are found.

5. (a) Create a payroll file called PAY FILE to store each of ten person's names (last name first), his or her hourly pay rate, the number of dependents, and deductions for medical and life insurance for each week. Supply appropriate data.
   (b) Use PAY FILE to prepare the payroll data sheet (supply the number of hours (H) each person worked during the week). The sheet should list the name, hours worked, gross pay, three deductions and net pay. Assume a tax rate of 25%, with 2% being subtracted from this rate for each dependent.

```
RUN
MENACE DENNIS -
HOURS WORKED:              40
GROSS PAY:            $  40
TAX:                 $  10
MEDICAL INSURANCE:   $  1
LIFE INSURANCE:      $  1
NET:                 $  28
```

6. (a) Write a program that will create the file FRAT FILE, which will contain the names, fraternities and ages of thirty college students.

(b) Write a program that will access FRAT FILE, and create the file SIGMA FILE, which contains the names and ages of only students who live in Sigma Chi.

(c) Write a program that accesses FRAT FILE and randomly selects sixteen students for seats in a classroom of four rows, four seats to a row. Have the computer print the seating plan for the class, placing each student's name at the correct seat location.

7. (a) Two persons, Sheryl and Carol, measured the Fahrenheit temperature (F) outside on February 12 at various times (T) during a ten-hour period. Their results are recorded here. Set up two sequential files, one for each person's data, naming each file after that person.

Sheryl			**Carol**	
T	**F**		**T**	**F**
0.0	18.1		1.0	20.9
2.1	24.0		1.9	23.3
3.8	27.2		3.5	26.1
6.0	29.3		6.0	28.8
8.0	26.6		8.2	26.2
9.0	16.1		10.0	16.0

(b) Write a program that will merge the two files into one file named MERGE. The times should be sequentially in order. However, when a value of (T) occurs in both Sheryl and Carol, the average of the two values of (F) should be placed in MERGE.

(c) Retrieve and print the contents of MERGE.

8. (a) You have just been hired to help produce a new dictionary. Write a program to create the file WORD FILE. The file is to contain twenty-five words in random order.

(b) Write a program to sort the contents of the file WORD FILE into alphabetical order. Hint: To sort the contents of the file, the program should:

      (1) read the contents of WORD FILE

      (2) sort the list of words in memory

      (3) write the sorted list to the file TEMP FILE

      (4) remove WORD FILE from the diskette

      (5) rename TEMP FILE as WORD FILE

The program should also print the sorted list on the display.

9. (a) Write a program to create the file NAME & AGE FILE. The file is to contain the first names and ages of fifteen people.

(b) Write a program to sort the contents of NAME & AGE FILE alphabetically. For example, given the list:

Rob	20
Don	19
Lester	21

The program should change to:

Don	19
Lester	21
Rob	20

Note the ages have been switched also.

(c) Write a program to sort the contents of NAME & AGE FILE by age. For example, given the above initial list, the computer should change it to:

Don	19
Rob	20
Lester	21

10. (a) Create a file named NUMBER FILE that contains a list of telephone numbers. The area codes are not to be included.

(b) Write a program to sort the contents of NUMBER FILE by *exchange only*. For example, given the list:

676-2004
609-4444
676-5112
867-5309
932-6840
867-1441

the computer should change it to:

609-4444
676-2004
676-5112
867-5309
867-1441
932-6804

11. The program fragment given below should be used as the data lines for the answer to this question. The names (N$()) and associated telephone numbers (T$()) should be sorted into alphabetical order by *last* name. For example, the first three names of the sorted list should be:

John Adams	555-1640
Bob Atkins	555-1964
Phil Colins	555-6498

```
900 DATA LARRY PELHAM,555-1234
910 DATA PHIL COLINS,555-6498
920 DATA LAWRENCE RUSSELL,555-5285
930 DATA ALICIA OSTRIKER,555-4788
940 DATA JOHN ADAMS,555-1640
950 DATA DEBORAH FALEY,555-7749
960 DATA LAURIE JOHNSON,555-0012
970 DATA GARY WALLACE,555-1537
980 DATA BOB ATKINS,555-1964
990 DATA DAVID NAUGHTON,555-5487
```

APPENDICES

SAVE
VERIFY
LOAD
SAVE
VERIFY
LOAD
SAVE
VERIFY
LOAD
SAVE
VERIFY
LOAD
SAVE
VERIFY
LOAD
SAVE
VERIFY
LOAD
SAVE
VERIFY
LOAD
SAVE
VERIFY
LOAD
SAVE

APPENDIX A
EDITING

The Commodore-64 and VIC-20 computers have an editing feature which helps the programmer correct a program currently in the computer's memory. The programmer can best learn the use of this feature by spending time becoming familiar with it. An outline of the editing controls is presented here:

KEY

FUNCTION

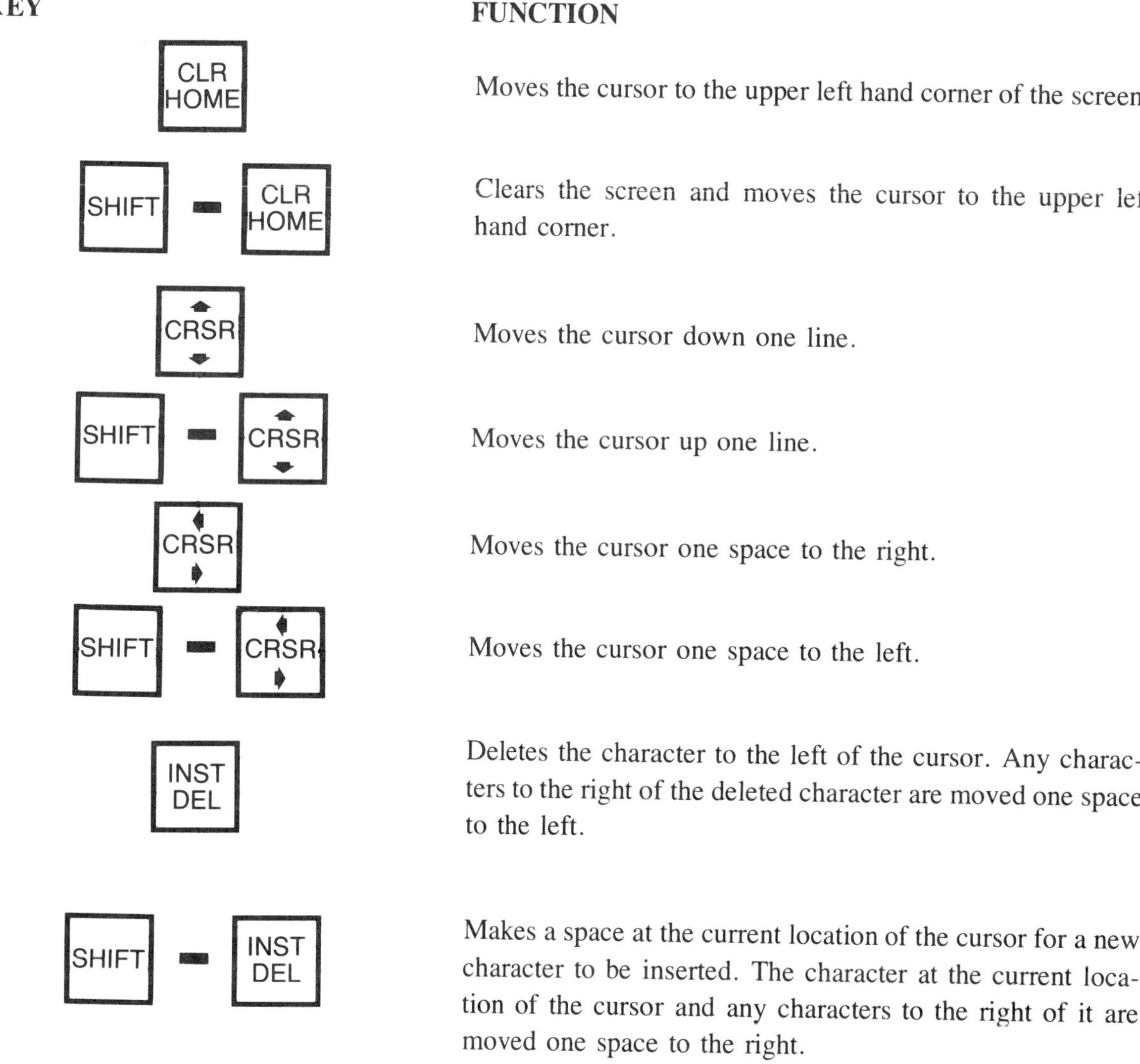

Moves the cursor to the upper left hand corner of the screen.

Clears the screen and moves the cursor to the upper left hand corner.

Moves the cursor down one line.

Moves the cursor up one line.

Moves the cursor one space to the right.

Moves the cursor one space to the left.

Deletes the character to the left of the cursor. Any characters to the right of the deleted character are moved one space to the left.

Makes a space at the current location of the cursor for a new character to be inserted. The character at the current location of the cursor and any characters to the right of it are moved one space to the right.

APPENDIX B
CASSETTE OPERATION

Program and File Names

Every program and file stored on a tape is identified by a unique name. The name may be from one to sixteen characters long. Any type of character, either standard or graphic, may be used in the name. To help distinguish between programs and files, it is useful to incorporate the word FILE in file names. For example, a program named PAYROLL might access a file named PAYROLL FILE. The following examples are valid program and file names:

```
MAIL
CODE FILE
NAMES & NUMBERS
```

SAVE

The SAVE command is used to store a program on a tape. Its form is:

```
SAVE "<file name>"
```

The program name must be within quotation marks.

To save a program on a tape, type SAVE followed by the program name. For example:

```
SAVE "TAXES"
```

The computer will print the message PRESS RECORD & PLAY ON TAPE and then wait for the buttons to be pressed before saving the program currently in memory on tape. To prevent the erasure of a previously stored program, position the tape at a blank section.

The user should keep a written record of the programs and files stored on a tape, along with their locations on the tape so that the tape may be correctly positioned when the user wishes to recall a program or file.

VERIFY

The VERIFY command is used to check a program in memory against a program that has been saved on tape. Its form is:

```
VERIFY "<program name>"
```

The program name must be enclosed within quotation marks.

To verify that the program TAXES has been saved properly, rewind the tape to the beginning of the program and type:

```
VERIFY "TAXES"
```

When the computer has found TAXES, it will print the message VERIFYING and proceed to compare the program on tape with the program in memory. If they are identical, the computer will print the message OK. If the message ?VERIFY ERROR is printed, the program has not been saved on the tape correctly. In this event, the programmer should attempt to save the program again.

LOAD

Programs previously saved on a tape may be recalled using the LOAD command. Its form is:

$$LOAD \ ``<program \ name>"$$

To recall a program from a tape and transfer it into the computer's memory, make sure the tape is at a point preceding the beginning of the program. Type LOAD followed by the program name. For example:

$$LOAD \ ``TAXES"$$

The computer will print the message PRESS PLAY ON TAPE and wait for the button to be pressed before attempting to load the program.

Removing Programs and Files

Programs and files are removed from a tape by recording over them. The user should guard against doing this accidentally. The computer will save a program or file at whatever position the tape happens to be located when the appropriate instructions are given.

APPENDIX C
DISKETTE OPERATION

Program and File names

Every program and file on a disk is identified by a unique name. The name may be from one to sixteen characters long, made up of any type of character, either standard or graphic. The only restriction is that @: cannot be used as the first two characters of the name. To help distinguish between programs and files, it is useful to incorporate the word FILE in file names. For example, a program named PAYROLL might access the file PAYROLL FILE. The following examples are valid program and file names:

> ADDRESS FILE
> COMMODORE
> NAMES & NUMBERS

Formatting Diskettes

The following procedure must be used, as given, to initialize or "format" a new diskette before the computer can use it for the first time:

> OPEN 15, 8, 15
> PRINT#15, ''N0: <name>, <id>''
> CLOSE 15

The name becomes part of the directory as the name of the entire diskette. The name appears only when the directory of the diskette is displayed. The ID code, which may be any two characters, is used by the computer to identify the disk.

> OPEN 15, 8, 15
> PRINT#15, ''N0:PAYROLL DISK,PD
> CLOSE 15

will instruct the computer to format the disk in the drive, giving it the name PAYROLL DISK and the ID code PD. The disk will then be ready to be used.

SAVE

The SAVE command is used to store a program on a diskette. Its form is:

> SAVE ''<program name>'', <device#>

The program name must be enclosed in quotation marks. The device number specifies which disk drive the program is to be stored on. For single drive systems this is 8. The examples in this appendix will assume single drive systems.

SAVE ''TAXES'',8

will save the program currently in memory on the diskette and give it the name TAXES.

VERIFY

The VERIFY command is used to check a program in memory against a program that has been saved on a diskette. Its form is:

VERIFY ''<program name>'', <device#>

To verify that the program TAXES has been saved properly type:

VERIFY ''TAXES'',8

When the computer has found TAXES, it will print the message VERIFYING and proceed to compare the program on the diskette with the program in memory. If they are identical, the computer will print the message OK. If the message ?VERIFY ERROR is printed, the program has not been saved correctly. In this event, the programmer should attempt to save the program again.

LOAD

Programs previously saved on a diskette may be recalled using the LOAD command. Its format is:

LOAD ''<program name>'', <divice#>

For example,

LOAD ''TAXES'',8

will load the program TAXES into memory from the diskette. Any program previously in memory will be erased.

Renaming Programs and Files

It is possible to change the name of files and programs that have been stored on a diskette with the following procedure:

                    OPEN 15, 8, 15
                    PRINT#15, ''R:<new name>=<old name>''
                    CLOSE 15

For example:

                    OPEN 15, 8, 15
                    PRINT#15, ''R:IRS=TAXES''
                    CLOSE 15

will give the program TAXES on the diskette the name IRS.

Copying Programs and Files

A program or file can be duplicated with the procedure:

                    OPEN 15, 8, 15
                    PRINT#15, ''C:<new>=<original>''
                    CLOSE 15

For example:

                    OPEN 15, 8, 15
                    PRINT#15, ''C:IRS BACKUP=IRS''
                    CLOSE 15

will instruct the computer to make an exact copy of IRS and place it on the same diskette with
the name IRS BACKUP.
    A similar procedure can be used to combine up to four files on the disk:

                    OPEN 15, 8, 15
                    PRINT#15, ''C:MASTER FILE=NAMES, ADDRESSES, NUMBERS''
                    CLOSE 15

will place the contents of NAMES, ADDRESSES and NUMBERS in that order, in the new file
MASTER FILE. The files NAMES, ADDRESSES and NUMBERS will not be affected.

Diskette Directories

To produce a catalogue of the programs and files stored on a diskette, type

LOAD ''$'', 8

and then

LIST

Note that this procedure will erase any program currently in memory:

```
LOAD "$",8

SEARCHING FOR $
LOADING
READY.
LIST

Ø  "TRANSFER          "  TG  2A
1       "C3P23"             PRG
1       "C3P25"             PRG
1       "C3P27"             PRG
1       "C3P33"             PRG
66Ø BLOCKS FREE.
READY.
```

Removing Programs and Files

Unwanted programs and files are removed from a diskette with the following procedure:

```
OPEN 15, 8, 15
PRINT#15, "S:<program or file name>"
CLOSE 15
```

For example,

```
OPEN 15, 8, 15
PRINT#15, "S:PAYROLL FILE"
CLOSE 15
```

will instruct the computer to remove the file PAYROLL FILE from the diskette.

The demonstration disk provided by Commodore with the disk drive contains a program that modifies the operating system of the computer. VIC-20 WEDGE will modify the VIC-20, and C-64 WEDGE will modify the COMMODORE-64. After running the appropriate program, the programmer can obtain a catalogue of a diskette by typing $. This will not cause any program currently in memory to be erased. In addition, a program can be loaded into memory by typing / followed by the program name.

```
>$
0  "TRANSFER         " TG 2A
1      "C3P23"              PRG
1      "C3P25"              PRG
1      "C3P27"              PRG
1      "C3P33"              PRG
660 BLOCKS FREE.
READY.
```

CHAPTER ONE

1.
```
10 X = 5
20 Y = 5*X + 7
30 PRINT Y
```

2.
```
10 A$ = "HARRY"
20 B$ = "SHERRY"
30 PRINT "HELLO, ";A$
40 PRINT B$;" IS LOOKING FOR YOU."
```

3.
```
10 READ X
20 Y = 3*X + 5
30 PRINT Y;
40 GOTO 10
50 DATA 3,5,12,17,8
```

4.
```
5 PRINT "NAME","FIRST GRADE"
10 READ N$, A, B, C, D
20 PRINT N$,A
30 GOTO 10
50 DATA WATERS,83,95,86,80,KANE,56,97,66,89,MIKAN,61,83,42,90
```

5.
```
10 INPUT "WHAT IS X"; X
20 Y = 5*X
30 PRINT "5*X ="; Y
40 PRINT "X/5 ="; X/5
50 GOTO 10
```

6.  ```
    10 INPUT "WHAT IS YOUR NAME";N$
    20 INPUT "WHAT IS YOUR FRIEND'S NAME";F$
    30 PRINT F$; "IS A FRIEND OF "; N$
    40 PRINT
    50 GOTO 10
    ```

CHAPTER TWO

1.  ```
    10 INPUT "ENTER TWO NUMBERS";A,B
    20 IF A>B THEN PRINT A : PRINT B : GOTO 10
    30 PRINT B : PRINT A : GOTO 10
    ```

2.  ```
    10 INPUT "ENTER TWO LAST NAMES";A$,B$
    20 IF A$<B$ THEN PRINT A$ : PRINT B$ : GOTO 10
    30 PRINT B$ : PRINT A$ : GOTO 10
    ```

3.  ```
    10 INPUT "ENTER A NUMBER";N
    20 IF N>25 AND N<112 THEN 40
    30 PRINT N;"IS OUT OF RANGE" : GOTO 10
    40 PRINT N;"IS BETWEEN 25 AND 112": GOTO 10
    ```

4.  ```
    10 INPUT "ENTER N$";N$
    20 IF N$ < "GARBAGE" OR N$ > "TRASH" THEN 40
    30 PRINT "NO" : GOTO 10
    40 PRINT "YES" : GOTO 10
    ```

5.  ```
    10 FOR I = 1 TO 25
    20    PRINT I;
    30 NEXT I
    ```

6.  ```
    10 FOR S = 20 TO 10 STEP -2
    20    PRINT S;
    30 NEXT S
    40 PRINT
    ```

7.  ```
    10 INPUT "STEP VALUE"; N
    20 FOR X = 8 TO 20 STEP N
    30    PRINT X;
    40 NEXT X
    50 PRINT
    ```

CHAPTER THREE

1.  ```
    10 N1 = INT(101 * RND(0) + 50)
    20 N2 = INT(101 * RND(0) + 50)
    30 PRINT N1;"MULTIPLIED BY";N2;"IS";N1*N2
    ```
    ```

```
2.  1 REM W = NUMBER OF WRONG GUESSES
    10 PRINT "I'M THINKING OF A RANDOM NUMBER FROM 1 TO 50."
    20 R = INT(50 * RND(0) + 1)
    30 FOR W = 1 TO 5
    40    INPUT "WHAT IS YOUR GUESS";G
    50    IF G=R THEN PRINT "CORRECT!!": END
    60    IF G>R THEN PRINT "TOO HIGH!"
    70    IF G<R THEN PRINT "TOO LOW!"
    80 NEXT W
    90 PRINT "YOU'VE HAD 5 GUESSES NOW."
    100 PRINT "THE NUMBER WAS";R


3.  10 FOR I = 1 TO 50
    20    N = INT(10 * RND(0))
    30    IF N<5 THEN L = L + 1
    40 NEXT I
    50 PRINT "THERE WERE";L;"NUMBERS BETWEEN 0 AND 4."
    60 PRINT "THERE WERE";50-L;"NUMBERS BETWEEN 5 AND 9."
```

CHAPTER FOUR

```
1.  10 FOR X = 20 TO 24
    20    PRINT "OUTER LOOP:"; X
    30    FOR Y = 1 TO 3
    40      PRINT "INNER:";Y,
    50    NEXT Y
    60    PRINT
    70 NEXT X


2.  10 FOR I = 1 TO 3
    20    INPUT N(I)
    30 NEXT I
    40 FOR I = 3 TO 1 STEP -1
    50    PRINT N(I)
    60 NEXT I


3.  10 REM READ 6 WORDS FROM KEYBOARD
    20 FOR X = 1 TO 6
    30    INPUT W$(X)
    40 NEXT X
    50 REM PICK 4 WORDS AND PRINT THEM AS A SENTENCE
    60 FOR P = 1 TO 4
    70    N = INT(5 * RND(0) + 1)
    80    PRINT W$(N);" ";
    90 NEXT P
    100 PRINT "." : REM PERIOD = END OF SENTENCE
```

4.
```
10 REM READ 6 WORDS FROM THE KEYBOARD
20 FOR X = 1 TO 6
30    INPUT W$(X)
40 NEXT X
50 REM PICK FOR DIFFERENT WORDS AND PRINT THEM AS A SENTENCE
60 C(1) = INT(5 * RND(Ø) + 1) : REM FIRST RANDOM NUMBER
70 PRINT W$(C(1));" "; : REM ALWAYS SHOW FIRST WORD
80 FOR P = 2 TO 4
90    C(P) = INT(5 * RND(Ø) + 1)
100    REM NOW CHECK FOR DUPLICATE RANDOM NUMBERS
110    FOR K = 1 TO P-1
120       IF C(K)=C(P) THEN 90 : REM PICK ANOTHER IF USED
130    NEXT K
140    PRINT W$(C(P)); " ";
150 NEXT P
160 PRINT "." : REM PERIOD = END OF SENTENCE
```

5.
```
10 REM ENTER THE SIX NUMBERS FROM KEYBOARD
20 FOR K = 1 TO 6
30    INPUT X(K)
40 NEXT K
50 REM PRINT THE SIX NUMBERS IN A COLUMN
60 FOR K = 1 TO 6
70    PRINT X(K)
80 NEXT K
90 REM PRINT THE SIX NUMBERS IN A ROW
100 PRINT
110 FOR K = 1 TO 6
120    PRINT X(K);
130 NEXT K
140 PRINT
```

6.
```
5 DIM X$(5,3)
10 FOR I = 1 TO 5
20    FOR J = 1 TO 3
30       READ X$(I,J)
40    NEXT J
50 NEXT I
60 REM OUTPUT X$(), MAKING THE ROWS BECOME COLUMNS
70 FOR I = 1 TO 3
80    FOR J = 1 TO 5
90       PRINT X$(J,I);" ";
100    NEXT J
110    PRINT
120 NEXT I
130 DATA A,B,C,D,E,F,G,H,I,J,K,L,M,N,O
```

CHAPTER FIVE

```
1.  10  INPUT "NAME";N$
    20  PRINT N$
    30  IF N$ = "DONALD" THEN GOSUB 100
    40  GOTO 10
    50  REM
    60  REM
    100 REM THIS IS THE CODE TO UNDERLINE
    110 FOR I = 1 TO 6
    120    PRINT "-";
    130 NEXT I
    140 PRINT
    150 RETURN


2.  10  FOR D = 1 TO 5
    20     C = INT(13*RND(Ø)+1)
    30     S = INT(4*RND(Ø)+1)
    40     PRINT "CARD";D;"IS THE ";C;"OF ";
    50     ON S GOTO 60,70,80,90
    60     PRINT "CLUBS": GOTO 100
    70     PRINT "DIAMONDS": GOTO 100
    80     PRINT "HEARTS": GOTO 100
    90     PRINT "SPADES"
    100 NEXT D


3.  10  INPUT "ENTER A (BETWEEN Ø AND 3)";A
    20  IF A>3 OR A<Ø THEN 10
    30  A = A+1
    40  ON A GOSUB 100,200,300,400
    50  END
    100 PRINT "YOU ARE A ZERO"
    110 RETURN
    200 PRINT "DANIELLE LOVES MICHAEL
    210 RETURN
    300 PRINT "MICHAEL LOVES DANIELLE
    310 RETURN
    400 PRINT "WHO IS DANIELLE?"
    410 RETURN
```

4a. The FOR-TO-NEXT loop in line 20 is
missing the STEP command. Line 20 should read:

20 FOR X =10 TO 1 STEP -1

4b. The product in line 30 is always positive. The best way to correct this error in logic
would be to eliminate line 40 and replace it with:

40 PRINT "THE PRODUCT IS POSITIVE"

CHAPTER SIX

1.
```
10 INPUT N
20 FOR I = 1 TO N
25    PRINT
30    PRINT
40    PRINT
50    PRINT
60 NEXT I
```

2.
```
COMPUTING IS VERY FUN
READY.
```

3.
```
10 INPUT A,B
20 POKE 53281,A
30 POKE 53280,B
40 GOTO 10
```

VIC-20:
```
10 INPUT A,B
20 POKE 36879,A*16+8+B
30 GOTO 10
```

4.
```
10 INPUT A,B,C
20 POKE 53281,A
30 POKE 53280,B
40 POKE 53272,21 : IF C=1 THEN POKE 53272,23
50 GOTO 10
```

VIC-20:
```
10 INPUT A,B,C
20 POKE 36879,A*16+8+B
30 POKE 36869,240 : IF C=1 THEN POKE 36869,242
40 GOTO 10
```

5.
```
5 PRINT "" : D = 3
10 FOR I = 0 TO 10
20    READ C(I)
30 NEXT I
40 J1 = 15-(PEEK(56321) AND 15)
50 IF J1=D THEN 40
55 POKE C(D),32 : POKE C(J1),81 : POKE 54272+C(J1),0
60 D = J1
70 GOTO 40
80 REM
100 DATA 1523,1043,2003,0,1504,1024,1984,0,1543,1063,2023
```

6.
```
5 PRINT ""
10 POKE 37139,0 : D=3
20 FOR I = 0 TO 10
30    READ C(I)
40 NEXT I
```

(Continued on next page)

```
50 POKE 37154,127
60 J = 15-((PEEK(37137) AND 28)/4 + (PEEK(37152) AND 128)/16)
70 POKE 37154,255
80 IF J=D THEN 50
85 POKE C(D),32
90 POKE C(J),81
100 POKE 30720+C(J),0
110 D=J
120 GOTO 50
130 REM
140 DATA 7932,7690,8174,0,7922,7680,8164,0,7943,7701,8185
```

7.
```
10 POKE 54296,15
20 A=12 : D=5 : REM ATTACK AND DECAY RATES
30 POKE 54277,A*16+D
40 S=8 : R=2 : REM SUSTAIN AND RELEASE VALUES
50 POKE 54278,S*16+R
60 C=1275 : REM D# IN 3RD OCTAVE
70 FOR I = 1 TO 2
80    POKE 54272,C-INT(C/256)*256
90    POKE 54273,INT(C/256)
100   POKE 54276,33
110   FOR D = 1 TO 500 : NEXT D : REM DELAY TO HEAR SOUND
120   POKE 54276,(PEEK(54276) AND 254)
130   C = 28871 : REM A IN 7TH OCTAVE
140 NEXT I
```

8.
```
10 POKE 36878,15
20 POKE 36876,167
30 FOR D = 1 TO 500 : NEXT D
40 POKE 36876,238
50 FOR D = 1 TO 500 : NEXT D
60 POKE 36878,0
```

CHAPTER SEVEN

1. (4)

2.
```
10 INPUT "FIRST COORDINATE (X1,Y1)";X1,Y1
20 INPUT "SECOND COORDINATE (X2,Y2)";X2,Y2
30 D = SQR((X1-X2)^2 + (Y1-Y2)^2)
40 PRINT "DISTANCE IS";D
```

3.
```
10 DEF FNR(D) = D * 3.14159265 / 180
20 DEF FND(R) = R * 180 / 3.14159265
30 INPUT "DEGREES";A
40 PRINT "THAT IS";FNR(A);"RADIANS."
50 PRINT
60 INPUT "RADIANS";B
70 PRINT "THAT IS";FND(B);"DEGREES."
```

CHAPTER EIGHT

1. (A)   16 BITS FOR THE INTEGER 6167

   (B)   72 BITS - 8 FOR EACH LETTER
          IN 'APRIL' PLUS 16 EACH FOR
          THE INTEGERS 1 AND 1963

   (C)   32 BITS - 42864 IS AN INTEGER,
          BUT IT IS OUTSIDE THE ALLOWABLE
          RANGE FOR INTEGER STORAGE, SO
          IT MUST BE STORED AS A FLOATING
          POINT NUMBER.

   (D)   32 BITS FOR THE FLOATING POINT
          NUMBER 35.78

2.
```
10 INPUT "INPUT A LETTER";A$
20 PRINT "THE ASCII OF '";A$;"' IS";ASC(A$)
30 PRINT "TWO LETTERS AFTER '";A$;"' IS ";
40 C=ASC(A$) : C=C+2 : IF C>90 THEN C=C-26
50 PRINT "'";CHR$(C);"'"
```

CHAPTER NINE

1.
```
10 OPEN 1,1,1,"MONTH FILE"
20 FOR X=1 TO 12
30   READ M$
40    PRINT#1,M$
50 NEXT X
60 CLOSE 1
70 DATA JANUARY,FEBRUARY,MARCH,APRIL
80 DATA MAY,JUNE,JULY,AUGUST,SEPTEMBER
90 DATA OCTOBER,NOVEMBER,DECEMBER
100 END
```

2.
```
10 OPEN 1,1,0,"MONTH FILE"
20 PRINT "ODD MONTHS OF THE YEAR -"
30 FOR X=1 TO 12
40    INPUT#1,M$
50    IF X/2 = INT(X/2) THEN 70
60    PRINT M$
70 NEXT X
80 CLOSE 1
90 END
```

CHAPTER ONE

```
1.  10 PRINT "A"
    20 PRINT " B"
    30 PRINT "  C"
    40 PRINT "ABCD"


3.  RUN
    THE VALUE OF B
     19

    READY.


5.  10 READ A,B
    20 PRINT "THE SUM IS"; A+B
    30 GOTO 10
    40 DATA 12,8,9,5


7.  10 INPUT "PRICE, NUMBER OF LOAVES";P,N
    20 PRINT "TOTAL SPENT = $";P*N/100


9.  10 INPUT X,Y
    20 PRINT "X =";X,"Y =";Y,"X*Y =";X*Y
    30 GOTO 10


11. RUN
     300        510
     .3     .51

    READY.


13. PRINT "AAA";111,222;"AAA","333";"    ";16-3*2
    AAA 111      222 AAA  333      10

    READY.
```

15. RUN
    ABCDXYZ
    ABCD 7
     7 XYZ
    -4 XYZ

    READY.

17. 10 PRINT "TOTAL MILEAGE FOR THE WEEK IS:";
    20 PRINT 2+3+4+3+5

19. 10 READ X,Y
    20 A = 12*X + 7*Y
    30 PRINT A
    40 GOTO 10
    50 DATA 3,2,7,9,12,-4

21. 10 INPUT "LENGTH, WIDTH, HEIGHT";L,W,H
    20 PRINT "VOLUME IS";L*W*H

23. 10 INPUT "HEIGHT";H
    20 INPUT "WIDTH";W
    30 INPUT "LENGTH";L
    40 INPUT "PRESENCE";P
    50 PRINT "YOUR OBJECT USES";H*W*L*P;"TESSERACTS IN FOUR SPACE."

25. 10 INPUT "HOW MANY BOOKS HAVE YOU BORROWED";B
    20 INPUT "HOW MANY DAYS LATE ARE THEY";L
    30 PRINT "YOU OWE $";.10*B*L

27. 10 INPUT "WHAT IS THE PLAYER'S NAME";P$
    20 PRINT "WHAT IS ";P$;"'S";
    30 INPUT " WAGE";W
    40 T = W*.44
    50 PRINT P$;" WOULD KEEP $";W-T
    60 PRINT "HE WOULD PAY $";T;"IN TAXES."

29. 10 INPUT "WHAT IS THE BASE";B
    20 INPUT "WHAT IS THE ALTITUDE";A
    30 PRINT
    40 PRINT "THE AREA IS";A*B/2

31. 10 READ S1,G1,S2,G2,S3,G3,S4,G4,S5,G5
    20 S = S1+S2+S3+S4+S5
    30 G = G1+G2+G3+G4+G5
    40 T = S+G
    50 PRINT "SLOTH'S TOTAL VOTE WAS";S
    60 PRINT "HIS TOTAL PERCENTAGE WAS";100*S/T
    70 PRINT
    80 PRINT "GRAFT'S TOTAL VOTE WAS";G
    90 PRINT "HIS TOTAL PERCENTAGE WAS";100*G/T
    100 DATA 528,210,313,721,1003,822,413,1107,516,1700

33.
```
10  INPUT "MONTH, DAY, AND YEAR OF BIRTH";M1,D1,Y1
20  D9 = Y1*365 + M1*30 + D1
30  INPUT "TODAY'S MONTH, DAY, AND YEAR";M2,D2,Y2
40  D8 = Y2*365 + M2*30 + D2
50  S = 8*(D8-D9)
60  PRINT "YOU HAVE SLEPT ABOUT";S;"HOURS."
```

CHAPTER TWO

1.
```
10  INPUT A,B
20  IF A<B THEN PRINT A;"IS LESS THAN";B
30  IF A>B THEN PRINT A;"IS GREATER THAN";B
40  IF A=B THEN PRINT A;"IS EQUAL TO";B
50  GOTO 10
```

3.

(a) PRINT 3^2^3
729.000003

(b) PRINT 5-4^2
-11

(c) PRINT 3*(5+16)
63

(d) PRINT 5+3*6/2
14

(e) PRINT 640/10/2*5
160

(f) PRINT 5+3*4-1
16

(g) PRINT 2^3^2
64

(h) PRINT 2^(3^2)
512.000002

(i) PRINT 64/4*0.5+((1+5)*2^3)*1/(2*4)
14

5.
```
10  INPUT A$,B$ : PRINT A$,B$ : PRINT B$,A$
```

7.
```
10  INPUT A$
20  IF A$>"DOWN" AND A$<"UP" THEN PRINT "A$ IS BETWEEN"
```

9.
```
10  INPUT X
20  IF X<=25 OR X>=75 THEN PRINT "NOT IN THE INTERVAL" : GOTO 10
30  PRINT "IN THE INTERVAL" : GOTO 10
```

11.
```
10  FOR I = 11 TO -11 STEP -2
20     PRINT I^3
30  NEXT I
```

13.
```
10  FOR I = 1 TO 20
20     PRINT "*";
30  NEXT I
```

15.
```
10  FOR I = 10 TO 97 STEP 3
20     PRINT I;
30  NEXT I
```

17. ```
10 INPUT "CREATURE";X$
20 RESTORE
30 FOR I = 1 TO 6
40   READ C$,W$
50   IF C$=X$ THEN 90
60 NEXT I
70 PRINT "CREATURE ";X$;" NOT FOUND."
80 GOTO 10
90 PRINT "YOU CAN KILL A ";C$;" WITH A ";W$
100 GOTO 10
110 DATA LICH,FIRE BALL,MUMMY,FLAMNG TORCH,WEREWOLF,SILVER BULLET
120 DATA VAMPIRE,WOODEN STAKE,MEDUSA,SHARP SWORD,TRIFFID,FIRE HOSE
```

19. ```
LINE:    10   20   30   40   50   60   10   20   30   40
         50   60   10   20   30   40   50
```

21. ```
10 FOR I = 1 TO 10
20   PRINT : PRINT "------------------------"
30   PRINT " HAPPY HOLIDAY MOTEL"
40   PRINT "   ROOM";I
50   PRINT "------------------------"
60 NEXT I
```

23. ```
10  PRINT " X","X^2","X^3"
20  PRINT
30  FOR I = 2 TO 10 STEP 2
40    PRINT I,I^2,I^3
50  NEXT I
```

25. ```
10 INPUT N
20 FOR H = 1 TO N : REM H IS HEIGHT OF TRIANGLE
30   IF W=H THEN 70 : REM W IS WIDTH
40   PRINT "*";
50   W = W+1
60   GOTO 30
70   PRINT : W = 0 : REM RESET WIDTH FOR EACH H
80 NEXT H
```

27. ```
10  FOR I = 1 TO 5
20    READ N$,P : REM GET NAME, PERFORMANCE
30    IF P>=75 THEN 120
40    PRINT:PRINT "DEAR ";N$;","
50    PRINT "  I AM SORRY THAT I MUST FIRE YOU."
60    PRINT "YOU HAVE BEEN SUCH A FINE EMPLOYEE"
70    PRINT "WITH A PERFORMANCE RATING OF";P;"%"
80    PRINT "I'M SURE YOU'LL HAVE NO TROUBLE"
90    PRINT "FINDING ANOTHER JOB."
100   PRINT TAB(20);"SINCERELY,"
110   PRINT : PRINT TAB(20);"GEORGE SHWABB" : PRINT
120 NEXT I
130 DATA OAKLEY,69,HOWE,92,ANDERSON,96,OLLEY,88,GOERZ,74
```

29.
```
10  INPUT "HOURS WORKED";H
20  INPUT "HOURLY WAGE";W
30  M = W*H
40  IF H>40 THEN M = M+W/2*(H-40)
50  PRINT "THE WAGE FOR THE WEEK IS $";M
```

31.
```
1 REM A = AMOUNT OF MONEY LEFT
10  A = 200 : REM INITIAL AMOUNT
20  INPUT "HOW MUCH DOES THE ITEM COST";C
30  IF C = 0 THEN END
40  A = A - 1.05*C : REM 1.05*C IS COST WITH TAX
50  IF A<0 THEN 90
60  PRINT "YOUR TOTAL IS NOW $";A
70  PRINT
80  GOTO 20
90  PRINT "YOU DON'T HAVE ENOUGH MONEY."
100 A = A + 1.05*C
110 GOTO 20
```

CHAPTER THREE

1.
```
10  FOR I = 1 TO 10
20    R = RND(0)
30     IF R>.5 THEN PRINT R
40  NEXT I
```

3.
```
10  INPUT N
20  IF N=INT(N) THEN PRINT N
30  GOTO 10
```

5.
```
10  N = INT(4*RND(0)+2)
20  D = INT(4*RND(0)+1)
30  Q = INT(4*RND(0))
40  F = .05*N + .1*D + .25*Q : REM TOTAL AMOUNT FOUND
50  PRINT "YOU FOUND $";F
60  IF F>.99 THEN PRINT "YOU CAN BUY LUNCH" : END
70  PRINT "SORRY, YOU CAN'T BUY LUNCH"
```

7.
```
10  REM A = AMOUNT IN BANK
20  REM I = WEEK NUMBER
30  A = 11 : REM INITIAL AMOUNT
40  FOR I = 1 TO 4
50    PRINT "WEEK";I;", HOW MANY PENNIES DO YOU HAVE"
60    INPUT N
70    A = A + N
80    PRINT "YOUR TOTAL IS NOW $";A/100
90  NEXT I
```

9.
```
10  FOR I = 1 TO 10
20    PRINT INT(21*RND(0)-10)
30  NEXT I
```

11a. RUN
   1
   3
   6
  10

    READY.

11b. RUN
  123.4   12.35
  123.45   123.46

    READY.

13.

X	Y
1	**5**
2	0
2	2
2	1
3	1
3	−1
3	**2**

15.
```
10 FOR I = 13 TO 147 STEP 2
20    S = S + I
30 NEXT I
40 PRINT "THE SUM =";S
```

17.
```
10 FOR I = 1 TO 1000
20    R = INT(9*RND(0)+1)
30    IF R/2 = INT(R/2) THEN E = E + 1
40 NEXT I
50 PRINT "THERE WERE";1000-E;"ODD INTEGERS."
60 PRINT "THERE WERE";E;"EVEN INTEGERS."
```

19.
```
10 PRINT "DATE",,"BALANCE"
20 B = 1000 : Y = 1984
30 B = B * 1.05 : Y = Y + 1
40 PRINT "JAN 1,";Y,"$";INT(100*B+.5)/100
50 IF B>2000 THEN END
60 GOTO 30
```

21.
```
10 READ V
20 PI = 3.14159
30 R = (.75*V/PI)^(1/3)
40 PRINT "A SPHERE WITH VOLUME";V;"CM.^3"
50 PRINT "HAS A RADIUS OF ABOUT";INT(100*R+.5)/100;"CM."
60 PRINT
70 GOTO 10
100 DATA 690,720,460,620
```

23.
```
10 INPUT "YOUR STRING";A$
20 PRINT A$;
30 P = POS(0)
40 PRINT
50 PRINT "THE LENGTH OF ";A$;" IS";P
```

25.
```
10 FOR I = 1 TO 20
20   N = INT(100*RND(0)+1)
23   IF N=1 THEN 70
25   IF N=2 THEN 60
30   FOR X = 2 TO SQR(N)
40     IF N/X = INT(N/X) THEN 70
50   NEXT X
60   PRINT N;
70 NEXT I
```

27.
```
10 Q = INT(8*RND(0))
20 D = INT(5*RND(0))
30 P = INT(10*RND(0))
40 V = .25*Q + .1*D + .01*P
50 T = Q + D + P
60 PRINT "THERE ARE";T;"COINS, TOTALLING $";V
70 PRINT "GUESS HOW MANY QUARTERS, DIMES, PENNIES"
80 FOR I = 1 TO 3
90   INPUT "GUESS";Q1,D1,P1
100    IF Q1=Q AND D1=D AND P1=P THEN PRINT "YOU GOT IT!" : END
110    PRINT "INCORRECT."
120 NEXT I
130 PRINT "HAH, YOU DIDN'T GET IT"
```

CHAPTER FOUR

1.
```
10 FOR I = 1 TO 8
20   FOR I1 = 1 TO 30
30     PRINT "*";
40   NEXT I1
50   PRINT
60 NEXT I
```

3.
```
10 FOR I = 1 TO 6
20   INPUT "ENTER X(I)";X(I)
30 NEXT I
40 FOR I = 1 TO 5 STEP 2
50   PRINT I,X(I)
60 NEXT I
70 FOR I = 2 TO 6 STEP 2
80   PRINT I,X(I)
90 NEXT I
```

5.
```
10 DIM A(4,12)
20 FOR I = 1 TO 4
30    FOR J = 1 TO 12
40       A(I,J) = 3*I + J*J
50    NEXT J
60 NEXT I
70 INPUT "N";N
80 FOR I = 1 TO 12
90    PRINT A(N,I);
100 NEXT I
110 PRINT
120 GOTO 70
```

7a.
```
RUN
 1        5
 1        6
 2        5
 2        6
 3        5
 3        6

READY.
```

7b.
```
RUN
 10
 10
 10
 12
 12
 11
 14
 13
 11

READY.
```

7c.
```
RUN
 45        89        35

READY.
```

9.
```
10 FOR X = 40 TO 1 STEP -1
20    FOR Y = 1 TO 10
30       READ N
40       IF N = X THEN PRINT N;
50    NEXT Y
55    RESTORE
60 NEXT X
70 DATA 5,27,37,16,27,8,2,40,1,9
```

11.
```
10 DIM N(100)
20 FOR X = 1 TO 100
25    REM    GET A RANDOM NUMBER
30    N(X) = INT(99*RND(0)+1)
35    REM    LOOP THROUGH ALL PREVIOUS NUMBERS
40    FOR Y = 0 TO X-1
45       REM    CHECK FOR ANY DUPLICATES
50       IF N(X) = N(Y) THEN 90
60    NEXT Y
70 NEXT X
80 END
90 PRINT "DUPLICATE AFTER";X;"NUMBERS"
100 FOR I = 1 TO X
110    PRINT N(I);
120 NEXT I
```

13.
```
10 FOR I = 3 TO 50
20    FOR J = I+1 TO 50
30       FOR K = J+1 TO 50
40          IF K*K > I*I + J*J THEN 70
50          IF K*K = I*I + J*J THEN PRINT I,J,K
60       NEXT K
70    NEXT J
80 NEXT I
```

15.
```
10 DIM N(20)
20 FOR I = 1 TO 20
30    N(I) = INT(90*RND(0)+10)
40 NEXT I
50 PRINT "ODD INTEGERS:";
60 FOR I = 1 TO 20
70    IF N(I)/2 <> INT(N(I)/2) THEN PRINT N(I);
80 NEXT I
90 PRINT: PRINT "EVEN INTEGERS:";
100 FOR I = 1 TO 20
110    IF N(I)/2 = INT(N(I)/2) THEN PRINT N(I);
120 NEXT I
```

17a.
```
10 DIM N$(5,6)
20 INPUT "WHAT DAY AND TIME WOULD YOU LIKE";D,T
30 IF N$(D,T) <> "" THEN PRINT "THAT TIME IS TAKEN." : GOTO 20
40 INPUT "WHAT IS YOUR NAME";N$(D,T)
50 PRINT "THANK YOU VERY MUCH."
60 GOTO 20
```

17b.
```
10 DIM N$(5,6)
15 INPUT "ARE YOU THE DOCTOR";A$
17 IF A$ = "YES" THEN 70
20 INPUT "WHAT DAY AND TIME WOULD YOU LIKE";D,T
30 IF N$(D,T) <> "" THEN PRINT "THAT TIME IS TAKEN." : GOTO 20
40 INPUT "WHAT IS YOUR NAME";N$(D,T)
50 PRINT "THANK YOU VERY MUCH."
60 GOTO 15
70 INPUT "WHICH DAY";D
80 FOR T = 1 TO 6
90    IF N$(D,T) = "" THEN PRINT "SANKA BREAK" : GOTO 110
100   PRINT N$(D,T)
110 NEXT T
120 GOTO 15
```

19.
```
10 DIM N(100)
20 R = INT(100*RND(0)+1)
30 FOR X = 1 TO 100
40    INPUT "GUESS";G
50    IF G=R THEN 150
60    FOR Z = 1 TO X-1
70      IF N(Z) = G THEN 130
80    NEXT Z
90    N(X) = G
100   IF G>R THEN PRINT "LOWER" : GOTO 120
110   PRINT "HIGHER"
120 NEXT X
130 PRINT "WAKE UP! YOU GUESSED THAT NUMBER BEFORE."
140 GOTO 40
150 PRINT "CORRECT."
```

21.
```
1 REM P() = POINT VALUES FOR THE BOARD
2 REM B() = P, WITH A ZERO ENTERED WHEN A PENNY HITS THE BOARD
3 REM
4 REM
10 DIM P(6,6),B(6,6)
20 REM SET UP OUTSIDE OF BOARD FOR 1 POINT
30 FOR I = 1 TO 6
40    P(1,I)=1 : P(6,I)=1 : P(I,6)=1 : P(I,1)=1
50 NEXT I
60 REM SET UP BOARD POSITIONS WORTH 2 POINTS
70 FOR I = 2 TO 5
80 P(2,I)=2 : P(5,I)=2 : P(I,2)=2 : P(I,5)=2
90 NEXT I
100 REM SET UP THE THREE POINT POSITIONS
110 P(3,3)=3 : P(3,4)=3 : P(4,3)=3 : P(4,4)=3
120 REM SET ARRAY B EQUAL TO ARRAY P
130 FOR Q = 1 TO 6
140    FOR W = 1 TO 6
150      B(Q,W) = P(Q,W)
160    NEXT W
170 NEXT Q
180 REM GET 10 RANDOM ROWS AND COLUMNS FOR PENNY TOSSES
190 FOR T = 1 TO 10
200    R = INT(6*RND(0)+1) : C = INT(6*RND(0)+1)
210    B(R,C) = 0 : REM SET HIT POSITIONS TO 0
220    S = S + P(R,C) : REM SUM OF POINT VALUES
230 NEXT T
240 REM PRINT OUT RESULTANT BOARD
250 FOR R = 1 TO 6
260    FOR C = 1 TO 6
270 IF B(R,C)=0 THEN PRINT " X "; : GOTO 290
280      PRINT B(R,C);
290    NEXT C
300    PRINT
310 NEXT R
320 PRINT : PRINT "SCORE = ";S
```

23.
```
1 REM A$() = LETTERS OF THE ALPHABET
2 REM W$() = THE WORD FORMED
10 DIM A$(26)
20 FOR I = 1 TO 26
30    READ A$(I)
40 NEXT I
50 FOR W = 1 TO 15
60    R = INT(7*RND(0)+1) : REM RANDOM LENGTH
70    FOR L = 1 TO R : REM GET WORD OF LENGTH R
80       W$ = W$+A$(INT(26*RND(0)+1))
90    NEXT L
100   PRINT W$
110   W$ = "" : REM BLANK W$ FOR NEXT WORD
120 NEXT W
200 REM
210 DATA A,B,C,D,E,F,G,H,I,J,K,L,M,N,O,P,Q,R,S,T,U,V,W,X,Y,Z
```

25.
```
10 M = 500
20 FOR X = 1 TO 21
30    FOR Q = 1 TO 4
40       M = M + M * .06/4
50    NEXT Q
60    PRINT "AT THE END OF YEAR";X;"THERE IS $";M
70    M = M + 60
80 NEXT X
```

CHAPTER FIVE

1.
```
10 GOSUB 200
20 FOR J=1 TO 30
30    PRINT "*";
40 NEXT J
50 GOSUB 200
60 FOR J=1 TO 3
70    PRINT "!",
80 NEXT J
90 GOSUB 200
100 FOR J=1 TO 15
110    PRINT "AB";
120 NEXT J
130 END
200 PRINT
210 I = I+1
220 PRINT "PART";I
230 RETURN
```

3.
```
10  INPUT "1,2,3, OR 4";X
20  IF X<1 OR X>4 THEN 10
30  ON X GOTO 40,60,80,100
40  PRINT "AVOID BEING A VICTIM"
50  END
60  PRINT "PROGRAMMING IS COMMON SENSE"
70  END
80  PRINT "A LITTLE VICE IS SOMETIMES NICE"
90  END
100 PRINT "A COMMON COMIC COMUTER COMMANDS HIS COMMODORE"
110 END
```

5a.
```
10, 20, 30, 70, 40
10, 20, 30, 50, 40
10, 20, 30, 60, 40
10, 20, 90, 100
```

5b. N= 3   Z= 1   P= 4

7.
```
10  READ A,B,C
20  GOSUB 200
30  IF L=1 THEN PRINT "NOT A RIGHT TRIANGLE": GOTO 10
40  R = A*B/2
50  PRINT "AREA=";R,"PERIMETER=";A+B+C
60  GOTO 10
200 L = 0
210 IF A+B <= C THEN 250
220 IF A+C <= B THEN 250
230 IF B+C <= A THEN 250
240 IF INT(A^2 + B^2) = INT(C^2) THEN 260
250 L = 1
260 RETURN
270 DATA 3,4,5,0,1,1,2,2,2,12,5,13
280 END
```

9.
```
10  PRINT "WITHDRAWAL(1),DEPOSIT(2),"
20  PRINT "CALCULATE INTEREST(3), OR EXIT(4)
30  INPUT "1,2,3, OR 4";D
40  IF D<1 OR D>4 THEN 30
50  ON D GOSUB 100,200,300,400
60  PRINT "YOUR BALANCE STANDS AT $";INT(100*B+.5)/100
70  PRINT: GOTO 10
100 REM    WITHDRAWAL ROUTINE
110 PRINT "HOW MUCH WOULD YOU LIKE TO WITHDRAW"
115 INPUT A
120 IF A >= 0 AND B-A > 0 THEN B = B-A: RETURN
130 GOTO 110
200 REM    DEPOSIT ROUTINE
210 PRINT "HOW MUCH WOULD YOU LIKE TO DEPOSIT"
215 INPUT A
220 IF A >= 0 THEN B = B+A : RETURN
230 GOTO 210
240 RETURN
```

(Continued on next page)

```
300 PRINT "HOW MANY MONTHS SINCE LAST CALCULATION"
305 INPUT M
310 Q = M/3
320 IF Q < 1 THEN PRINT "TOO SOON": RETURN
330 FOR C = 1 TO Q
340    B = B+.0575/4*B
350 NEXT C
360 RETURN
400 END
```

11. Label1: Deal Player two cards
             Deal Dealer two cards
             Reveal both of Player's cards
             Reveal one of Dealer's cards

     Label2: Does the Player want more cards?
             If not, goto Label3
             Deal Player another card
             If Player's TOTAL >21 then Dealer wins : goto Label5
             Goto Label2

     Label3: REM Dealer takes cards routine
             If Dealer's TOTAL >16 and Dealer's TOTAL <21
                then goto Label14
             Deal Dealer another card
             If Dealer's TOTAL >21 then Player wins : goto Label5
             Goto Label3

     Label4: REM Compare card totals
             If Dealer's TOTAL >= Player's TOTAL then
                Dealer wins : goto Label5
             Player wins

     Label5: Does the Player want to play again?
             If the Player wants to play again then goto Label1
             END

13. (a) This program will generate an "?OUT OF DATA ERROR IN 10". Line 10 attempts to
     read a fourth data element from line 40. A possible correction might read:

                              40 DATA 2,3,4,5

     where the value 5 becomes the fourth data element.

     (b) This program will endlessly print .5 because no new data is read in at line 10. Correct
     line 40 as follows:

                              40 GOTO 10

(c) Lines 20 and 30 each contain syntax errors. The function "$*$ /" referenced at line 20 is illegal. The statement may be corrected to read:

20 PRINT A$*$B+C

to indicate multiplication, or:

20 PRINT A/B+C

to indicate division of A by B. Line 30 may be corrected by placing quotation marks around "D/F=" to read:

30 PRINT ''D/F='';D/F

In addition, the variables D and F should be defined, or else a division by zero will result in line 30.

(d) The conditional clause at line 20 is incomplete. The user has not specified what variable should be less than 10. The obvious variable is F, so that line 20 reads:

20 IF F>5 OR F<10 THEN 40

A comma or a semicolon must be inserted between the variables F and G at line 40 so that the computer understands that they are two separate elements:

40 PRINT F,G

(e) The FOR . . . TO . . . NEXT loops are improperly nested:

```
10   FOR X=1 TO 8
20      FOR Y=1 TO 3
30         X=X+Y
40            NEXT X
50   NEXT Y
60   PRINT X
70   END
```

Line 40 and 50 may be corrected as follows:

```
40   NEXT Y
50   NEXT X
```

Also, changing the value of variables used in FOR . . . TO . . . NEXT loops is not recommended practice such as at line 30.

(f) This program will continuously print the sum of 3, 6 and 9 since new data is not being read at line 10. Correct line 40 as follows:

```
40   GOTO 10
```

15. RUN
  −6   6

  READY.

17. The computer will return the error "?SYNTAX ERROR IN 20". Since it appears that the variable "X" is intended to contain formula weight, line 20 may be corrected to read:

$$20 \text{ INPUT ''FORMULA WEIGHT'';X}$$

(b) When this program attempts to branch to line 50 at line 35, it will not find lin 50, and the error message "?UNDEF'D STATEMENT ERROR IN 35" will be printed. Change line 35 to:

$$35 \text{ IF } Y=X \text{ THEN } A=A-1 : \text{GOTO } 55$$

(c) Note that both lines 10 and 20 do not contain the same number of closing parentheses as opening parentheses, thereby causing an "?ILLEGAL QUANTITY ERROR IN 10". The computer reports the first error encountered so the errors in line 20 and 30 go undiscovered. The first opening parenthesis is not necessary in either line 10 or 20. Line 30 should read:

$$\text{IF } X1>X2 \text{ THEN } 50$$

(d) Upon encountering line 30, the computer will print the error message "?SYNTAX ERROR IN 30". The line in question should read:

$$30 \text{ IF } X>200 \text{ THEN } 10$$

(e) When the computer runs this program, it will print "?TYPE MISMATCH IN 20" and terminate the run. The problem arises from trying to add a floating point variable to a string variable. Variables can be of several types. They can be integers (which means they have no decimal places), floating point or real (which means they have decimal places), or string variables. Assuming the intent of the program was to sum all the numbers between 1 and 26, the best way to correct this program is to change all occurrences of "A$" to "A".

$$20 \qquad A=A+X$$
$$40 \quad \text{PRINT } A$$

19. The computer stores all decimal numbers in binary form. Because of this, small "rounding errors" are introduced into stored numbers. When these errors are compounded as in the large summation at lin 30 (100 and 1000 times), it leads to very visible miscalculations as seen when this program is run. In this case the error was small.

CHAPTER SIX

Due to the difficulty of the material in Chapter 6, both odd and even answers are given here. Each question is answered with the Commodore-64 solution. In addition, alterations are included where necessary so that the program can run on the VIC-20 computer.

```
1.  10 PRINT "[clr]"
    20 PRINT "[graphics]"
    30 FOR I = 1 TO 10
    40 PRINT "        [R]"
    50 NEXT I

2.  10 PRINT "[clr]"
    20 FOR Y = 0 TO 23
    30    PRINT "                 |"
    40 NEXT Y
    50 PRINT "[graphics]"
    60 FOR X = 0 TO 4
    70    PRINT "-";
    80 NEXT X
    90 PRINT "+";
    100 FOR X = 6 TO 39
    110    PRINT "-";
    120 NEXT X
```

VIC-20 Alterations:

```
20  FOR Y = 0 TO 22
50  PRINT "[graphics]"
100 FOR X = 6 TO 21
130 PRINT "[graphics]"
```

```
3.  5 PRINT "[clr]"
    10 POKE 53280,5 : POKE 53281,12
    20 PRINT "TODAY ONLY!"
    30 PRINT "  UNCLE BILL'S"
    40 PRINT "WHAMBURGERS!"
    50 PRINT "      ONLY $0.79"
    60 FOR D = 1 TO 100 : NEXT D
    70 PRINT "[clr]"
    80 FOR D = 1 TO 100 : NEXT D
    90 GOTO 20
```

VIC-20 Alterations:

```
10 POKE 36879,6*16+8+5
```

```
4.  5 PRINT "[clr]" : REM CLEAR SCREEN
    9 REM VERTICAL PIECES
    10 FOR Y = 1 TO 13
    20    POKE 1024+3+40*Y,103 : POKE 55296+3+40*Y,1
    30    POKE 1024+10+40*Y,93 : POKE 55296+10+40*Y,1
    40    POKE 1024+17+40*Y,101 : POKE 55296+17+40*Y,1
    50 NEXT Y
    60 REM
    90 REM HORIZONTAL PIECES
    100 FOR X = 3 TO 8
    110    POKE 1024+X+1+40*14,99 : POKE 55296+X+1+40*14,1
    120    POKE 1024+X+8+40*1,99 : POKE 55296+X+8+40*1,1
    130 NEXT X
```

(Continued on next page)

```
190 REM DIAGONAL
200 FOR I = 1 TO 13
210    POKE 1024+3+I+40*I,77 : POKE 55296+3+I+40*I,1
220 NEXT I
230 PRINT "◘◘◘◘◘◘◘◘◘◘◘◘"
```

VIC-20 Alterations:

```
20    POKE 7680+3+22*Y,103 : POKE 38400+3+22*Y,0
30    POKE 7680+10+22*Y,93 : POKE 38400+10+22*Y,0
40    POKE 7680+17+22*Y,101 : POKE 38400+17+22*Y,0
110   POKE 7680+X+1+22*14,99 : POKE 38400+X+1+22*14,0
120   POKE 7680+X+8+22*1,99 : POKE 38400+X+8+22*1,0
210   POKE 7680+3+I+22*I,77 : POKE 38400+3+I+22*I,0
```

5a.
```
5 PRINT "◻" : REM CLEAR SCREEN
7 REM FILL LEFT HALF OF SCREEN WITH RANDOM COLORS
10 FOR X = 0 TO 19
20    FOR Y = 0 TO 24
30       POKE 1024+X+40*Y,160
40       POKE 55296+X+40*Y,INT(8*RND(0)+1)
50    NEXT Y
60 NEXT X
70 REM
90 REM DUPLICATE LEFT HALF OF SCREEN ON RIGHT HALF
100 FOR X = 0 TO 19
110    FOR Y = 0 TO 24
120       C = PEEK(55296+X+40*Y) AND 15
130       POKE 1024+X+20+40*Y,160
140       POKE 55296+X+20+40*Y,C
150    NEXT Y
160 NEXT X
170 GOTO 170 : REM SUPPRESS READY.
```

VIC-20 Alterations:

```
10 FOR X = 0 TO 10
20    FOR Y = 0 TO 22
30       POKE 7680+X+22*Y,160
40       POKE 38400+X+22*Y,INT(8*RND(0)+1)
100 FOR X = 0 TO 10
110    FOR Y = 0 TO 22
120       C = PEEK(38400+X+22*Y) AND 15
130       POKE 7680+X+11+22*Y,160
140       POKE 38400+X+11+22*Y,C
```

5b.
```
5 PRINT "◻" : REM CLEAR SCREEN
7 REM FILL LEFT HALF OF SCREEN WITH RANDOM COLORS
10 FOR X = 0 TO 19
20    FOR Y = 0 TO 24
30       POKE 1024+X+40*Y,160
40       POKE 55296+X+40*Y,INT(8*RND(0)+1)
50    NEXT Y
60 NEXT X
```

```
90 REM MIRROR LEFT HALF OF SCREEN ON RIGHT HALF
100 FOR X = Ø TO 19
110   FOR Y = Ø TO 24
120     C = PEEK(55296+X+40*Y) AND 15
130       POKE 1024+39-X+40*Y,160
140       POKE 55296+39-X+40*Y,C
150   NEXT Y
160 NEXT X
170 GOTO 170 : REM SUPPRESS READY.
```

VIC-20 Alterations:

```
10 FOR X = Ø TO 10
20   FOR Y = Ø TO 22
30     POKE 7680+X+22*Y,160
40     POKE 38400+X+22*Y,INT(8*RND(Ø)+1)
100 FOR X = Ø TO 10
110   FOR Y = Ø TO 22
120     C = PEEK(38400+X+22*Y) AND 15
130       POKE 7680+21-X+22*Y,160
140       POKE 38400+21-X+22*Y,C
```

6.
```
1 REM   B = BOX NUMBER WITH BOMB
2 REM   G = GUESS OF PLAYER OR COMPUTER
3 REM   X = NUMBER OF PREVIOUS GUESSES
4 REM   A() = NUMBERS GUESSED ALREADY
10 PRINT "I HAVE SIX BOXES, AND ONLY"
20 PRINT "ONE OF THE SIX BOXES CONTAINS"
30 PRINT "A BOMB. THE PLAYER PICKS ANY"
40 PRINT "BOX AND THE COMPUTER DETERMINES"
50 PRINT "WHETHER OR NOT THERE IS A BOMB INSIDE"
60 POKE 54277,9:POKE 54278,Ø: REM SOUND INIT
70 B = INT(6*RND(Ø)+1)
80 X = 1
100 PRINT "YOUR TURN, PICK A BOX"
110 GET G
120 IF G > 6 OR G < 1 THEN 110
130 FOR I = 1 TO X
140   IF G = A(I) THEN PRINT "PICK AGAIN": GOTO 110
150 NEXT I
160 GOSUB 300
170 PRINT
180 PRINT "IT'S MY TURN"
190 FOR D = 1 TO 200: NEXT D: REM DELAY LOOP
200 G = INT(6*RND(Ø)+1)
210 FOR I = 1 TO X
220   IF G = A(I) THEN 200 : REM DUPLICATE NUMBER
230 NEXT I
240 GOSUB 300
250 GOTO 100
300 PRINT G
310 IF G <> B THEN PRINT "CLICK.":A(X)=G:X = X+1:GOTO 370
320 PRINT "BANG!!!"
330 REM   EXPLOSION NOISE
340 REM SET VOLUME,WAVE FORM,NOTE
350 POKE 54296,15:POKE 54276,129:C=8000: GOTO 390
```

(Continued on next page)

```
360 REM  CLICK NOISE
370 REM SET VOLUME,WAVE FORM,NOTE
380 POKE 54296,8:POKE 54276,17:C=1300
390 REM POKE NOTE
400 POKE 54272,C-INT(C/256)*256:POKE 54273,INT(C/256)
410 FOR D=1 TO 300:NEXT D:POKE 54276,PEEK(54276) AND 254
420 POKE 54296,0
430 IF G <> B THEN RETURN
440 IF X/2 <> INT(X/2) THEN PRINT"HA HA,YOU LOSE": END
450 PRINT "ARG!!- YOU WIN TOUGH GUY"
460 FOR D = 1 TO 300 : NEXT D
470 POKE 53280,0:POKE 53281,0 : REM TURN SCREEN BLACK
480 PRINT "    " : REM CLEAR SCREEN, SET
    CURSOR BLACK
```

VIC-20 Alterations:

```
310 IF G <> B THEN PRINT "CLICK.":A(X)=G:X = X+1:GOTO 400
340 POKE 36878,15
350 FOR Z = 1 TO 255
360 POKE 36877,Z
370 NEXT Z
380 POKE 36878,0
390 GOTO 430
400 REM  CLICK NOISE
410 POKE 36878,5: POKE 36877,200
420 FOR D = 1 TO 300: NEXT D: REM DELAY
425 POKE 36878,0
470 POKE 36879,8: REM TURN SCREEN BLACK
```

```
7. 10 REM CLEAR SCREEN, SET CURSOR WHITE, P
   RINT HEADER
   20 PRINT"       OCCURRENCES OF 100 RANDOM
      NUMBERS"
   40 FOR I = 1 TO 100
   50    R = INT(10*RND(0)+1)
   60    N(R) = N(R) + 1
   70 NEXT I
   120 REM
   130 REM
   140 REM  NOW PLOT BAR FOR EACH NUMBER
   160 FOR I = 1 TO 10
   170    X0 = (I-1)*4
   180    FOR Y0 = 20-N(I) TO 19
   190       GOSUB 300: REM POSITION CURSOR
   200       PRINT "   "; : REM PRINT A SIN
   GLE BAR
   220    NEXT Y0
   225    REM POSITION CURSOR, PRINT NUMBER
   230    PRINT "      ";I;
   240 NEXT I
   250 PRINT "  ": : GOTO 600
   300 REM  POSITION CURSOR AT (X0,Y0)
   310 PRINT "S";: REM PUT CURSOR AT (0,0)
   320 IF X0 = 0 THEN 360
   330 FOR L = 0 TO X0-1
   340    PRINT "U";: REM MOVE CURSOR RIGHT
   350 NEXT L
   360 IF Y0 = 0 THEN RETURN
   370 FOR L = 0 TO Y0-1
   380    PRINT "U";: REM MOVE CURSOR DOWN
   390 NEXT L
   400 RETURN
   600 END
```

VIC-20 Alterations:

```
10 REM CLEAR SCREEN, SET CURSOR BLACK, P
RINT HEADER
20 PRINT"  PLOT OF 100 RANDOM #'S";
170 X0 = (I-1)*2
180 FOR Y0 = 19-N(I) TO 18
200 PRINT "   "; : REM PRINT A SINGLE BA
R
230 PRINT "    ";I;
250 PRINT "  "; : GOTO 600
```

8.
```
10 REM CLEAR SCREEN,SET CURSOR WHITE,PRI
NT HEADER
20 PRINT"   ";TAB(9);"CHERYL'S SHOE SHOP
"
30 REM   FIVE EMPLOYEES
40 FOR E = 1 TO 5
45    S = 0
50    READ N$(E)
60    FOR X = 1 TO 7
70       READ N
80       S = S+N
90    NEXT X
100   A(E) = S/7 : REM CALCULATE AVERAGE
120 NEXT E: PRINT
125 FOR I = 19 TO 0 STEP -1
130    PRINT I
135 NEXT I
140 REM   NOW PLOT BAR FOR EACH EMPLOYEE
160 FOR E = 1 TO 5
170    X0 = (E-1)*7+4
180    FOR Y0 = 22-A(E) TO 21
190       GOSUB 300: REM POSITION CURSOR
200       PRINT "   "; : REM PRINT A SI
NGLE BAR
220    NEXT Y0
225    REM POSITION CURSOR,PRINT NAME
230    PRINT"    ";N$(E)
240 NEXT E
250 PRINT "  "; : GOTO 600
300 REM   POSITION CURSOR AT (X0,Y0)
310 PRINT "  "; : REM PUT CURSOR AT (0,0)
320 IF X0 = 0 THEN 360
330 FOR L = 0 TO X0-1
340    PRINT "  ";: REM MOVE CURSOR RIGHT
350 NEXT L
360 IF Y0 = 0 THEN RETURN
370 FOR L = 0 TO Y0-1
380    PRINT "  ";: REM MOVE CURSOR DOWN
390 NEXT L
400 RETURN
500 DATA HOWARD,7,10,10,10,8,9,7
510 DATA JASON,11,20,18,15,27,20,20
520 DATA JOSH,17,20,12,18,10,15,22
530 DATA JARED,21,25,17,16,20,14,22
540 DATA JESS,17,11,8,10,14,21,13
600 END
```

VIC-20 Alterations:

```
10 REM CLEAR SCREEN,SET CURSOR BLACK,PRI
NT HEADER
20 PRINT"   CHERYL'S SHOE SHOP"
125 FOR I = 18 TO 0 STEP -1
170 X0 = (E-1)*4+3
200 PRINT "   "; : REM PRINT A SINGLE B
AR
230 PRINT"    ";: IF E/2=INT(E/2) THEN P
RINT "  ";
235 PRINT N$(E);
250 PRINT "  "; : GOTO 600
```

9.
```
5 DIM N$(14),N(14)
10 FOR I = 1 TO 13
20    READ N$(I)
30 READ N(I)
40 NEXT I
50 POKE 54277,15 : POKE 54278,255
60 GET L$ : IF L$="" THEN 60
65 IF L$ = N$(I) THEN POKE 54296,0
70 GOSUB 100 : GOTO 60
80 REM
90 REM
100 FOR I = 1 TO 13
110    IF L$=N$(I) THEN 150
120 NEXT I
130 POKE 54296,0
140 GOTO 210
150 POKE 54276,33: POKE 54296,8
160 C = N(I)
170 POKE 54272,C-INT(C/256)*256
180 POKE 54273,INT(C/256)
200 POKE 54276,32
210 RETURN
300 REM    NOTE DATA
310 DATA Z,4291,S,4547,X,4817,D,5103
320 DATA C,5407,V,5728,G,6069,B,6430
330 DATA H,6812,N,7217,J,7647,M,8101
340 DATA ",",8583
```

VIC-20 Answer:

```
5 DIM N$(14),N(14)
10 FOR I = 1 TO 13
20    READ N$(I)
30 READ N(I)
40 NEXT I
60 GET L$ : IF L$="" THEN 60
65 IF L$ = N$(I) THEN POKE 36878,0
70 GOSUB 100 : GOTO 60
80 REM
90 REM
100 FOR I = 1 TO 13
110    IF L$=N$(I) THEN 150
120 NEXT I
130 POKE 36878,0
140 GOTO 210
150 POKE 36878,8
160 C = N(I)
170 POKE 36876,C
210 RETURN
300 REM    NOTE DATA
310 DATA Z,225,S,227,X,228,D,229
320 DATA C,231,V,232,G,233,B,235
330 DATA H,236,N,237,J,238,M,239
340 DATA ",",240
```

```
10a. 10 PRINT "�def"
     20 PRINT "≫≫≫──────────≻"
     30 PRINT "≫≫≫──────────≻"

10b. 10 FOR I = 0 TO 24
     20    PRINT "◦"
     30    PRINT TAB(I);"≫≫≫─────────≻"
     40    PRINT TAB(I);"≫≫≫─────────≻"
     50 NEXT I
     60 GOTO 10
```

VIC-20 Alterations:

```
10 FOR I = 0 TO 10
45 FOR D = 1 TO 50 : NEXT D : REM DELAY
```

```
11a. 90  FOR D = 1 TO 50 : NEXT D : PRINT "◦"
     100 PRINT"          "
     110 PRINT"    O     "
     130 PRINT"          "
     140 PRINT
     145 PRINT"          "
     150 PRINT"          "
     160 PRINT"          "
     170 PRINT"          "
     180 PRINT"          "
     190 FOR D = 1 TO 50 : NEXT D : PRINT "◦"
     200 PRINT"          "
     210 PRINT"    O     "
     230 PRINT"          "
     240 PRINT"          "
     245 PRINT"          "
     250 PRINT"          "
     260 PRINT"          "
     270 PRINT"          "
     280 PRINT"          "
     290 FOR D = 1 TO 50 : NEXT D : PRINT "◦"
     300 PRINT"          "
     310 PRINT"    O     "
     330 PRINT"          "
     340 PRINT"          "
     345 PRINT"          "
     350 PRINT"          "
     360 PRINT"          "
     370 PRINT"          "
     380 PRINT"          "
     390 FOR D = 1 TO 50 : NEXT D : PRINT "◦"
     400 PRINT"          "
     410 PRINT"    O     "
     430 PRINT"          "
     440 PRINT"          "
     445 PRINT"          "
     450 PRINT"          "
     460 PRINT"          "
     470 PRINT"          "
     480 PRINT"          "
     490 FOR D = 1 TO 50 : NEXT D : PRINT "◦"
     500 PRINT"          "
     510 PRINT"    O     "
     530 PRINT"          "
     540 PRINT
     545 PRINT"          "
     550 PRINT"          "
     560 PRINT"          "
     570 PRINT"          "
     580 PRINT"          "
     590 GOTO 90
```

11b.
```
89 IF X > 30 THEN X=0
90 FOR D = 1 TO 1 : NEXT D : PRINT "[clr]"
100 PRINT TAB(X);"..."
110 PRINT TAB(X);"..."
130 PRINT TAB(X);"..."
140 PRINT TAB(X);"..."
145 PRINT TAB(X);"..."
150 PRINT TAB(X);"..."
160 PRINT TAB(X);"..."
170 PRINT TAB(X);"..."
180 PRINT TAB(X);"..."
190 FOR D = 1 TO 1 : NEXT D : PRINT "[clr]"
200 PRINT TAB(X);"..."
210 PRINT TAB(X);"..."
230 PRINT TAB(X);"..."
240 PRINT TAB(X);"..."
245 PRINT TAB(X);"..."
250 PRINT TAB(X);"..."
260 PRINT TAB(X);"..."
270 PRINT TAB(X);"..."
280 PRINT TAB(X);"..."
290 FOR D = 1 TO 1 : NEXT D : PRINT "[clr]"
300 PRINT TAB(X);"..."
310 PRINT TAB(X);"..."
330 PRINT TAB(X);"..."
340 PRINT TAB(X);"..."
345 PRINT TAB(X);"..."
350 PRINT TAB(X);"..."
360 PRINT TAB(X);"..."
370 PRINT TAB(X);"..."
380 PRINT TAB(X);"..."
390 FOR D = 1 TO 1 : NEXT D : PRINT "[clr]"
400 PRINT TAB(X);"..."
410 PRINT TAB(X);"..."
430 PRINT TAB(X);"..."
440 PRINT TAB(X);"..."
445 PRINT TAB(X);"..."
450 PRINT TAB(X);"..."
460 PRINT TAB(X);"..."
470 PRINT TAB(X);"..."
480 PRINT TAB(X);"..."
490 FOR D = 1 TO 1 : NEXT D : PRINT "[clr]"
500 PRINT TAB(X);"..."
510 PRINT TAB(X);"..."
530 PRINT TAB(X);"..."
540 PRINT TAB(X);"..."
545 PRINT TAB(X);"..."
550 PRINT TAB(X);"..."
560 PRINT TAB(X);"..."
570 PRINT TAB(X);"..."
580 PRINT TAB(X);"..."
590 X = X+2 : GOTO 89
```

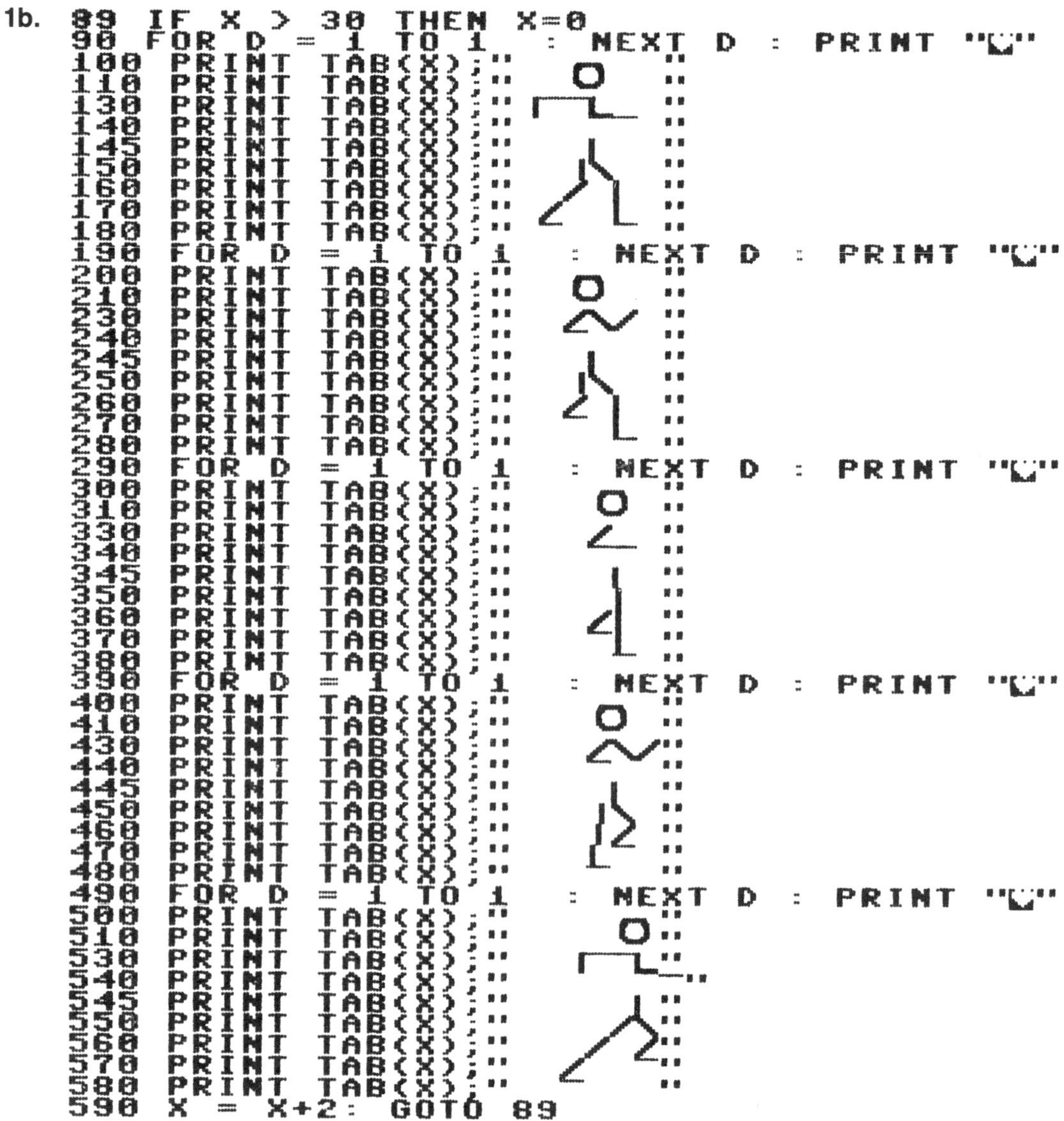

VIC-20 Alterations:
```
89 IF X > 15 THEN X=0
```

12.
```
10 PRINT " [clr] " : REM CLEAR SCREEN
20 DIM C(21,2)
30 POKE 53280,1 : POKE 53281,0
40 FOR I = 1 TO 7
50   READ L(I):REM LOCATION OF START OF DATA FOR ROLL "I" IN C()
60 NEXT I
70 FOR I = 1 TO 21
80   READ C(I,1) : REM X COORDINATE OF DOT
90   READ C(I,2) : REM Y COORDINATE OF DOT
100 NEXT I
110 R = INT(6*RND(0)+1)
120 C1=1 : GOSUB 200 : REM C1=1 FOR DRAWING
130 GET N$ : IF N$="" THEN 130
140 C1=0 : GOSUB 200 : REM C1=0 FOR ERASING
150 GOTO 110
```

(Continued on next page)

```basic
200 FOR I = L(R) TO L(R+1)-1
210   X = C(I,1)
220   Y = C(I,2)
230   POKE 1024+X+40*Y,81  : REM DRAW A DOT
240   POKE 55296+X+40*Y,C1 : REM SET COLOR OF DOT TO C1
250 NEXT I
260 RETURN
270 REM
299 REM INDEX DATA
300 DATA 1,2,4,7,11,16,22
310 REM
400 REM COORDINATE DATA
410 DATA 19,12,11,4,27,20
420 DATA 11,4,19,12,27,20
430 DATA 11,4,27,4,27,20,11,20
440 DATA 11,4,27,4,27,20,11,20,19,12
450 DATA 11,4,27,4,27,20,11,20,11,12,27,12
```

VIC-20 Alterations:

```basic
30 POKE 36879,0*16+8+0
230 POKE 7680+X+22*Y,81  : REM DRAW A DOT
240 POKE 38400+X+22*Y,C1 : REM SET COLOR OF DOT TO C1
410 DATA 10,11,5,5,15,17
420 DATA 5,5,10,11,15,17
430 DATA 5,5,15,5,15,16,5,17
440 DATA 5,5,15,5,15,17,5,17,10,11
450 DATA 5,5,15,5,15,17,5,17,5,11,15,11
```

13a.
```basic
10 PRINT " ▚ " : REM CLEAR SCREEN
15 REM READ IN SCREEN POSITION DATA
20 FOR I = 0 TO 6
30   READ P(I,1)
40   READ P(I,2)
50 NEXT I
55 REM READ SEGMENT DATA
60 READ N
65 REM DECODE SEGMENT DATA
70 FOR I = 0 TO 6
80   N - N/2 : REM IS N DIVISIBLE BY 2?
90   IF N = INT(N) THEN 120
95   REM POSITION BAR AT (X1,Y1)
100   X1 = P(I,1) : Y1 = P(I,2)
110   ON I+1 GOSUB 200,300,200,300,300,200,300
120   N = INT(N)
130 NEXT I
140 FOR D = 1 TO 500 : NEXT D : REM DELAY
150 PRINT " ▚ " : REM CLEAR SCREEN
160 GOTO 60
170 REM
200 REM PRINTS HORIZONTAL BAR AT (X1,Y1)
210 FOR X = X1+1 TO X1+3
220   POKE 1024+X+40*Y1,64
230   POKE 55296+X+40*Y1,1
240 NEXT X
250 RETURN
```

(Continued on next page)

```
300 REM PRINTS VERTICAL BAR AT (X1,Y1)
310 FOR Y = Y1+1 TO Y1+3
320    POKE 1024+X1+40*Y,66
330    POKE 55296+X1+40*Y,1
340 NEXT Y
350 RETURN
360 REM
400 REM   POSITION DATA
410 DATA 14,11,18,7,14,7,14,7
420 DATA 14,11,14,15,18,11
430 REM
500 REM   SEGMENT DATA
510 DATA 126,66,55,103,75,109,125,70,127,111
```

VIC-20 Alterations:

```
15 POKE 36879,8
220    POKE 7680+X+22*Y1,64
230    POKE 38400+X+22*Y1,1
320    POKE 7680+X1+22*Y,66
330    POKE 38400+X1+22*Y,1
410 DATA 8,11,12,7,8,7,8,7
420 DATA 8,11,8,15,12,11
```

13b.
```
5 PRINT " ⬚ " : REM CLEAR SCREEN
10 POKE 53281,0 : REM SET BACKGROUND BLACK
15 REM READ IN SCREEN POSITION DATA
20 FOR I = 0 TO 6
30    READ P(I,1)
40    READ P(I,2)
50 NEXT I
55 REM READ IN ENCODED SEGMENT DATA
60 FOR I = 0 TO 9
70    READ D(I)
80 NEXT I
90 FOR S1 = 0 TO 9
100   N = D(S1) : F = 0 : C = 1 : GOSUB 400
110   FOR S2 = 0 TO 9
120     N = D(S2) : F = 6 : C = 1 : GOSUB 400
130     FOR D = 1 TO 50 : NEXT D : REM   DELAY
135     REM ERASE DISPLAY S2 UNLESS A NINE
140     N = D(S2) : C = 0
150     IF S2 <> 9 THEN GOSUB 400
160   NEXT S2
170 PRINT " ⬚ " : REM CLEAR SCREEN
180 NEXT S1
190 END
200 REM PRINT HORIZONTAL BAR AT (X1,X1)
210 FOR X = X1+1 TO X1+3
220    POKE 1024+X+40*Y1,64
230    POKE 55296+X+40*Y1,C
240 NEXT X
250 RETURN
```

(Continued on next page)

```
300 REM PRINT VERTICAL BAR AT (X1,Y1)
310 FOR Y = Y1+1 TO Y1+3
320    POKE 1024+X1+40*Y,66
330    POKE 55296+X1+40*Y,C
340 NEXT Y
350 RETURN
360 REM
400 REM ROUTINE TO DECODE SEGMENT DATA
410 FOR I = 0 TO 6 : REM 7 SEGMENTS
420    N = N/2 : REM IS N DIVISIBLE BY 2?
430    IF N = INT(N) THEN 460
435    REM  POSITION BAR AT (X1,Y1)
440    X1 = P(I,1) + F : Y1 = P(I,2)
450 ON I+1 GOSUB 200,300,200,300,300,200,300
460    N = INT(N)
470 NEXT I
480 RETURN
490 REM
500 REM    POSITION DATA
510 DATA 12,11,16,7,12,7,12,7
520 DATA 12,11,12,15,16,11
530 REM
600 REM    SEGMENT DATA
610 DATA 126,66,55,103,75,109,125,70,127,111
```

VIC-20 Alterations:

```
10 POKE 36879,8 : REM SET BACKGROUND BLACK
220    POKE 7680+X+22*Y1,64
230    POKE 38400+X+22*Y1,C
320    POKE 7680+X1+22*Y,66
330    POKE 38400+X1+22*Y,C
510 DATA 5,11,9,7,5,7,5,7
520 DATA 5,11,5,15,9,11
```

CHAPTER SEVEN

1.
```
10 INPUT N
20 IF N < 0 THEN PRINT "NO NEGATIVE NUMBERS ALLOWED." : GOTO 10
30 PRINT "N =";N,"SQUARE ROOTS = + OR -";SQR(N) : GOTO 10
```

3.
```
10 PRINT "COS(X)"; TAB(20);"SIN(X+90)"
20 FOR X = 0 TO 360 STEP 10
30    R = X * π / 180 : REM CVT TO RADIANS
40    PRINT COS(R); TAB(20); SIN(R +/2)
50 NEXT X
```

5.
```
10 INPUT N
20 PRINT SGN(N) * N : REM THIS IS EQUIVALENT TO ABS(N)
```

7.  ```
10 PRINT "RADIANS","DEGREES"
20 FOR A = 0 TO 3 STEP .25
30   PRINT A,A*180/π
40 NEXT A
```

9.  ```
10 INPUT N
15 N = N/180
20 C = COS(N)
30 S = SIN(N)
40 T = TAN(N)
50 IF C>S AND C>T THEN PRINT "COSINE =";C
60 IF S>T AND S>C THEN PRINT "SINE =";S
70 IF T>S AND T>C THEN PRINT "TANGENT =";T
```

11. ```
10 DEF FNF(X) = 9*X^3 - 7*X^2 + 4*X - 1
20 INPUT "A,B";A,B
30 PRINT FNF(B)-FNF(A)
```

13. ```
10 DEF FNR(X) = INT(100*X + .5)/100
20 PRINT " X","LN(X)","EXP(X)"
30 FOR I = 1 TO 15
40 PRINT I,FNR(LOG(I)),FNR(EXP(I))
50 NEXT I
```

15. ```
RUN
 5   -4   3   4

READY.
```

17. ```
RUN
FNF(-4 ) IS NEGATIVE
FNF(-2 ) IS NEGATIVE
FNF( 0 ) IS NEGATIVE
FNF( 2 ) IS ZERO
FNF( 4 ) IS POSITIVE
FNF( 6 ) IS POSITIVE

READY.
```

19. ```
RUN
-3
-2
-1
 0
 1
 2
 3
 4

READY.
```
```

21. 10 INPUT "R AND THETA (IN DEGREES) :";R,T
    20 T = T*π/180
    30 X = R*COS(T)
    40 Y = R*SIN(T)
    50 PRINT "(X,Y) = (";X;",";Y;")"

23. 10 FOR X = 1 TO 100
    20   Y = ABS(SIN(X)*1000)
    30   R = INT(Y)/16 - INT(INT(Y)/16)
    40   PRINT R
    50 NEXT X

25. 10 FOR N = 0 TO 6.2 STEP .2
    20   U = SIN(N)
    30   PRINT TAB(16*U+17);"SHAZAM!"
    40 NEXT N

CHAPTER EIGHT

1. 10 INPUT "A$";A$
   20 FOR I=1 TO LEN(A$)
   30   PRINT ASC(MID$(A$,I,1));
   40 NEXT I

3. 10 READ X
   20 PRINT CHR$(X);
   30 GOTO 10
   40 DATA 65,83,67,73,73,32,68,73
   50 DATA 68,32,84,72,73,83,33

5. 1 REM   A$ = ORIGINAL STRING
   2 REM   L$,M$,R$ = LEFT,MID,RIGHT STRINGS OF ORIGINAL
   3 REM
   4 REM
   10 A$ = "THREE!@#$%STRING!@#$%FUNCTIONS"
   20 L$=LEFT$(A$,5)
   30 M$=MID$(A$,11,6)
   40 R$=RIGHT$(A$,9)
   50 PRINT L$;" ";M$;" ";R$

7. 1 REM   N$ = NAME BEING EXAMINED
   2 REM   A() = NUMBER OF OCCURRENCES OF EACH LETTER
   3 REM   S = ASCII CODE FOR THE LETTERS IN A$
   4 REM   F = 1 IF THERE IS A TIE BETWEEN LETTERS, ELSE F=0
   5 REM
   6 REM
   10 REM   GET NAME AND COUNT OCCURRENCES
   20 DIM A(26)
   30 INPUT "NAME";N$

(Continued on next page)

```
40 FOR I=1 TO LEN(N$)
50    S=ASC(MID$(N$,I,1))
60    A(S-64)=A(S-64)+1
70 NEXT I
80 REM
89 REM
100 REM   FIND MOST COMMON LETTER
110 REM
120 M=1
130 FOR I=1 TO 26
140    IF A(I)=M THEN F=1
150    IF A(I)>M THEN M=A(I):V=I:F=0
160 NEXT I
170 REM
180 REM
200 REM    PRINT MOST COMMON LETTER
210 IF F=0 THEN PRINT CHR$(V+64);
                  " IS THE MOST COMMON LETTER" : END
220 PRINT "THE FOLLOWING LETTERS HAVE AN"
230 PRINT "EQUAL OCCURRENCE:"
240 FOR I=1 TO 26
250    IF A(I) = M THEN PRINT CHR$(I+64);" ";
260 NEXT I
```

```
9.  10 READ W$
    20 FOR I = 1 TO LEN(W$)
    30    T$ = MID$(W$,I,1)
    40    IF T$<>"E" THEN PRINT T$;
    50 NEXT I
    60 PRINT : GOTO 10
    100 DATA QUEEN,LENGTH,REMEMBER
```

11.

BINARY	DECIMAL
1011	11
10100	20
1111	15
1110	14
1010011	83
110011	51
1011100	92
1101111	111
11000000	192
100000111	135

```
13.  10 A$ = "ABCDEFGHIJKL"
     20 FOR I = 1 TO 12
     30    PRINT LEFT$(A$,I)
     40 NEXT I
```

15. RUN
    87
    72
    55
    54

READY.

17. 10 FOR X=1 TO 15
    20   I=INT(26*RND(Ø)+65)
    30   PRINT CHR$(I);
    40 NEXT X

19. 10 FOR X=1 TO 100
    20   A$=A$+CHR$(INT(95*RND(Ø)+32))
    30 NEXT X
    40 PRINT : PRINT A$: PRINT
    50 FOR Y=1 TO 100
    60   C=ASC(MID$(A$,Y,1))
    70   IF (C>64 AND C<91) THEN L=L+1 : GOTO 100
    80   IF (C>47 AND C<58) THEN N=N+1 : GOTO 100
    90   M=M+1
    100 NEXT Y
    110 PRINT "THERE ARE";L;"LETTERS,";N
    120 PRINT "NUMBERS AND";M;"MISC. CHARACTERS."

21a. 10 INPUT "MESSAGE TO ENCODE";M$
     20 FOR I=1 TO LEN(M$)
     30   C=ASC(MID$(M$,I,1))
     40   IF C=32 THEN 80
     50   IF C<65 OR C>90 THEN 100
     60   C=C+2
     70   IF C>90 THEN C=C-26
     80   A$=A$+CHR$(C)
     90 NEXT I
     100 PRINT "ENCODED MESSAGE:"
     110 PRINT A$

21b. 10 INPUT "MESSAGE TO DECODE";M$
     20 FOR I=1 TO LEN(M$)
     30   C=ASC(MID$(M$,I,1))
     40   IF C=32 THEN 80
     50   IF C<65 OR C>90 THEN 90
     60   C=C-2
     70   IF C<65 THEN C=C+26
     80   A$=A$+CHR$(C)
     90 NEXT I
     100 PRINT "MESSAGE:"
     110 PRINT A$

23.
```
1 REM   T$ = A WORD FROM THE SENTANCE
2 REM   W$() = UP TO 30 WORD SENTENCE
3 REM   S$ = ORIGINAL SENTENCE
4 REM
5 REM
10  DIM W$(30)
20  INPUT "YOUR SENTENCE";S$
30  S$=CHR$(32)+S$+CHR$(32)
40  FOR X=1 TO LEN(S$)
50     T$=MID$(S$,X,1)
60     IF ASC(T$)=32 THEN C=C+1:GOTO 80
70  W$(C)=W$(C)+T$
80  NEXT X
90  FOR L=30 TO 1 STEP -1
100    IF W$(L)<>"" THEN PRINT W$(L);" ";
110 NEXT L
```

25.
```
10  INPUT "ENTER A BINARY NUMBER";N$
20  FOR N=1 TO LEN(N$)
30     D=D+VAL(MID$(N$,N,1))*2^(LEN(N$)-N)
40  NEXT N
50  PRINT D
```

CHAPTER NINE

Tape Files

1a.
```
1 REM CASSETTE FILE
10 OPEN 1,1,1,"RANUM FILE"
20 FOR X=1 TO 50
30    PRINT#1,INT(21*RND(0))
40 NEXT X
50 CLOSE 1
60 END
```

1b.
```
1 REM CASSETTE FILE
10 OPEN 2,1,0,"RANUM FILE"
20 FOR I=1 TO 50
30    INPUT#2,R
40    S=S+R
50 NEXT I
60 CLOSE 2
70 PRINT "THE SUM IS";S
80 END
```

3a.
```
1 REM CASSETTE FILE
10 OPEN 2,1,1,"SEQ FILE"
20 FOR I=1001 TO 1128
30    PRINT#2,I
40 NEXT I
50 CLOSE 1
60 END
```

3b.
```
1 REM CASSETTE TAPE
10 OPEN 2,1,0,"SEQ FILE"
20 INPUT "WHICH MEMBER OF SEQUENCE";P
30 FOR I=1 TO P
40    INPUT#2,N
50 NEXT I
60 CLOSE 2
70 PRINT "THAT IS";N
80 END
```

5a.
```
1 REM CASSETTE FILE
2 REM N$ = NAME
3 REM R = HOURLY PAY RATE
4 REM D = NUMBER OF DEPENDENTS
5 REM M = MEDICAL INSURANCE DEDUCTION
6 REM L = LIFE INSURANCE DEDUCTION
7 REM
8 REM
10 OPEN 1,1,1,"PAY FILE"
20 FOR X=1 TO 10
30    READ N$,R,D,M,L
40    PRINT#1,N$;",";R;",";D;",";M;",";L
50 NEXT X
60 CLOSE 1
70 REM
80 REM
100 DATA MENACE DENNIS,1,0,1,1
110 DATA BEAVER LEAVITTO,2.25,0,1,1
120 DATA ISLAND GILLIGAN,4.50,0,2,1
130 DATA WILSON MISTER,4.95,2,5,3
140 DATA HOGAN COLONEL,40,2,3,3
150 DATA SCHULTZ SEARGENT,30,1,1,2
160 DATA KIRK JIM,78.50,1,1,1
170 DATA BUNNY BUGS,12.45,2,5,3
180 DATA SERLING ROD,55.90,2,2,1
190 DATA BOND JAMES,9.25,3,0,0
200 END
```

5b.
```
1 REM CASSETTE FILE
2 REM N$ = NAME
3 REM R = HOURLY PAY RATE
4 REM D = NUMBER OF DEPENDENTS
5 REM M = MEDICAL INSURANCE DEDUCTION
6 REM L = LIFE INSURANCE DEDUCTION
7 REM G = GROSS PAY
```

(Continued on next page)

```
10 REM FUNCTION TO ROUND TO NEAREST 100TH
20 REM
30 DEF FNR(X)=INT(100*X+.5)/100
40 REM
50 REM
100 OPEN 2,1,0,"PAY FILE"
110 FOR X=1 TO 10
120 INPUT#2,N$,R,D,M,L
130   READ H : REM GET HOURS WORKED
140   G=H*R : T=(25-2*D)*G/100
150   IF T<0 THEN T=0
160   P=G-T-M-L
170   PRINT N$;" - "
180   PRINT "HOURS WORKED:";TAB(25);H
190   PRINT "GROSS PAY:";TAB(24);"$";FNR(G)
200   PRINT "TAX:";TAB(24);"$";FNR(T)
210   PRINT "MEDICAL INSURANCE:";TAB(24);"$";FNR(M)
220   PRINT "LIFE INSURANCE:";TAB(24);"$";FNR(L)
230   PRINT "NET:";TAB(24);"$";FNR(P)
240   PRINT
250 NEXT X
260 CLOSE 2
270 REM
280 REM
300 REM DATA SECTION
310 DATA 40,37.1,51,48,39.21,18,6,59.8
320 DATA 45.3,68.3,41
330 END
```

Diskette Files

1a.
```
1 REM DISKETTE FILE
10 OPEN 3,8,3,"RANUM FILE,S,W"
20 FOR X=1 TO 50
30 PRINT#3,INT(21*RND(0))
40 NEXT X
50 CLOSE 3
60 END
```

1b.
```
1 REM DISKETTE FILE
10 OPEN 3,8,3,"RANUM FILE,S,R"
20 FOR I=1 TO 50
30   INPUT#3,R
40 S=S+R
50 NEXT I
60 CLOSE 3
70 PRINT "THE SUM IS";S
80 END
```

3a.
```
1 REM DISKETTE FILE
10 OPEN 3,8,3,"SEQ FILE,S,W"
20 FOR I=1001 TO 1128
30   PRINT#3,I
40 NEXT I
50 CLOSE 3
60 END
```

3b.
```
1 REM DISKETTE FILE
10 OPEN 7,8,7,"SEQ FILE,S,R"
20 INPUT "WHICH MEMBER OF SEQUENCE";P
30 FOR I=1 TO P
40   INPUT#7,N
50 NEXT I
60 CLOSE 7
70 PRINT "THAT IS";N
80 END
```

5a.
```
1 REM DISKETTE FILE
2 REM N$ = NAME
3 REM R = HOURLY PAY RATE
4 REM D = NUMBER OF DEPENDENTS
5 REM M = MEDICAL INSURANCE DEDUCTION
6 REM L = LIFE INSURANCE DEDUCTION
7 REM
8 REM
10 OPEN 9,8,9,"PAY FILE,S,W"
20 FOR X=1 TO 10
30   READ N$,R,D,M,L
40   PRINT#9,N$;",";R;",";D;",";M;",";L
50 NEXT X
60 CLOSE 9
70 REM
80 REM
100 DATA MENACE DENNIS,1,0,1,1
110 DATA BEAVER LEAVITTO,2.25,0,1,1
120 DATA ISLAND GILLIGAN,4.50,0,2,1
130 DATA WILSON MISTER,4.95,2,5,3
140 DATA HOGAN COLONEL,40,2,3,3
150 DATA SCHULTZ SEARGENT,30,1,1,2
160 DATA KIRK JIM,78.50,1,1,1
170 DATA BUNNY BUGS,12.45,2,5,3
180 DATA SERLING ROD,55.90,2,2,1
190 DATA BOND JAMES,9.25,3,0,0
200 END
```

5b.
```
1 REM DISKETTE FILE
2 REM N$ = NAME
3 REM R = HOURLY PAY RATE
4 REM D = NUMBER OF DEPENDENTS
5 REM M = MEDICAL INSURANCE DEDUCTION
6 REM L = LIFE INSURANCE DEDUCTION
7 REM G = GROSS PAY
```

(Continued on next page)

```basic
10 REM FUNCTION TO ROUND TO NEAREST 100TH
20 REM
30 DEF FNR(X)=INT(100*X+.5)/100
40 REM
50 REM
100 OPEN 7,8,7,"PAY FILE,S,R"
110 FOR X=1 TO 10
120    INPUT#7,N$,R,D,M,L
130    READ H : REM GET HOURS WORKED
140    G=H*R : T=(25-2*D)*G/100
150    IF T<0 THEN T=0
160    P=G-T-M-L
170    PRINT N$;" - "
180    PRINT "HOURS WORKED:";TAB(25);H
190    PRINT "GROSS PAY:";TAB(24);"$";FNR(G)
200    PRINT "TAX:";TAB(24);"$";FNR(T)
210    PRINT "MEDICAL INSURANCE:";TAB(24);"$";FNR(M)
220    PRINT "LIFE INSURANCE:";TAB(24);"$";FNR(L)
230    PRINT "NET:";TAB(24);"$";FNR(P)
240    PRINT
250 NEXT X
260 CLOSE 7
270 REM
280 REM
300 REM DATA SECTION
310 DATA 40,37.1,51,48,39.21,18,6,59.8
320 DATA 45.3,68.3,41
330 END
```

7a.

```basic
1 REM DISKETTE FILE
2 REM H = TIME IN HOURS
3 REM F = TEMP IN DEGREES (F)
4 REM
10 OPEN 7,8,7,"SHERYL FILE,S,W"
20 PRINT "ENTER SHERYL'S DATA"
30 GOSUB 200
40 CLOSE 7
50 PRINT
60 OPEN 7,8,7,"CAROL FILE,S,W"
70 PRINT "ENTER CAROL'S DATA"
80 GOSUB 200
90 CLOSE 7
100 GOTO 300
110 REM
120 REM
200 REM COLLECT DATA & WRITE TO FILE
210 REM
220 FOR A=1 TO 6
230 INPUT "TIME";H
240 INPUT "TEMPERATURE";F
250 PRINT#7,H;",";F
260 NEXT A
270 RETURN
280 REM
290 REM
300 END
```

7b.
```
1 REM DISKETTE FILE
2 REM  T() = ARRAY WHICH HOLDS TEMP IN
3 REM         POSITION TIME*10
4 REM  H = TIME IN HOURS
5 REM
10 DIM T(100)
20 OPEN 3,8,3,"SHERYL FILE,S,R"
30 OPEN 4,8,4,"CAROL FILE,S,R"
40 OPEN 5,8,5,"MERGE FILE,S,W"
50 FOR L=1 TO 6
60    INPUT#3,H,F : GOSUB 100
70    INPUT#4,H,F : GOSUB 100
80 NEXT L : GOTO 200
90 REM
100 REM IF T(TIME*10) IS EMPTY THEN PUT
110 REM THE TEMP IN IT, ELSE AVERAGE
120 REM THE VALUES
130 REM
140 IF T(H*10)=0 THEN T(H*10)=F:RETURN
150 T(H*10)=(T(H*10)+F)/2 : RETURN
160 REM
170 REM
200 REM WRITE TO MERGE FILE
210 REM
220 FOR Z=0 TO 100
230 IF T(Z)<>0 THEN PRINT#5,Z/10;",";T(Z)
240 NEXT Z
250 CLOSE 3 : CLOSE 4 : CLOSE 5
260 END
```

7c.
```
1 REM DISKETTE FILE
10 OPEN 4,8,4,"MERGE FILE,S,R"
20 IF (STATUS AND 64)=64 THEN 60
30    INPUT#4,H,F
40    PRINT H,F
50 GOTO 20
60 CLOSE 4
70 END
```

9a.
```
10 OPEN 4,8,4,"NAME & AGE FILE,S,W"
20 FOR X=1 TO 15
30    INPUT "NAME";N$
40    INPUT "AGE";A
50 PRINT#4,N$;",";A
60 NEXT X
70 CLOSE 4
80 END
```

9b.
```
100 REM  INPUT SECTION
110 REM
120 DIM N$(15),A(15)
130 OPEN 3,8,3,"NAME & AGE FILE,S,R"
140 FOR X=1 TO 15
150    INPUT#3,N$(X),A(X)
160 NEXT X
170 CLOSE 3
```

(Continued on next page)

```
200 REM   BUBBLE SORT
210 REM
220 FOR T=1 TO 14
230   FOR I=15 TO T+1 STEP -1
240     IF N$(I)>N$(I-1) THEN 270
250     T$=N$(I):N$(I)=N$(I-1):N$(I-1)=T$ : REM  SWAP NAMES
260     T1=A(I):A(I)=A(I-1):A(I-1)=T1 : REM  SWAP AGES
270   NEXT I
280 NEXT T
300 REM
400 REM   OUTPUT SECTION
410 REM
420 OPEN 6,8,6,"TEMP FILE,S,W"
430 FOR X=1 TO 15
440   PRINT#6,N$(X);",";A(X)
450 NEXT X
460 CLOSE 6
480 REM
500 REM    FILE MANAGEMENT SECTION
510 REM
520 OPEN 15,8,15
530 PRINT#15,"S:NAME & AGE FILE"
540 PRINT#15,"R:NAME & AGE FILE=TEMP FILE"
550 CLOSE 15
560 END
```

9c.
```
100 REM   INPUT SECTION
110 REM
120 DIM N$(15),A(15)
130 OPEN 3,8,3,"NAME & AGE FILE,S,R"
140 FOR X=1 TO 15
150   INPUT#3,N$(X),A(X)
160 NEXT X
170 CLOSE 3
190 REM
200 REM   BUBBLE SORT
210 REM
220 FOR T=1 TO 14
230   FOR I=15 TO T+1 STEP -1
240     IF A(I)>A(I-1) THEN 270
250     T$=N$(I):N$(I)=N$(I-1):N$(I-1)=T$ : REM  SWAP NAMES
260     T1=A(I):A(I)=A(I-1):A(I-1)=T1 : REM  SWAP AGES
270   NEXT I
280 NEXT T
300 REM
400 REM   OUTPUT SECTION
410 REM
420 OPEN 6,8,6,"TEMP FILE,S,W"
430 FOR X=1 TO 15
440   PRINT#6,N$(X);",";A(X)
450 NEXT X
460 CLOSE 6
```

(Continued on next page)

```
500 REM    FILE MANAGEMENT SECTION
510 REM
520 OPEN 15,8,15
530 PRINT#15,"S:NAME & AGE FILE"
540 PRINT#15,"R:NAME & AGE FILE=TEMP FILE"
550 CLOSE 15
560 END
```

11.

```
1 REM   N$() = ARRAY TO HOLD NAMES
2 REM   T$() = ARRAY TO HOLD NUMBERS
3 REM   B1,B2 = POSITION OF BLANK IN NAME
4 REM   L1,L2 = LAST NAMES
5 REM
10 DIM N$(10),T$(10)
20 FOR X=1 TO 10
30    READ N$(X),T$(X)
40 NEXT X
50 REM
100 REM   BUBBLE SORT
110 REM
120 FOR T=1 TO 9
130    FOR I=10 TO T+1 STEP -1
140       REM   FIND BLANK IN FIRST NAME
150       FOR P=1 TO LEN(N$(I))
160          IF ASC(MID$(N$(I),P,1))=32 THEN B1=P
170       NEXT P
180       REM   FIND BLANK IN SECOND NAME
190       FOR P=1 TO LEN(N$(I-1))
200          IF ASC(MID$(N$(I-1),P,1))=32 THEN B2=P
210       NEXT P
220       REM   COMPARE LAST NAMES ONLY
230       L1$=RIGHT$(N$(I),LEN(N$(I))-B1)
240       L2$=RIGHT$(N$(I-1),LEN(N$(I-1))-B2)
250       IF L1$>L2$ THEN 280
260       Q$=N$(I):N$(I)=N$(I-1):N$(I-1)=Q$
270       Q$=T$(I):T$(I)=T$(I-1):T$(I-1)=Q$
280    NEXT I
290 NEXT T
300 REM
400 REM   DISPLAY SORTED LIST
410 REM
420 FOR X=1 TO 10
430    PRINT N$(X),T$(X)
440 NEXT X
450 END
460 REM
900 DATA LARRY PELHAM,555-1234
910 DATA PHIL COLINS,555-6498
920 DATA LAWRENCE RUSSELL,555-5285
930 DATA ALICIA OSTRIKER,555-4788
940 DATA JOHN ADAMS,555-1640
950 DATA DEBORAH PALEY,555-7749
960 DATA LAURIE JOHNSON,555-0012
970 DATA GARY WALLACE,555-1537
980 DATA BOB ATKINS,555-1964
990 DATA DAVID NAUGHTON,555-5487
```

INDEX